The Craftsman
in Early America

The Craftsman
in Early America

EDITED BY

Ian M. G. Quimby

PUBLISHED FOR
The Henry Francis du Pont Winterthur Museum
WINTERTHUR, DELAWARE

W · W · Norton & Company
NEW YORK   LONDON

Copyright © 1984 by The Henry Francis du Pont Winterthur Museum
Published simultaneously in Canada by Stoddart Publishing.
Printed in the United States of America.

The text of this book is composed in Electra, with
display type set in Garamond. Composition and
manufacturing by The Maple-Vail Book Manufacturing Group.

First Edition

Library of Congress Cataloging in Publication Data
Main entry under title:

The Craftsman in early America.

        Includes index.
        1. Artisans—United States—History.   I. Quimby,
Ian M.G.   II. Henry Francis du Pont Winterthur Museum.
HD2346.U5C67 1984   331.7'94   94–1562

ISBN 0-393-61856-3

ISBN 0-393-95449-8 (pbk.)

W. W. Norton & Company, Inc., 500 Fifth Avenue, New York, N.Y. 10110
W. W. Norton & Company Ltd., 37 Great Russell Street, London WC1B 3NU

1 2 3 4 5 6 7 8 9 0

Contents

The Craftsman
in Early America

Introduction:
Some Observations on the
Craftsman in Early America
Ian M. G. Quimby

It was a felicitous coincidence that the 1979 Winterthur conference, the event for which the papers in this volume were originally prepared, marked the thirtieth anniversary of the completion of Carl Bridenbaugh's important book *The Colonial Craftsman*. The book is still in print and is likely to remain so for the foreseeable future.[1] His was the first major scholarly attempt to examine the role of the craftsman in early American society rather than the products of the craftsman. Instead of discussing just the cabinetmakers, the silversmiths, and the practitioners of other luxury crafts, he embraced the full range of crafts necessary to sustain life in eighteenth-century America. Thus he included carpenters, coopers, cordwainers, and tailors—the four largest crafts in Philadelphia in 1773. Bridenbaugh provided a wealth of specific details on the lives and work of all manner of artisan. The book is loosely organized into two chapters on rural and village craftsmen, two on urban craftsmen, and a chapter each on craftsmen at work and craftsmen as citizens. He relied heavily on eighteenth-century newspaper advertisements and on secondary sources.

In retrospect, of course, *The Colonial Craftsman* suffers from myopia.

---

[1] Carl Bridenbaugh, *The Colonial Craftsman* (1950; reprint ed., Chicago: University of Chicago Press, Phoenix Books, 1961). The author's preface is dated September 1949.

It is too obviously a cut-and-paste collection of information from colonial newspapers accepted at face value. It lacks a sense of movement as if, somehow, things really did not change much from 1700 to 1776, and the author ignored the seventeenth century. It also lacks a transatlantic context, assumes too much continuity of British traditions, and is fairly oblivious to the larger forces shaping Western society. Finally, of course, it seems unsatisfactory because we have been treated to so much more sophisticated scholarship in the last three decades. Although it may seem unfair, it is hard to avoid comparing Bridenbaugh's *Colonial Craftsman* with E. P. Thompson's *Making of the English Working Class* published only thirteen years later (1963). Bridenbaugh's book is a modest though welcome contribution. Thompson's is a monumental and original study of great importance to social historians on both sides of the Atlantic. Thompson's subject is not merely craftsmen; it is the process by which one group of Englishmen came to see their interests as distinct from those of other Englishmen. Class, Thompson says, is not a matter of structure; it is a set of historical relationships. These relationships are not abstract, for, as he says in his preface, "the relationship must always be embodied in real people and in a real context. . . . We cannot have love without lovers, nor deference without squires and labourers."[2]

Thompson is deeply concerned with the impact of technological change on working people, as indeed he must be since he focuses on the period 1780 to 1832. The book could easily have been called "The Impact of the Industrial Revolution on British Labor." Such a title suggests a narrower study which Thompson's is not. It is in fact an analysis of cultural change where radical protestantism is at least as important as technological change. Thompson does not merely chronicle change; he explains how and why. With all the fine American scholarship on industrialization, labor history, modernization, and so on, we still lack a comparable major synthesis of the American experience. Americans specialize in case studies which, I hasten to add, are essential too. Such specific studies as those of Howard Rock on New York City, Susan Hirsch on Newark, and Bruce Laurie on Philadelphia are admirable contributions. These studies suggest, however, that the thrust of American historical research has shifted to the nineteenth century when the

---

[2] E. P. Thompson, *The Making of the English Working Class* (1963; reprint ed., New York: Random House, Vintage Books, 1966), p. 9.

impact of industrialization was the greatest. They tell us relatively little of the fate of the traditional craftsman discussed by Bridenbaugh.[3]

Who was this traditional craftsman? He is easy enough to describe in the abstract. In a preindustrial society he was a workman who possessed specialized skills that set him apart from a common laborer. These skills were his most valuable possession, for they gave him varying degrees of independence, mobility, and status. In the ritualistic language found in the indentures of apprenticeship, the craft skills to be learned by the apprentice are referred to as "the art and mystery"—no matter what the craft. Here *art* is used in its now obsolete sense of practicing technical skills with the aid of magic. *Mystery* connotes more than something unknown or a puzzle to be solved; it suggests the spiritual element, the essential knowledge without which the artisan would be a mere automaton. *Mystery* also smacks of secret rites, and, indeed, the process of apprenticeship is one long rite of passage that earned the apprentice special privileges in society. Apprenticeship assured the continuity of technical skills from one generation to another, but it served other purposes as well. Its primary purpose was educational in the broadest sense and involved the intergenerational transfer of culture itself. Masters stood in loco parentis to their apprentices and servants which, together, helped to constitute the extended family. The craftsman with his leather apron was thus more than a mere producer of goods. All members of the extended family were well advised to heed the biblical exhortation to "Obey them that have the rule over you, and submit yourselves: for they watch for your souls, as they that must give account."[4]

At least that was the ideal. Any serious treatment of the craftsman in early America, however, has to take into consideration the fact that the traditions of preindustrial society were disintegrating under the impact of New World conditions and those technological and commercial changes that we call the industrial revolution—even in the eighteenth century. Full terms of apprenticeship were difficult to enforce in an economy with a chronic labor shortage. No effective municipal or guild

[3] Howard B. Rock, *Artisans of the New Republic: The Tradesmen of New York City in the Age of Jefferson* (New York: New York University Press, 1979); Susan E. Hirsch, *Roots of the American Working Class: The Industrialization of Crafts in Newark, 1800–1860* (Philadelphia: University of Pennsylvania Press, 1978); Bruce Laurie, *Working People of Philadelphia, 1800–1850* (Philadelphia: Temple University Press, 1980).

[4] Ian M. G. Quimby, "Apprenticeship in Colonial Philadelphia" (M.A. thesis, University of Delaware, 1963). Heb. 13:17; a somewhat altered version appeared in *American Weekly Mercury* (Philadelphia), November 1–7, 1772.

ordinances governed who could practice a craft in any colonial American city. Attempts to control the quality of goods and their prices were, by and large, unsuccessful. And then there was always land to be had by those willing to work hard enough to clear it and make it productive. The lure of land was irresistible for many immigrants fresh from countries where holdings were often too small to support a family. Such freedoms and such opportunities were destabilizing to the social structures of a preindustrial society.

How the craftsman was affected by modernization and industrial capitalism is a complicated story that varies considerably from one craft to another. It was not just a question of substituting machines for manual labor. From the 1790s to the 1830s Philadelphia cordwainers experienced declining real income. They fell victim to competition between masters for wider markets. The expanding export market should have insured their prosperity, but instead it had the opposite effect. The shoe industry mechanized late, and when it did Lynn, Massachusetts, led the way—not Philadelphia. Mechanization of the textile industry is a familiar story, but there are some less familiar aspects. Philadelphia and its northeastern suburbs became a major center for the production of textiles and textile machinery. As elsewhere, power-loom operatives were mostly women. But the Philadelphia carpet industry continued to use hand looms until about 1860. These looms required the brawn of male weavers. It was not considered a highly skilled craft, and, indeed, the pay was low. By 1850, not surprisingly, 76 percent of those weavers were Irish immigrants.[5] Textile manufacturing did not move from home production for home use directly to factory production; in fact, the industry mechanized in stages and relied heavily on outwork. Cotton was fully integrated very early, but the production of woolens was industrialized at a much slower rate because of the nature of the fiber itself. Water-powered carding mills served families making their own woolen cloth before there were woolen mills. Massachusetts had carding mills in abundance from at least the 1790s, and some of them remained in operation into the twentieth century. Unlike cotton, which was spun by a continuous process from the time of Sir Richard Arkwright in the eighteenth century, woolen spinning remained a discontinuous and, hence, a slower process until the twentieth century.

[5] Richard A. McLeod, "The Philadelphia Artisan, 1828–1850" (Ph.D. diss., University of Missouri, 1971).

Thompson noted fundamental changes in English society between 1780 and 1832, England's period of industrialization. A comparable fifty-year period in the United States is less easily identifiable. Herbert Gutman uses 1843–93 as the critical half century that changed America from a preindustrial to a major industrial society. He identifies the period 1815–43 as "predominantly preindustrial," noting that "most workers drawn to its few factories were products of rural and village preindustrial culture." Gutman also identifies a third period, 1893–1920, in which he compares the expectations and work habits of first-generation immigrant factory workers with those of pre-1843 American factory workers who were predominantly native-born. His point is, of course, that throughout all three periods, covering the years from 1815 to 1920, preindustrial customs and attitudes were present and were a significant factor in labor unrest.[6]

While most of the crafts and the social structure they represented were headed for virtual extinction, this state of affairs was little understood at the time. Many traditional urban crafts continued to prosper, and there appeared little reason to suppose that they would one day disappear. Indeed, there was in the 1790s and the early decades of the nineteenth century a flowering of mechanics' associations and libraries. One of the most prominent among these was the Massachusetts Charitable Mechanic Association organized in 1795 with eighty-two founding members led by Paul Revere, the venerable goldsmith who was unanimously chosen president. Among the artisans were bricklayers, blacksmiths, coopers, cordwainers, housewrights, ropemakers, printers, and tailors. Other crafts were represented as well. Most members appear to have been artisans in the classical sense. This would not be surprising were it not for the fact that their constitution called for the association to consist of "mechanics and manufacturers." Few manufacturers or merchants joined, and a petition to twenty of the latter specifically inviting their support was coldly rejected, ostensibly on the grounds that such an organization could only be a "combination to extort extravagant prices for labor."[7]

The association had some of the attributes of earlier artisan benev-

[6] Herbert G. Gutman, "Work, Culture, and Society in Industrializing America, 1815–1919," *American Historical Review* 78, no. 3 (June 1973): 531–87.

[7] Joseph T. Buckingham, comp., *Annals of the Massachusetts Charitable Mechanic Association* (Boston: Crocker and Brewster, 1853). All subsequent references to the association are derived from this source.

olent societies, but its goals were more ambitious and its concerns more serious. While its general purposes were subsumed in such phrases as "promoting mutual good offices and fellowship by assisting the necessitous, encouraging the ingenious, and rewarding the faithful," the organization had very specific interests. Number one among those interests was the matter of apprenticeship. It is probable that the organization grew out of the failure of a petition from Boston mechanics in December 1794 to the legislature asking for legislation "to better regulate apprenticeship." When the legislature failed to respond, the mechanics took matters into their own hands by organizing an association with coercive powers. Built into the constitution of the association were the requirements that mechanics be "master workmen" (that is, have served a full apprenticeship) and, as a condition of membership, that they agree not to employ any apprentice still bound to another master. The latter point was precisely what had been requested in the way of new legislation. The association further provided that every apprentice upon reaching the age of twenty-one and who had faithfully complied with the terms of his indenture would receive a certificate from the association which in effect provided the young man with a stamp of approval. Should any member of the association "employ or entertain any bound apprentice, who shall have left the person he was bound to, without said person's consent," that member automatically forfeited his membership. The better regulation of apprenticeship, therefore, was the primary reason for the existence of the association.

In a society dedicated to the inviolability of contracts, something had clearly gone awry. The terms of the contracts between masters and servants were being violated with impunity. Traditionally the time of servants or apprentices was considered property, and upon the death of a master unexpired portions of that time were assigned a cash value and became part of the decedent's estate. If an apprentice could depart before completing the term of years specified in the indenture, then the master was deprived of property as well as inconvenienced. The master craftsman's importance in the social structure diminished as his power over his servants declined. Notions of individual freedom assumed greater importance and took precedence over the bonds of voluntary servitude. And finally, of course, short, unstable apprenticeships had to affect technical training adversely. The Boston mechanics tried through their association to put things right. Even without the cooperation of government they hoped to gain control over the apprenticeship issue. It seemed possible, they assumed, because the regulations were in the interest of all mechanics.

Gradually the Massachusetts Charitable Mechanic Association came to take on a different character. By 1817 the goals of the association were defined as *"the diffusion of benevolence; the encouragement of improvements in the mechanic arts and manufactures; the reward of fidelity in apprentices;* and *the promotion of fellowship and good feeling among the associates."* It will be noticed that the once all-important question of apprenticeship, while given lip service, is no longer the preeminent issue that it was in 1795. In fact, the certificates were awarded only to those apprentices who had been bound to members of the association. This seems perverse because the constitution of the association clearly intended them to be awarded to *every* apprentice completing his term. During the 1820s, after a generous donor provided books for an apprentices' library, the officers fretted over the trouble and expense of operating it. In 1832 the library was turned over to the apprentices themselves to run for their own benefit and for as long as they exercised good judgment. An 1843 report commended the apprentices for their success in maintaining, supporting, and using it. The report recommended the establishment of a library "to which *all* the members of the association could have free access . . . for their moral and intellectual improvement."[8]

One suspects that these enterprising apprentices who ran a library for their own benefit—and actually used it—were a far different lot from their earlier counterparts. Although the ideal of the learned mechanic had existed at least since the establishment of the American Philosophical Society in Philadelphia in the 1740s, it was a remote prospect indeed for most craftsmen. These Boston apprentices of the 1830s had far more in common with modern craft apprentices than with their eighteenth-century brethren. They were, for the most part, paid employees who lived not with their masters but elsewhere. They were no longer children to all-powerful surrogate fathers. James Alexander, writing under the pen name of Charles Quill, in *The Working-Man* (1839), commented:

The relation of master and apprentice was a closer and warmer one in former days. The lad was willing to allow that he had a *master*, for a certain time and a certain purpose, and in expectation of being one day a master himself. He

[8] Buckingham, *Annals of the Association*, pp. 146, 323 (emphasis added).

thought this was no more disgraceful than the subordination of the scholar to his teacher, or the soldier to his captain. And, in return, the employer felt a responsibility proportioned to his authority. Good men were accustomed to treat their apprentices as their sons. . . . It is unnecessary to say, that the state of things is very much altered. . . . The whole affair of indentures, as my readers very well know, is in some places becoming a mere formality. It is less common than it used to be for boys to serve out their whole time. Many influences are at work to make lads impatient, and loath to continue in one place, however good. And when they abscond from their proper service, it is not every employer who now thinks it worth his while to take the legal measures for recovering their time. . . . The old-fashioned system is found to be ineffectual.

Alexander went on to lament the decline of craft training and the loss of jobs requiring high skills to well-trained immigrants. His final concern was with the moral consequences of the new system whereby the apprentice lacked the constructive influences of home life. The apprentice lived neither with his own family nor with that of his employer, "at least under the system prevailing in our cities and large towns."

In great manufactories, where there are at least a dozen boys—these of course cannot be allowed to overrun the employer's house: they are often put out to board elsewhere. In neither case have they a *home.*—Even where there is only an ordinary number, as the master is no longer a parent, the apprentice feels no longer like a son. Where can he spend his evenings? Not in the garret or loft where he sleeps: in winter it is cold; in summer it is suffocating.—Not in the kitchen: he would be in the way. Not in the sitting-room: that would be too familiar.—Where can he spend the long hours of his Sunday? Let us look the truth in the face: *The apprentice has no home.* . . . Is it any wonder that they crowd our oyster-houses, porter-cellars, bar-rooms, shows, and wait for checks about the doors of our theatres?[9]

One man's definition of social decay may be another's prescription for opportunity. Austrian immigrant Francis J. Grund found conditions for the craftsman far better in America than in Europe. In *The Americans in Their Moral, Social, and Political Relations* (1837), he extolled the prosperity and ingenuity of the American mechanic.

On entering the house of a respectable mechanic, in any of the large cities of the United States, one cannot but be astonished at the apparent neatness and comfort of the apartments, the large airy parlours, the nice carpets and mahog-

[9]Charles Quill [James Alexander], *The Working-Man* (Philadelphia: Henry Perkins, and Boston: Perkins and Marvin, 1839), pp. 114–15, 117–18.

any furniture, and the tolerably good library, showing the inmates' acquaintance with the standard works of English literature. These are advantages which
but few individuals of the same class enjoy . . . in Europe.

Grund noted the lack of "a certain *mechanical* perfection" in American
machines and products, unlike England where "a greater division of
labour and long-followed practice in a narrow circumscribed trade"
assured a nicety of execution. What the American mechanic lacked in
perfecting his mechanical skills was more than compensated for by his
willingness to innovate.

An American mechanic does not exercise his trade as he has learned it: he is
constantly making improvements, studying out new and ingenious processes
either to perfect his work or to reduce its price, and is, in most cases, able to
account for the various processes of his art in a manner which would do credit
to a philosopher.

According to Grund, the genius of the mechanic flowered because the
primary needs of life were met with time to spare for thought and reflection.

In America not only the master mechanic, but also his journeymen have the
means of earning more than is required for a mere living; they are able to
procure for themselves comforts which would hardly enter the imagination of
similar orders in Europe. They are enabled to command a portion of their time;
and their minds being free from the anxieties of a precarious life . . . are better
qualified for study or improvement, the only sure means by which they can
hope to better their conditions.[10]

The fact is, it is hard to get a grip on the American craftsman, who
becomes increasingly hard to identify in the early nineteenth century.
The traditional craft structure of apprentice, journeyman, and master
was breaking up. Stuart Blumin in his study "Mobility and Change in
Ante-Bellum Philadelphia" identifies a tripling in the number of journeymen relative to masters between 1820 and 1860. At the same time,
the number of masters relative to the total work force declined to less
than half. The total manual-labor work force grew in the forty-year
period, but the number of masters did not. According to Blumin,

In 1820 . . . there was a skilled, proprietary position for almost every skilled
and unskilled wage-earning position. . . . The demand for master craftsmen

[10] Francis J. Grund, *The Americans in Their Moral, Social and Political Relations*,
2 vols. (1837; reprint ed., New York: Augustus M. Kelley, 1971), 1:47, 2:158, 161–62.

was great enough to provide any ambitious and competent journeyman with the opportunity to set up his own shop. . . . During the next forty years, the number of shops remained substantially the same. But at the same time the population had quadrupled, and in this new city of a half-million people . . . a few thousand proprietorships [could not] give much hope to forty or fifty thousand journeymen.[11]

There appears to be some confusion in Blumin's study between journeymen and the unskilled which makes his reference to forty or fifty thousand journeymen somewhat suspect. One might also ask where all these journeymen had come from if the masters no longer had need of them. There had to be apprentices before there could be journeymen, and the apprenticeship system was breaking down. Journeymen are notoriously difficult to identify in the records because they usually did not own property and, earlier at least, did not have the ballot. Hence, questions concerning their social, economic, and political status remain difficult to answer.

Another element in the labor picture that has received insufficient attention is the merchant capitalist who, because of his access to capital and credit, was often in a position to dictate the price of labor. While many a merchant capitalist was no doubt a merchant in the eighteenth-century sense, that is, one who bought and sold goods in foreign trade, at least some of them were master craftsmen whose growing wealth gave them access to loans and credit so that they, in turn, were in a position to extend credit. The master cordwainers of Philadelphia during the first decade of the nineteenth century had at one time been craftsmen, and perhaps some still were. That they had become merchant capitalists, however, is evident from their many disputes over wages with journeymen, a conflict that resulted in the trial for conspiracy of key journeymen in 1809. The transcript of the trial sets forth with great eloquence the economic views of both parties.[12] This was the first major confrontation between labor and capital in the United States, and labor lost.

---

[11] Stuart Blumin, "Mobility and Change in Ante-Bellum Philadelphia," in *Nineteenth-Century Cities: Essays in the New Urban History*, ed. Stephen Thernstrom and Richard Sennett (New Haven: Yale University Press, 1969), pp. 199–200, 165–208.

[12] John R. Commons et al., eds., *A Documentary History of American Industrial Society*, vol. 3 (Cleveland: Arthur H. Clark, 1910), pp. 59–248. See also Ian M. G. Quimby, "The Cordwainers Protest: A Crisis in Labor Relations," in *Winterthur Portfolio* 3, ed. Milo M. Naeve (Winterthur, Del.: Winterthur Museum, 1967), pp. 83–101. For Commons's theory of the merchant capitalist, see John R. Commons et al., *History of Labour in the United States*, vol. 1 (New York: Macmillan Co., 1926), pp. 338f.

The journeymen were found guilty of conspiracy to regulate wages, and an important impetus to union organization was effectively blunted. The master cordwainers were no longer craftsmen in the classical sense, in spite of the fact that they insisted on being identified as cordwainers; they were merchant capitalists. How often was this practice repeated in other trades? Was the housewright or bricklayer who belonged to the Massachusetts Charitable Mechanic Association still framing houses or laying bricks, or had he become a general contractor? By the 1820s or 1830s, and perhaps earlier as in the case of the cordwainers, many craft designations were not necessarily accurate. Scholars are advised to check against other records before deciding whether someone who called himself a craftsman was so in fact.

With the realization that this discussion has included neither factory operatives nor the unskilled laboring classes, perhaps the changing nature of the Massachusetts Charitable Mechanic Association can become the paradigm for the fate of the preindustrial craftsman. There were few if any leather aprons left in 1860 when the compiler of the annals of the association noted with satisfaction that, in contrast to the early years, the membership was approaching a thousand, "chiefly men of substance,—many are men of wealth,—all are enterprizing and prosperous, except a few, on whom adversity has laid its iron hand."[13] Merchants and manufacturers may have looked upon the association with suspicion in its early days, but they soon learned there was little to fear, and many of them joined. Professional men too came into the association. When in the 1820s it was proposed that the association hold a series of lectures on chemistry and other sciences, some of the members objected on the grounds that such subjects were not suitable for mechanics. But by that time, and increasingly thereafter, the association was dominated by the better educated and the more well heeled. In the face of at least a generation of heavy immigration, the ethnic composition of the association remained steadfastly Waspish. It was a private club of small businessmen that came increasingly to resemble a twentieth-century Rotary club more than a late eighteenth-century artisans' association.

In some ways the Massachusetts Charitable Mechanic Association fulfilled a dream of eighteenth-century mechanics by according recognition and status to working men. The image of the literate and articulate mechanic who provided society with its comforts and improvements

---

[13] Buckingham, *Annals of the Association*, p. 588.

was a compelling one, as the annals of the association show, and it lingered long after it ceased to have meaning. In retrospect all the attempts to organize the life of urban artisans were aimed at staving off change, at preserving what were perceived as the traditional features of craftsman life: dignity and status because they possessed special skills, a sturdy apprenticeship system to assure intergenerational continuity of those skills, and, perhaps most important of all, economic opportunity to become an independent entrepreneur (that is, a master) with relative ease. The two generations of craftsmen following national independence also inherited the heady rhetoric of freedom and equality. Their speeches and writings are laced with references to their rights as free men, and any policies that limited their economic freedom are regarded as assaults on the broader freedoms due them as American citizens. Starting with the great processions celebrating ratification of the federal constitution on every Independence Day, craftsmen marched in parades segregated by craft. Each group of craftsmen used such occasions to demonstrate the importance to society of their particular craft. Underlying the bravado of such occasions was the fear of slipping in the social order, of falling back into a servile condition.[14] And while some continued to prosper, others found their way barred. As Stephen Mayer put it, "The journeyman of the 1820s and 1830s was in a perilous position. He was caught on the middle rung of the crumbling apprentice system. The promise of upward mobility had vanished." According to a contemporary source quoted by Mayer this was so because " 'monopolists and capitalists' " had "usurped the rights of journeymen, 'abridging their privileges with the advantage of large capital.' " If Stuart Blumin's assertions about Philadelphia hold for other urban centers, that the loss of opportunity by journeymen contributed to the emergence of a large wage-earning lower class by midcentury, then craftsmen were everywhere divided into sheep and goats, some to prosper as tradesmen but most others doomed to dependency as wage slaves. Blumin calculated that economic change in Philadelphia between 1820 and 1860 resulted in lessened opportunity for working people but vastly expanded opportunity for a few people of means. "Philadelphia, on the eve of the Civil War, was a society of extreme economic stratification." Thus the worst

[14]Howard B. Rock, "The American Revolution and the Mechanics of New York City: One Generation Later," New York History 57, no. 3 (July 1976): 367–94.

fears of Rock's "artisans of the new republic" were realized. For all
practical purposes the craftsman had ceased to exist.[15]

Literature on the craftsman in early America has greatly expanded
since Carl Bridenbaugh's book was published in 1950, and yet with all
the fine scholarship done since then the craftsman remains an elusive
figure. As David Montgomery has astutely noted, "Our concern has
been either with the journeyman's economic circumstances (where there
is still much to be learned) or with whether he voted for Andrew Jackson," and he called for further research in a number of potentially interesting areas.[16] Certainly, one of the problems is the great diversity of
crafts and the vastly different circumstances between those crafts that
required only a few hand tools and those that required major capital
investment. The tailor required a set of needles and a tailor's goose, but
a glassmaker required a plant, a labor force, fuel, and raw materials, all
of which required the outlay of considerable funds before the production of the first piece of glass.

The contributors to this volume provide insights into a wide variety
of crafts over a 200-year span of American history: seventeenth-century
woodworkers in Massachusetts and Rhode Island; goldsmiths in early
eighteenth-century Boston; peripatetic glassblowers of the eighteenth and
early nineteenth centuries; the ceramics industry during the years 1780–
1840; the industrialization of shoemaking in Lynn, Massachusetts;
America's first professional architect and his working relations with his
builders and stonecutters; and the craft structure of a religious community. Complementing the specific craft studies are four papers of a broader
nature: the social and political role of mechanics in colonial Philadelphia, the historiography of craftsmen in early America, a review of primary documents for the study of craftsmen, and a complementary study
on the pitfalls of visual evidence for studying the craftsman. The range
of techniques used in these papers is suggested by the types of scholars
represented: historians, art historians, a folklorist, American-studies
specialists, and museum curators. The emphasis on specific crafts reaf-

[15] Stephen Mayer, "*People v. Fisher:* The Shoemakers' Strike of 1833," *New-York
Historical Society Quarterly* 62, no. 1 (January 1978):13, 6–21; Blumin, "Mobility and
Change," pp. 204–6.

[16] David Montgomery, "The Working Classes of the Pre-Industrial American City,
1780–1830," *Labor History* 9 (1968): 21, 3–22.

firms the necessity for understanding the peculiarities existing in crafts which industrialized at different times, different rates, and in different ways. These papers also demonstrate the complexities of the preindustrial period for craft study and suggest that an oversimplified view has warped our understanding of the preindustrial period, a failing that inevitably skews any attempts to analyze the process of industrialization itself.

Documentary Sources for the Study of the Craftsman
Stephanie Grauman Wolf

In 1958 E. McClung Fleming proposed the use of artifacts as social documents to enrich the historian's understanding, since "the verified object and the verified text serve to supplement and fortify each other and should be used together." Some years later he outlined a method of approach to artifactual study that would facilitate this goal. His model for study differentiated between the informational level of object understanding—that is, traditional museum concerns of identification, description, and evaluation—and the conceptual levels of understanding which include cultural analysis and interpretation. These categories are roughly equivalent to those a historian asks of written sources, such as tax lists, land records, and census returns, when attempting to use specific data in explaining the more abstract problems of process and relationship. Fleming felt it was necessary to present a carefully articulated plan for working with objects since "it is the rare historian who can read the museum's artifact as freely and accurately as he can read the library's printed book or written manuscript."[1] Granted it requires a great deal of background and training before the historian—or anyone else for that matter—can "read" the artifact, but does it follow that the document is readily accessible to anyone with the ability to recognize

[1] E. McClung Fleming, "Early American Decorative Arts as Social Documents," *Mississippi Valley Historical Review* 45, no. 2 (September 1958): 277, 276. See also E. McClung Fleming, "Artifact Study: A Proposed Model," in *Winterthur Portfolio* 9, ed. Ian M. G. Quimby (Charlottesville: University Press of Virginia, 1974), pp. 153–73.

words as they appear on a piece of paper? I would like to suggest that it does not: that the written record itself is a very special sort of artifact, all the more susceptible to misunderstanding because it seems to be obvious and available.

As a material object—in this case a piece of paper marked upon by a person often unknown and long since departed from a society whose ways are not known with certainty but are, in fact, the object of the study itself—the written record shares most of the basic problems of other bits of material culture which have drifted down to us across time and which bid us to explore them for their long-kept secrets. Like the object, the document does not really "speak for itself." It must be identified, to borrow the vocabulary of artifact analysis, as to its maker, its method, time, and place of construction, and the use for which it was intended. To misconstrue, as does James Deetz, the purpose of early American estate inventories as having been "taken for tax purposes" at the time of an individual's death, is inevitably to misinterpret the information included therein.[2] To take at face value the signature of, for example, a Simple Cobbler of Agawam on a religious tract or a Mechanic on a political letter to the *Pennsylvania Gazette* is to add false information to an understanding of the *mentalité* of the craftsman in American society. Second, the vocabulary used in the document must be understood within its own context, just as the student of material culture must compile a vocabulary of construction techniques and artistic styles. The problems are even greater because the words themselves are still readable and do have a meaning in our own vocabulary. But what did the people of seventeenth-century Massachusetts or Maryland mean by a looking glass, a bedstead, a burning glass? Did the definition of the word *coarse* or even of the most basic terms for the purposes of this paper—*artisan, mechanic, craftsman*—change over time? The logic of the past must be understood in terms of the present to make documentary sources speak to us intelligibly.

Furthermore, it is of significance—again, obvious in relation to objects, less so for documentary sources—in what form the information comes to us. The original document offers the most fruitful material; small marginal marks or changes in ink might provide clues to its manufacture and meaning. Of course, the condition of the document must

---

[2] James Deetz, *In Small Things Forgotten: The Archaeology of Early American Life* (Garden City, N.Y.: Anchor Books, 1977), p. 8.

be considered. Just as the replaced stretchers on a chair may change its value as artifactual document, so do missing or rewritten parts affect our judgment of the document. Xerox or microfilm copies are next best, just as a good picture of an object is useful when the original itself is unobtainable. But readability as well as subtlety can be lost through distance from the original. Since mechanical copying procedures often reduce the opacity of paper, documents written on both sides appear as totally undecipherable rows of crosses, while the original document itself may be quite readable. Finally, a transcription is least satisfactory: it is a reproduced artifact. So many questions of authenticity arise; so many errors are perpetrated by filtration through the mind and pen of an intermediary; so much may be lost in the translation. The transcriber might even have been trying to help—correcting arithmetic errors, making guesses on illegible words, alphabetizing tax lists to make the search for individual names easier when the original was written on a geographical basis or through some contemporary gradation of social standing. Each of these changes diminishes the value of the source. One would expect that the sensitivity of editors to the importance of *exact* reproduction, akin to using eighteenth-century tools and materials to recreate eighteenth-century furniture, had increased with changing notions of the purposes of historical research, so that the more recent the transcription, the more faithful it would be to the original. But the recently published version of the diary of Philadelphia merchant Thomas Cope, in which editorial discretion was exercised (without even the use of deletion marks) over material that, in the opinion of the editor, was felt to be repetitious or unnecessary, illustrates that a serious problem of accuracy and completeness still exists in the use of printed or transcribed material.[3]

By far the most serious difficulty to overcome in the use of documents, as in the use of objects, is the problem of survival. While all of us work on specific materials—since evidence is only available in concrete unique examples—we hope somehow to be able to transmute the particular into the universal, to transform the study of *a* craftsman into knowledge of *the* craftsman, to turn the life experience of some weavers in Pennsylvania into the situation of all weavers in colonial America. In the same way, the object analyst looks at surviving court cupboards

[3] Eliza Cope Harrison, ed., *Philadelphia Merchant: The Diary of Thomas Cope, 1800–1851* (South Bend, Ind.: Gateway Editions, 1978).

from Essex County, Massachusetts, and hopes to see them as representative of a much larger body of no longer existing furniture. This works, perhaps, if we can be assured of the typicality of our sample and if selection by accident of time is truly as mathematically random as the sample of the modern statistician. But, of course, it is not. It does not, unfortunately, even represent the idiosyncratic selection made by a tornado when it leaves one house standing in a ten-block area. Historical survivals, both artifactual and documentary, are highly selective. This is obvious for artifacts if one merely counts the number of known surviving high-style chairs from the colonial period and compares it to the number of authenticated plain benches and stools. A simple tally in combination with basic common sense informs us that we cannot use this body of data to generalize about the universe of seating furniture in colonial America.

The bias of documents extends much further than the numbers of their survival; it extends to their inherent qualities as well. Up to the last generation, documents used by historians were almost entirely selective in terms of elite orientation; that is, so-called literary evidence—diaries, journals, travel accounts, and newspaper articles—were conscious attempts to set down facts and impressions of the contemporary scene. It was not as if benches were rare because they had not been preserved; it was as if they had never existed at all. Diaries and journals were not kept by the illiterate nor travel accounts by those who moved in search of work rather than pleasure. The life of the craftsman, when described at all, was filtered through the perceptions of one who was attempting to describe the unique or the picaresque rather than the commonplace and average. Thus, it is Benjamin Franklin, Plunkett Fleeson, and Paul Revere who become "typical" artisans, lending credence to the mythology that the American experience was one of opportunity and advancement for those who worked with their hands; that in a land of labor scarcity, society was primarily made up of an undifferentiated middle class of independent craftsmen and yeomen whose lives were characterized by the dignity of ownership and access to modest competency, if not to abundance. To be sure, there was the dark side of the picture: newspaper and diary accounts of rowdy mobs of mean and vicious mechanics, references to growing numbers of poor, especially in the cities, requiring poorhouses, hospitals, and jails. But these allusions have barely touched the deeply ingrained belief in the favored position of the craftsman in early American life.

With the introduction of a social-science methodology to study the lives of the inarticulate and an interest in questions that focus on the typical rather than the exceptional, historians began, some fifteen or twenty years ago, to develop what they called the new history. No longer new and now incorporated into the mainstream of American historiography, this discipline, using models derived from the Annales school of French historians and the Cambridge group for population studies in England, has sought the answers to its questions through exploitation of a long, underutilized body of nonliterary sources. Broadly defined, these sources include all materials susceptible of quantification. They contain "bits" of hard data, to borrow the language of the computer, and can be not only measured as simple frequencies but also compared by holding some factors constant and working with others as variables. Since they involve "objective" rather than "impressionistic" material, they may be handled by a computer, making possible a whole range of potentially interesting considerations denied to the pencil-and-paper researchers on the grounds of time alone.

It is to a consideration of these sources, their advantages and limitations, that I will devote the rest of this paper. Although many of these materials had long been used by genealogists and antiquarians in searching out specific individuals or families, they were for the historians what the discovery of King Tut's tomb was for the archaeologist. And they enjoyed the same kind of instant popularity—one might almost say superstardom. They have been, perhaps, overexploited in much the same way as that once-obscure deity, and, for the most part, little thinking has gone into a real examination of their nature.

While escaping the biases of personal idiosyncracy and elitism so often condemned in literary sources, nonliterary sources have their own built-in problems that must be understood and taken into account before we dare to use them in the quest for historical "truth." The broadest criticism of such sources has been made by the radical French historian Jean Chesneaux who charges that quantifiable materials "originate with the state or its adjuncts" and are therefore imbued with institutional, if not individual, selectivity.

The historian's territory is completely marked out by the apparatus of repression . . . the power structure . . . functions as a gigantic recording machine, using the official archives of Government services (Tax Offices, Treasury, etc.), church archives (ecclesiastical accounts, hospitals, parish records, etc.), the archives of powerful private interests (trusts, big commercial firms, etc.). We know nothing of reality except what can be inferred from the information the power structure has recorded and made available.

Furthermore, according to Chesneaux, the state may control the past by withholding information, keeping certain facts secret, and even destroying embarrassing material.[4]

It is neither necessary nor desirable to accept Chesneaux's view which would condemn the entire range of institutional documents and a priori render suspect any results based on its use. His polemic does, however, serve to alert the researcher to the biases lurking within apparently objective materials. Since the nature of all institutional records tends to place undue emphasis on the wealthy, the stable, and the urban, such records may be especially prone to skew the results of those working specifically on early America, where the vast majority of the population was nonaffluent, mobile, and rural. Moreover, European methods and models are frequently unadaptable to the needs of American scholars because of the vagaries of record taking and record retention in the New World. Sheer geographic size and cultural variation may make generalization from a localized collection of documents impossible. A heavy leaning in American historiography toward both New England studies in particular and a general interpretation of the American experience as New England writ large is at least partially explained by a mania for record keeping among New Englanders, unmatched in any other region.

Biases of survival, region, and socioeconomics aside, nonliterary sources differ in basic composition and, therefore, are not all equally useful in answering the same kinds of questions or in testing the same large-scale hypotheses. To return to the artifactual metaphor of Fleming's model, it is necessary to understand their basic design, construction, and functional properties before attempting to subject them to cultural analysis and interpretation.

Nonliterary sources may be divided into three general categories. The first group is composed of genuinely aggregative data which present a limited body of information about most of the inhabitants of a community at the same time. Tax lists, census records, and business directories are the most widely available survivors in this group. Using methods of quantification, aggregate sources allow the researchers to form a pro-

---

[4] Jean Chesneaux, *Pasts and Futures: Or What Is History For?* (New York: Thames and Hudson, 1978), p. 19.

file of the whole population in cross section, to compare the relation-ships among its members, and to make visible those formerly invisible groups who established no family lines, signed no masterworks of high-style craftsmanship, and, in general, left no "footprints on the sands of time." Depending on the nature and quality of such aggregative sources, they can provide a great deal of information about the life of craftsmen in colonial America.

Tax lists are, perhaps, the most obviously rewarding, particularly where they are the raw work of assessors who itemized property rather than final lists which tend to contain merely names and amounts owed. A really fruitful tax assessment, such as the Massachusetts list of 1771 (now available in computer printout), the Philadelphia County lists of 1767 and 1780, or the Federal Direct Tax of 1798 (where it still sur-vives) can enlighten us on the economic standing, shop practices, and material life of early craftsmen. Sometimes these lists give occupational status; sometimes they indicate it by enumeration of a shop or work space and the kinds of goods on hand contained therein. Since these early lists are usually compiled geographically rather than alphabeti-cally, they can also be made to reveal shop size as well as the economic spread between the master and his workmen. A carriagemaker, owner of substantial property, may be followed on the list by a couple of other men, also listed as carriagemakers but designated renters or boarders and with little real property to declare. They, in turn, may be followed by men of related occupations—trimmers or wheelwrights perhaps—but of less economic status. If the shop is quite large, there may be a day laborer or two, occupations unspecified and property nonexistent, assessed at the lowest tax provided for by law and levied on their wages rather than on their holdings. The move to the next property is indi-cated by the list of another person of property, engaged in another occu-pation, accompanied or not by another set of dependents. Some assessments provide interesting extra details on life-styles by indicating slaves held or the possession of investment property or such status-bear-ing luxuries as plate, carriages, and vacation houses. Since this infor-mation is given on a communitywide basis, it becomes possible to compare craftsmen in an overall evaluation of their position with other segments of society—merchants and farmers, for example. On the level of material life, the 1798 Federal Direct Tax offers a detailed picture of housing and property arrangement. It included building dimensions, number of stories, construction materials, number of windows (including number of lights), and outbuildings in proximity to the dwelling, with their usage and construction details also noted. As the earliest compilation of this kind of information on a common base across the entire breadth of the young Republic, this particular list allows a rare opportunity to make comparisons from state to state.

During the course of the nineteenth century, the federal census became an even more complete source for understanding the economic life of craftsmen as well as presenting a picture of their family structure and household makeup. Early state and local census lists and the earliest of the national censuses, 1790 and 1800, while they frequently list occupation, thereby making it possible to identify craftsmen, generally produce the skimpiest outline of their lives. Those local lists that enumerate only heads of households require certain dubious assumptions by the researcher to arrive at so-called conversion figures for estimating total population size. These very loose results give their tentative answers for community rather than family size. Even on this level, one need only compare total population figures for pre-Revolutionary Philadelphia produced by Carl Bridenbaugh, Sam Bass Warner, and John Alexander—they range from 23,000 to 40,000 and are based on essentially similar data—to see how dangerously misleading such extrapolations can be.[5] The early national census is also frustrating for those who seek information concerning individual craftsmen since, again, only heads of household are listed by name, and females are not even separated into the most general age divisions of over and under sixteen.

A third major type of aggregate document can be used in combination with the census lists to throw more light on otherwise elusive topics. Take, for example, the importance and extent of female artisanship in early national economic life. Business or street directories of urban areas, which began to appear in the 1790s, have long been used by the researcher in hot pursuit of the life movements of a given individual. In addition, as data fulfilling the most stringent requirements for quantifiable material, they may be used to help form a generalized picture of craftsmen as well as for tracing the single example. Philadelphia

[5] Carl Bridenbaugh, *Rebels and Gentlemen: Philadelphia in the Age of Franklin* (New York: Oxford University Press, 1962), p. 3; Sam Bass Warner, Jr., *The Private City: Philadelphia in Three Periods of Its Growth* (Philadelphia: University of Pennsylvania Press, 1968), p. 12; John K. Alexander, "The Philadelphia Numbers Game: An Analysis of Philadelphia's Eighteenth-Century Population," *Pennsylvania Magazine of History and Biography* 98 (1974): 314–24.

census lists and business directories for the last decade of the eighteenth century were examined by two University of Delaware graduate students who were investigating female occupations. Their research not only provided a model for integration of these nonliterary sources but also drew a rough outline of the craft and working orientation of Philadelphia women at the turn of the nineteenth century. They indicated what kinds of work were done by women who had to support themselves and traced, in preliminary form, the extent to which a woman's occupation was dependent on that of her husband or father. Tracing several of these documents over a period of years helped to point out the way in which women frequently maintained their husbands' businesses as a holding action until their sons were old enough to take over.[6]

One of the major flaws of the business directories as a source is that they are essentially urban based and, therefore, tend to exaggerate the urban bias of early American studies. Only 10 percent of eighteenth-century Americans lived in cities, but research on this minority far exceeds the amount of work done on the other 90 percent of the population. This aspect of the survival bias may be as serious a defect in the work of new social historians as the bias toward elite sources was for an earlier generation that worked primarily with literary sources.

The urban bias unfortunately extends to most other documents within the aggregative category. These other sources cannot be readily catalogued. Each is a fortuitous survival having escaped file consolidation or house cleaning by falling behind the cabinet, by being kept as a souvenir by some nineteenth-century antiquarian, or by being relegated to someone's attic with a lot of old papers nobody wanted to deal with at the time. These unique bits of jetsam might include such items as ship passenger lists, communion lists of a church, sheets of subscriptions (including amounts) to a local charity, or petitions to open roads or undertake other civic improvements. The possibilities are endless. One excellent example of how useful the discovery of such a cache of documents can be—equivalent perhaps to finding the entire contents of an eighteenth-century craft shop locked up in a shed and forgotten— is the jury lists for some of the wards of New York City in the second decade of the nineteenth century that were used to great advantage by

[6] Dona McDermott and Carolyn Stallings, "Female Occupations in Philadelphia, 1790–1800" (Paper presented at Artifact in American History seminar, Winterthur Museum, 1979), Office of Coordinator, Winterthur Program in Early American Culture.

Howard Rock in *Artisans of the New Republic*. While the social picture of craftsmen's lives presented in this work is largely used as a background for focusing on political participation, the reader has more confidence in the description of that life because it is drawn from broadbased documentation in the jury lists. The lists include information on age, family and household size and structure, servants and slaves, occupational status, race, and general wealth and property holding for whole neighborhoods of potential jurors.[7]

No matter how excellent and complete a source of aggregative data may appear to be, however, it must be carefully weighed and checked against as many other sources as possible to insure its objectivity. In the first place, it may be just plain wrong as Gary Nash illustrated so graphically when he described how a slip of a clerical pen inadvertently added 2,000 persons to the population of New York in 1737. Only by referring to other sources, both nonliterary and literary, was it possible to expose the error, correct it, and make a valid interpretation of population growth and its relationship to economic change. Second, the same biases toward the survival of upper-class data existing in other sources are present in aggregate data, although to a lesser degree. Those persons most likely to be skipped by the tax collector are the numerous poor who have the least to give, those least apt to appear on the census are the faceless and mobile members of the lowest socioeconomic class, and these same groups are the ones who are eliminated from business and street directories. Still, where the total population of these groups is not systematically eliminated by the nature of the document, we can obtain some information about the structure of their lives even if in the end we underestimate their numbers.[8]

The second major category of documentary sources is even more prone to the biases of survival and elitism. This category might be called one of false aggregation, since it involves bodies of data which on the surface appear to be collective but in reality are collections of individual materials. Included here are church records of baptisms, marriages, and deaths, newspaper advertisements, and court records of all sorts: land grants and deeds, wills, inventories, and estate accounts. Groups of these

---

[7] Howard B. Rock, *Artisans of the New Republic: The Tradesmen of New York City in the Age of Jefferson* (New York: New York University Press, 1979).

[8] Gary B. Nash, "The New York Census of 1737: A Critical Note on the Integration of Statistical and Literary Sources," *William and Mary Quarterly*, 3d ser., 36, no. 1 (July 1979): 428–35.

materials have been gathered together into collections either in their own time, as in the case of wills and inventories, or later, as is frequently true of newspaper ads. Once gathered they are treated as true aggregative material, and quantitative methods are employed to derive the percents, medians, and averages of—what? Certainly not of the population at any given moment, because the essence of these compilations is that they are made up of documents representing a span of time, usually many years, frequently several decades, and occasionally more than a century. Once the time factor has entered into the equation, the common base of measurement is lost.

Let us use as an example the typical collection of household inventories, so popular with scholars of material culture, as evidence for the nature of craft production, the usage and popularity of objects, and the life-style of past generations. There is no question that as a baseline for the actual existence of objects and collections of objects by specific individuals, and even as representations of the contents of particular rooms at particular times, the inventories are invaluable. They represent the closest thing to a photograph of the past that we possess; they are far more inclusive than paintings, for example. The problem is that they are so rich in evidence that we find it impossible to resist the temptation to overgeneralize from them. But the time element alone raises a host of difficulties that cannot be factored out. Some of these difficulties include changing monetary systems across time, changing perceptions of the value of things, and the changing nature and purpose of the inventories and of the people who took them. In different times, even in the same place, the standard of what items should be included may change radically. How, for example, does one compare wealth across time in eighteenth-century Philadelphia based on inventories that cease to include land holdings by the 1730s? Can one really be sure that very few beds were available because they were not regularly listed in inventories of certain places at certain times? Is it not possible that, as large and not easily moved pieces, bedsteads were considered part of the house just as stoves are today? A person who had lived in rental quarters might not have one listed as part of his possessions even though bedding might clearly form part of his personal estate.

Where inventories provide the only real evidence available, they may, through injudicious use, involve the researcher in a variety of logical fallacies, the most serious of which is a tautology. Here the hypothesis and its proof rest on exactly the same material. For example, take the proposition that the wealthier a person has become, the most likely he or she is to own a good deal of expensive porcelain. First, a wealth ranking of estates is made by total value of the inventories. The inventories are then quantified to see what percentage of each estate's value is represented by porcelain. But if porcelain is, in fact, a significant part of the estate, it will have seriously affected the original wealth structure, and the result that one finally obtains merely indicates that wealthy people had more valuable possessions, including porcelain, than poorer folk, which is why they were rated rich in the first place.

A second problem of quantifying collections that represent a long span of time is functional. In order to have enough material to work with, the time factor is collapsed, and what emerges is a static picture. An average number of tools (representing the possessions of no real person) is derived for the colonial period. But an even more important historical question might concern itself with exactly that information that the process has destroyed; namely, to what extend did the craftsman's ownership of his tools change over time? Dividing the material by shorter time periods may remove the possibility of quantification altogether. Representative samples for decades are too small, other decades seem not to list contents of shops at all, or the changing nature of the craft may make the items considered in one decade irrelevant to another.

A sophisticated and subtle method for transforming collections of inventories into truly quantifiable material was successfully attempted by Alice Hanson Jones in *American Colonial Wealth*. Three volumes of inventories—a total of 919 documents for the thirteen original colonies in 1774—were chosen by careful mathematical techniques to insure the valid nature of the sample. Jones's sampling and weighting procedures are explained in the appendix of her interpretive work *Wealth of a Nation to Be*, which analyzes the inventories of the earlier volumes. By restricting the time period of the collection and using weighting factors to correct for variation in the number of inventories from one place to another, Jones was able to eliminate the time variable as a source of error; by developing a constant standard for currency valuation throughout the colonies, she was able to measure the economic status of various groups, including artisans and craftsmen, on an accurately comparative scale. Although Jones pursued only the goal of outlining wealth as expressed in monetary values, former Winterthur fellow Nancy Carlisle outlined a method for dealing directly with the material objects listed in inventories through the use of a specially developed object classification system. Of course, the results obtained are only as good as the sample on which they rest; in this case validity is supported by the use of the Jones collection.[9]

Where the collection of such individual sources rests at least on an attempt by its compilers to be all inclusive, as is the case with inventories from early Maryland or church records in colonial New England, it may be possible to derive from them an overall picture of contemporary life. Valid examples of this process may be seen in the results of the work sponsored by St. Mary's City Commission or in Philip Greven's exploration of four generations of family experience in colonial Andover, Massachusetts. In most other cases, it is necessary to stop and ask ourselves some hard questions about why and how the collection exists at all. Land records, after all, produce conclusions only about the condition of craftsmen who actually owned, sold, or deeded land and wills and inventories about those who had property to leave; church records tell only of those who maintained membership in a religious institution; and newspaper advertisements deal with those, usually, urban craftsmen who had come to recognize and make use of this modern opportunity to enlarge their pool of customers beyond an immediate circle of acquaintances and their contacts.[10]

Finally, the most serious drawback to the category of false aggregation or, to put it more positively, of collections, lies in the very richness of its individual detail. After looking over hundreds of deeds, inventories, or newspaper ads, the researcher is apt to pluck out one to use as an example. There is no doubt that a little personal detail enlivens a page filled with tables, graphs, and other statistical generalizations. But an illustration of typicality already proved by other methods is different from a one-quotation proof, or, as David Hackett Fischer more colorfully labeled it, the "fallacy of the lonely fact." Beware of sentences or paragraphs that begin "there is no reason to consider

[9] Alice Hanson Jones, *American Colonial Wealth: Documents and Methods*, 3 vols. (New York: Arno Press, 1977); Alice Hanson Jones, *Wealth of a Naton to Be: The American Colonies on the Eve of the Revolution* (New York: Columbia University Press, 1980); Nancy Carlisle, "A Methodology for Inventory Use" (Independent study course paper, 1982), Office of Coordinator, Winterthur Program in Early American Culture.

[10] For example, see Lois Green Carr and Lorena S. Walsh, "Changing Life Styles in Colonial St. Mary's County," *Working Papers from the Regional Economic History Research Center* 1, no. 3 (1979): 73–118; Philip J. Greven, Jr., *Four Generations: Population, Land, and Family in Colonial Andover, Massachusetts* (Ithaca, N.Y.: Cornell University Press, 1970).

untypical" and then go on to cite a single newspaper advertisement showing that such and such an upholsterer was willing to rent bed hangings or curtains in the 1780s. If the examination of decades of colonial newspapers has turned up only one such ad, there is, in fact, every reason in the world to consider the craftsman, his modern grasp of the leasing phenomenon, and his emphasis on status consumerism highly untypical. The same holds true of the "typical" inventory or any other source that is really chosen, not because there are so many like it, but rather because it is the only document available that illustrates a point the researcher believes and wants to make.[11]

The third and final general category of documentary sources, which must be used in still different ways to arrive at different sorts of insights, is made up of individual materials that cover a significant period of time. Many literary forms fall within this area—diaries, letter books, and travel accounts, for example—but there are a great many nonliterary ones as well. Most important of these are the financial records of public institutions, businesses, and individuals. In structural composition, these documents are the opposite side of the aggregative data coin; that is, they deal with a single member (whether personal or institutional) of a society across time in contrast to aggregative data which provide information for a whole community at a single time. Since the individual sources possess a time dimension, they have the great advantage of being useful in investigating the all-important historical questions of continuity and change. Aggregative data require more than one source to perform this function. On the other hand, without supporting evidence from other material, the individual records operate in a kind of vacuum outside the totality of the social structure.

Nonliterary individual documents are, perhaps, most often abused by assuming that the accounting numbers in the right-hand columns can be used as measures of value. That so-and-so turned out expensive chairs worth $15 or £13 has no significance for so-and-so's standing within the community as a craftsman and is only marginally useful when compared to other chairs listed at other times in the same daybook. After all, the value of a cow in Pennsylvania went from £6 in 1779 to £120 in 1780 because of a change in the value of the pound,

[11] David Hackett Fischer, *Historians' Fallacies: Toward a Logic of Historical Thought* (New York: Harper & Row, 1970), pp. 109–10.

not in the value of the cow relative to other cows and to other items
appearing on the tax list.

When supporting information from other categories of documents
is available, however, the nonliterary documents have a special role to
play in illuminating craftsmen of the past. They help to enrich the
socioeconomic analysis of the individual within the larger environment, since they involve transactions between the record keeper and
other members of the community. A seminar paper by one of my former students may be used to illustrate a point. In her study of the business records of Rea and Johnston Company of Boston, Susan Mackiewicz
was able to show in great detail the way in which the economic function
of a firm of decorative painting artisans was directly affected by the
political events and economic conditions in that major city between
1773 and 1802. Primary and secondary materials on the general situation were combined to form a backdrop against which the craftsman's
work would be studied. Quantitative analysis of the kinds of work performed and the amount of profit it produced allowed measurement among
three different types of work. The first, staple production, included house,
shop, and ship painting. The second, decorative-utilitarian jobs, added
material "beyond necessity" to the painting of a floor or a wall as in, for
example, the addition of a trompe l'oeil dog to the floor or a curtain to
the wall. The third, suprautilitarian work, covered items which in
themselves filled ceremonial or status roles rather than necessary ones.
When Boston was evacuated in 1775/76 house painting dropped 84
percent; in 1777/78, when privateers were being outfitted at the docks,
ship painting expanded from 15 percent of the firm's total business to
86 percent; and in the healthier economic climate of the years between
1793 and 1802, suprautilitarian work grew from 4.2 percent to 32 percent of total production. These are just a few of the conclusions drawn
from this remarkable work. Nowhere has the direct relationship between
the overall condition of the larger economic sphere and the working life
of a producer-artisan, whose numbers comprised up to 40 percent of
Boston's total population, been so clearly revealed. For the historian,
the study suggests methods for approaching the large and fascinating
questions of political process; for example, relationships between day-
to-day economic life and political participation and radicalization. For
the student of material culture, a combination of documentary evidence with artifactual survivals provides an opportunity for relating value,

technique, and style to employer-employee job division and shop practices. A good deal is revealed about material and marketing.[12]

The important thing to remember, however, is that comparable
studies must be done on many other specific cases before the model
becomes acceptable as more than an illustration. The transformation of
a particular craftsman into a representative of his class can never be
achieved from the single source, even when supported by other evidence about the same individual. And when the creation of generalization is accomplished by using several documents taken from different
individuals perceived as "typical," a totally false picture is obtained, one
that is not only untrue to the universal but irrelevant to the specific as
well. No degree of generalization can be created by combining one
man's diary with someone else's account book, the probate record of
still another, and, perhaps, to lend a spurious air of reality, pictures of
yet another's shop. One does violence to every aspect of historical unity:
time, place, and person. Again Fischer has named this not uncommon
procedure. Under the category of fallacies of statistical nonsense it appears
as the fallacy of shifting bases.[13]

The sloppy combination of noncompatible sources does not advance
the goal of generalization for either the expert in material culture, who
uses history to illustrate the background of the artifact and its makers,
or the historian who seeks to illustrate history by the inclusion of artifactual study. No document or artifact can speak to us a cappella. Each
requires a supporting chorus of other materials for contrast and comparison. The ways in which such a chorus can be formed and the kinds
of documents that go into its makeup are as varied as the goal of the
researcher and the surviving documents that pertain to the answers he
seeks. This paper has discussed the advantages and disadvantages of three
distinct types of nonliterary documents out of the many different possible sources. Within these categories are vast numbers of survivals, each
of which must be adapted to the special procedures most likely to produce general results. Even when carefully used these materials are not
enough. The artifacts themselves, the literary manuscript sources, and

---

[12] Susan Mackiewicz, "A Case Study in Early American Economics: The Rea and
Johnston Company of Boston, 1773–1802" (Paper presented at Artifact in American History seminar, Winterthur Museum, 1979), Office of Coordinator, Winterthur Program
in Early American Culture.
[13] Fischer, *Historians' Fallacies*, p. 117.

published material from the period under consideration must all go into the equation as well. Only through this synthesis can we hope to understand the craftsman, his world, and his production in a way that transcends the individual experience.

Artisans and Craftsmen:
A Historical Perspective
Thomas J. Schlereth

As Carl Bridenbaugh suggested almost thirty years ago, "crafts—and the artisans who practice them—played an important part in early American life; even more than historians have generally supposed. Next to husbandmen, craftsmen comprised the largest segment of the colonial population; whereas the former made up about eighty per cent of the people, artisans constituted about eighteen per cent." While Bridenbaugh's statistics pertained almost solely to the white, male, adult population, his claim still commands our attention three decades after the publication of his short, but seminal, study of the colonial craftsman. [1]

As the study of the colonial craftsman provided the rationale and focus for the papers, commentaries, and discussions of the twenty-third Winterthur conference, so the study of the *studies* of the colonial craftsman is the subject of this bibliographical survey. Fully cognizant of Alfred Young's admonitions about the dangers of historiographical "mailboy pigeonholing" and John Higham's caveats regarding the "occupational narcissism of the historiographer," I maintain that a brief

For assistance in the preparation of this essay, the author wishes to thank Alfred F. Young, Arlene Palmer Schwind, Charles F. Hummel, and Howard B. Rock.
[1] Carl Bridenbaugh, *The Colonial Craftsman* (1950; reprint ed., Chicago: University of Chicago Press, Phoenix Books, 1966), p. 1. Bridenbaugh offered token acknowledgment of colonial America's women artisans (pp. 105–8), but for a more extended treatment, see Frances Magnes, "Women Shopkeepers, Tavernkeepers and Artisans in Colonial Philadelphia" (Ph.D. diss., University of Pennsylvania, 1955); and Linda Grant Depauw, *Remember the Ladies: Women in America, 1750–1815* (New York: Viking Press, 1976).

intellectual history of the scholarship on the craftsman can afford us a useful perspective by which to evaluate several lines of inquiry that have emerged on this topic in the past half century and that continue to inform the field today. We who use the historical perspective on others assuredly ought also to apply it to our own past. For, as L. P. Curtis reminded us, we are all toilers in the "historian's workshop," laboring at what Marc Bloch aptly labeled the "historian's craft."[2]

Permit me to state here at the outset what I have deliberately excluded from my analysis. Although husbandmen were occasionally called "artisans of the fields" and "craftsmen of the soil," no assessment of the writing about their role will be proposed here. Also, a more comprehensive essay should give a broader account of the French, Spanish, and African colonial and regional traditions in artisan research.[3] Finally, my evidence has been primarily books, monographs, and journal literature written by an assortment of historians. I recognize that such a singular angle of vision neglects a significant body of data: that is, the museum historian's "curatorial publications" that have been conceptualized, researched, and mounted as gallery exhibitions or museum installations tracing the history of the early American artisan. Merrimack Valley Textile Museum's *Homespun to Factory Made* and Brockton Art Center's *The Wrought Covenant* are recent examples of this important genre of historical research which is published in a three-dimensional format.[4] A comparative study should be done on what might

[2] Alfred F. Young, *The American Revolution: Explorations in the History of American Radicalism* (DeKalb: Northern Illinois University Press, 1976), p. xiv; John Higham, *Writing American History: Essays on Modern Scholarship* (Bloomington: Indiana University Press, 1970), pp. ix, 157; L. P. Curtis, *The Historian's Workshop: Original Essays by Sixteen Historians* (New York: Alfred A. Knopf, 1970); Marc Bloch, *The Historian's Craft* (New York: Alfred A. Knopf, 1953). The historian-as-artisan motif recurs in a historiographical survey by Richard E. Beringer, *Historical Analysis: Contemporary Approaches to Clio's Craft* (New York: John Wiley & Sons, 1978).

[3] On the impact of French culture on artisanry in America, consult Detroit Institute of Arts, *The French in America, 1520–1880* (Detroit, 1951); and Antoine Roy, *Les lettres, les sciences et les arts en Canada sous le regime français* (Paris: Jouve, 1930); George Kubler and Martin Soria, *Art and Architecture in Spain and Portugal and Their American Dominions, 1500–1800* (Baltimore: Johns Hopkins University Press, 1959), provided a solid introduction to crafts practiced in the Spanish tradition. John Michael Vlach, *The Afro-American Tradition in Decorative Arts* (Cleveland: Cleveland Museum of Art, 1978), is superb in its context; and still useful is Leonard P. Stravicky, "Negro Craftsmanship in America," *American Historical Review* 54 (1949): 315–25.

[4] E. McClung Fleming, "The Period Room as a Curatorial Publication," *Museum News* 60, no. 10 (June 1972): 39–43; Merrimack Valley Textile Museum, *Homespun to Factory Made: Woolen Textiles in America, 1776–1876* (North Andover, Mass., 1977);

be termed the historiography of the early American craftsman in history museums in contrast to the historiography of that craftsman in history books.

Three types of investigators wrote those books: academic historians, museum historians, and avocational historians. By academic historians I simply mean those men and women who, since the beginning of institutional study of American history in the country's universities in the 1880s, have "done history" in the academy. An example of such a scholar interested in the American artisan is Thomas Jefferson Wertenbaker who, for most of his career, taught at Princeton University. For the museum historian (such as C. Malcom Watkins at the Smithsonian Institution), the historical society or the historical museum provided an institutional identity. Henry Mercer, author of *Ancient Carpenter's Tools* (1929) and other early studies on American tools, is my prototype for the avocational historian. Mercer is an example of a man who made the tile business his living and craftsman history his life. Widespread interest in the personalities, the processes, and the products of the early American craftsman has preoccupied all three research cadres for the past half century; appropriately, all three constituencies were represented at the Winterthur conference on the craftsman in early America and are, to various degrees, represented in this volume's essays.

Such a diversity of scholars and scholarship has, understandably, prompted some confusion as to nomenclature. No one has been able to agree, for example, which is the more proper or the more precise term, *craftsman* or *artisan.* Essayists in the following studies will use both. To muddle the issue still further, who are tradesmen and mechanics? Are they the same as craftsmen and artisans? In this volume Barbara Ward speaks of Boston silversmiths (she also calls them craftsmen), but in *The London Tradesman* such individuals are called "goldsmiths, the most genteel of any in the Mechanic Way."[5]

To put the issue another way, what do Marlowe's Faust, William Sawyer (a member of the Philadelphia Carpenter's Company in 1772), the Choice Tool Set described on page 533 of the 1902 Sears, Roebuck catalogue, and the second rank earned by members of the Horizon Club

---

Robert Blair St. George, *The Wrought Covenant: Source Materials for the Study of Craftsmen and Community in Southeastern New England, 1620–1700* (Brockton, Mass.: Brockton Art Center, Fuller Memorial, 1979).

[5] R. Campbell, *The London Tradesman* (1747; reprint ed., Newton Abbot: David and Charles, 1969), pp. 141–42.

of the Camp Fire Girls of America have in common? Answer: Each is called artisan. Or, what links an eighteenth-century Boston shoemaker named Elizabeth Shaw, Gustave Stickley's furniture, and the stationary drill press found on page 742 of the 1979 Sears, Roebuck catalogue? Answer: All are craftsmen.

In seventeenth-, eighteenth-, and nineteenth-century parlance, as in twentieth-century book titles and conference programs, the terms *artisan, craftsman, tradesman,* and *mechanic* are frequently used interchangeably. Is this accurate? It has been suggested that there is a progression of usage that would accord *artisan* more popularity in the seventeenth and early eighteenth centuries, *craftsman* continually in vogue from the eighteenth century onward, with *mechanic* gaining ascendancy in the late eighteenth and early nineteenth centuries. In any event, a tentative consensus seems to exist among modern scholars that during most of eighteenth-century American history, the terms *artisan, mechanic,* and *craftsman* are roughly synonymous.[6] I will also use them.

In craftsman research, some scholars blithely assume that the subjects about which they write—artisans or craftsmen—are individuals of the same social, economic, political, religious, or cultural background; others, such as Charles Olton, spend a book chapter attempting to define what they mean by an artisan or a craftsman in the particular time (for example, Revolutionary America, 1765–83) and the particular place (for example, Philadelphia) they are investigating. In addition to locating the craftsman/artisan within definite chronological and geographical limits, a definition should also include (1) occupational identity, (2) technological sophistication, (3) level of economic wealth, and (4) rank in social status. In order to give some precision to their discussions of occupational identity, scholars such as Olton, Stephanie Wolf, Edwin Tunis, Warren Roberts, and Howard Rock have prepared classification systems wherein distinctions are made, for instance, between furniture crafts and forging crafts, between comb crafts and construction crafts.[7]

[6] Bridenbaugh, *Colonial Craftsman,* p. 1. Contemporary scholar Herbert Gutman also adheres to the artisan/craftsman synonymity; see his essay, "Work, Culture, and Society in Industrializing America, 1815–1919," *American Historical Review* 78, no. 3 (June 1973): 558.

[7] Charles S. Olton, *Artisans for Independence: Philadelphia Mechanics and the American Revolution* (Syracuse, N.Y.: Syracuse University Press, 1975), pp. 7–18, 4–5; Stephanie G. Wolf, "Artisans and the Occupational Structure of an Industrial Town: 18th-Century Germantown, Pa.," *Working Papers from the Regional Economic History*

However, the major methodological difficulties inherent in devising an adequate classification system must be recognized, as Michael Katz and Thomas Smith deftly point out in two studies on the techniques of reconstructing occupational structures. Katz and Smith question, for example, whether one should define artisanry or craftsmanship in a fairly narrow sense, say, limiting it rigidly to hand production alone, to the craftsman's production of the entire object, or to a production process that is wholly controlled by the workman.[8]

Ascertaining the exact economic and social status of the artisan, craftsman, or mechanic has bedeviled many a modern historian of colonial America. A degree of consensus, however, seems to exist as to what the eighteenth-century craftsman was *not*: part of the preindustrial, preproletariat lower class of unskilled laborers (for example, sailors, free blacks, many new immigrants, servants, slaves) who lived solely by manual work, did not own their own tools, moved readily from job to job (and often from city to city), were excluded from craft organizations, and, in general, could not vote. On the other hand, the master-craftsman population in most colonial American cities constituted a broad and indeterminate stratum ranging from master artisans in highly skilled trades like instrumentmaking and silversmithing to the "inferior sort" of craftsmen such as coopers and soap boilers. Conscious of their social rank below the merchants, government officials, clergy, and attorneys, but clearly above the status of journeymen and apprentices, most artisans apparently were able to escape dire want, acquire some property, educate their children, and take part in politics. Moreover, as Rock argues, master craftsmen shared several social and economic experiences that gave them common cause and identity whether they worked in Boston, New York, or Philadelphia. Such experiences included an apprenticeship of some sort, a shared mode of functional dress, often a clearly differentiated workers' neighborhood in which to live within a city, fra-

---

Research Center 1, no. 1 (1977): 33–56; Edwin Tunis, *Colonial Craftsmen and the Beginnings of American Industry* (Cleveland and New York: World Publishing Co., 1965), pp. 7–8; Warren Roberts, "Material Culture: Folk Crafts," in *Folklore and Folklife: An Introduction*, ed. Richard Dorson (Chicago: University of Chicago Press, 1972), pp. 242–49; Howard B. Rock, *Artisans of the New Republic: The Tradesmen of New York City in the Age of Jefferson* (New York: New York University Press, 1979), p. 13.

[8] Michael Katz, "Occupational Classification in History," *Journal of Interdisciplinary History* 3, no. 1 (Summer 1972): 63–88; Thomas Smith, "Reconstructing Occupational Structures: The Case of the Ambiguous Artisans," *Historical Methods Newsletter* 8, no. 1 (June 1975): 34–46.

ternal craft-oriented societies and clubs devised as social and recreational outlets but which periodically became the forum for voicing political and economic grievances, and, finally, a definite political identity in that "mechanics were without question the single group to whom most [local] election appeals were addressed."[9]

Interconnected with the methodological issues of terminology and definition is the question of historical periodization in artisan/craftsman studies. When does the age of the early American craftsman begin? Was it with the early achievements of the native Americans, with the first arrival of Europeans, or only when the first native-born artisans reach their majority? Even more difficult to pin down is a terminal date for the era of the American craftsman: Does it peak, as Charles Hummel has argued, around 1760 and then enter "the time of its rapid decline" until the 1840s? Or, can we identify, as Kenneth Ames claimed, "unsung artisans at work in American industry thoughout the nineteenth century"? Of course, the National Conference of American Craftsmen and the American Crafts Council, through publications such as *Craft Horizons,* labor to persuade us that the great American artisan is still very much alive and running two-harness looms and potter's kick wheels all over modern suburbia.[10] The cultural history of the craftsman in the contemporary United States is, I propose, an important research area to which sociologists, social psychologists, museologists, and cultural historians might profitably turn since an abundance of literature on the topic has surfaced in pre- and postbicentennial America.[11] Contemporary crafts have also infiltrated the college curriculum, and artisans now practice in the academy. For example, Boston University's accredited Program in Artisanry offers courses in the traditional crafts of metals, wood, ceramics, and textiles. To successful apprentices in the program, the university awards a certificate of mastery. So prolific

[9] Rock, *Artisans of the New Republic,* p. 9.

[10] Charles F. Hummel, *With Hammer in Hand: The Dominy Craftsmen of East Hampton, New York* (Charlottesville: University Press of Virginia, 1968), p. 3; Kenneth L. Ames, "Meaning in Artifacts: Hall Furnishings in Victorian America," *Journal of Interdisciplinary History* 9, no. 1 (Summer 1978): 36. For a rapid survey of the role of these organizations, see Patricia Raymer, "The Scene Today," in *The Craftsman in America* (Washington, D.C.: National Geographic Society, 1975), pp. 164–75.

[11] See, for instance, Julie Hall, *Tradition and Change: The New American Craftsman* (New York: E. P. Dutton, 1977); Edward Lucie-Smith, *The World of the Makers: Today's Master Craftsmen and Craftswomen* (New York: Paddington Press, 1974); and Martin Lawrence, *The Compleat Craftsman: Yesterday's Handicrafts for Today's Family* (New York: Universe Books, 1979).

have craft courses become in modern America that the American Crafts Council now publishes an annual directory of craft courses. [12]

I raise these modern instances only to point up the complexity that the historian faces in deciding upon the end of a historical period. When, for example, does craft production stop and industrial production begin in America? Should this be the chronological watershed by which to differentiate the artisan in colonial America from the worker in Victorian America? Obviously, such a transition does not take place simultaneously in all crafts nor with the same velocity, as we see in this volume's essays by William Mulligan on shoemakers and by Susan Myers on potters. Advanced mechanization of craftsmanship came in different ways and at different times. Hand coopers, as Herbert Gutman has documented, continued to work in distinctly preindustrial patterns well beyond Gutman's cutoff date of 1843 as the advent of American industrialization. Roberts, an American folk-crafts scholar, thinks that in most areas of the United States it was not "the progress of manufacturing but the progress of transportation" that terminated the traditional craft era. "As long as transportation costs were high, the purchaser who lived some distance away from a factory could often buy an item made locally by a craftsman more cheaply than the manufactured item. During the second half of the nineteenth century, cheap and efficient transportation spelled doom for the age-old system of craft production wherein the craftsman produced items as needed for his own neighbors." In patiently sorting out the intricate chronology of different craftsmen's responses to industrialization, we need to recognize, as have British labor historians such as Sidney Pollard, E. P. Thompson, and Eric Hobsbawm, that such a transition often meant nothing short of "a severe restructuring of working habits—new disciplines and new incentives" whereby "a society of peasants, craftsmen, and versatile labourers became a society of modern industrial workers."[13] In short, considerable careful

---

[12] *Craft Courses* (available from American Crafts Council, 44 W. 53rd St., New York, N.Y. 10019); also consult John Coyne and Tom Herbert, *By Hand: A Guide to Schools and Careers in Crafts* (New York: E. P. Dutton, 1975).

[13] Gutman, "Work, Culture, and Society," p. 559; Roberts, "Material Culture," p. 237; Sidney Pollard, "Factory Discipline in the Industrial Revolution," *Economic History Review* 16, no. 2 (June 1963): 254–71; Sidney Pollard, *Genesis of Modern Management* (Cambridge: At the University Press, 1965); E. P. Thompson, "Time, Work-Discipline, and Industrial Capitalism," *Past & Present*, no. 38 (December 1967): 56–97; E. P. Thompson, *The Making of the English Working Class* (New York: Pantheon Books, 1963); Eric J. Hobsbawm, *Labouring Men: Studies in the History of Labour* (London: Weidenfeld and Nicolson, 1964).

research needs to be done in charting the post eighteenth-century evolution (and, sometimes, extinction) of the assorted craft activities we label colonial or early American.

Most scholarship since the Encyclopédistes (whom I consider to be the first significant historians of the transatlantic artisan) has, with a few exceptions, primarily focused on the American craftsman in the eighteenth century.[14] Since Diderot and his fellow philosophes first published their detailed entries, ranging from bookbinder to wainwright, in some seventeen volumes containing illustrations of 1,700 working figures and 1,100 types of equipment, a substantial literature (itself evidential of the the printer's craft) has described, romanticized, classified, and analyzed the craftsman and his works. Since I know that I cannot conquer this corpus, I propose to divide this published material, like Caesar's Gaul, into three parts; that is, I am persuaded that the significant contours of American craftsman scholarship can be separated into three major historiographical configurations depending on which facet of the artisan's life the historian decides to give primary emphasis in his research design, in his interpretation of his data, and in his mode of communicating that data's significance to others (table 1).

In brief, these three approaches consider, first, the craftsman as principally a creative *artiste*, producing an identifiable object, often highly valued as either classic, folk, or vernacular art; second, the craftsman as participant in a specific craft tradition, wherein he practices his *artisanry* by means of his mental and manual acumen aided by an assortment of tools; and, third, the craftsman as historical *actor* in society, principally as a citizen and as a consumer. This typology can be further explained by noting that in the craftsman-as-artiste tradition it is the *works* of the craftsman that the historian primarily chronicles, whereas in the craftsman-and-his-artisanry tradition it is principally the *working* of the craftsman that is studied, and while in the craftsman-as-historical-actor tradition it is the craftsman as a *worker* that primarily concerns the researcher. I recognize that the symmetry in these three categories of the craftsman and his products, his technological processes, and his social and political involvements cannot accommodate all the published scholarship in the field. Like any abstraction, my analytical schema cannot accurately characterize the nuances of craftsman history. The

[14] As early as 1950, Bridenbaugh claimed that "the great age of the colonial craftsman began with the eighteenth century" (*Colonial Craftsman*, p. 6).

TABLE 1. Artisan and Craftsman Scholarship in America, 1876–1976: Three

	A. Researching the product (Emphasis on the work)
Biographical emphasis	Craftsman practicing his *art*
Sociological focus	*Artiste* creating artifacts
Disciplinary divisions	Research by art/decorative arts historians
Pioneering scholars	Irving W. Lyon
Serial publications	*Antiques, EAIA Chronicle*
Publication genres	Museum exhibition catalogues/monographs
Research centers	Winterthur/Cooperstown programs
Professional organizations	Decorative Arts Society/Society of Architectural Historians
Bibliographical digests	Whitehill, *Arts in Early American History* (1965)
Iconographic symbols	Copley, *Paul Revere*, ca. 1764

NOTE.—Both the categories and their examples proposed in this diagram merely can indicate.

best work done in any of the three traditions singled out for study has almost always involved components of the other two traditions as well. Artifact-centered studies of any value deal with process because an understanding of how an object is made is vital to knowing whether the object in question is what it purports to be. Benno Forman's work on furniture and furniture craftsmanship is an outstanding example of what can be learned about craft techniques from a direct study of the furniture.[15] His scholarship should rightly be included in both of the first categories. The issue of overlap can also be noted when discussing a publication such as *Winterthur Portfolio* which has been consciously not included in any one of the three categories under representative

[15] Benno M. Forman, "Delaware Valley 'Crookt Foot' and Slat-Back Chairs: The Fussell-Savery Connection," *Winterthur Portfolio* 15, no. 1 (Spring 1980): 41–64; Benno M. Forman, "German Influences in Pennsylvania Furniture," in Scott T. Swank et al., *Arts of the Pennsylvania Germans*, ed. Catherine E. Hutchins (New York: W. W. Norton, 1983); see also his forthcoming publication on seventeenth-century furniture.

Historiographical Traditions

B. Researching the process (Emphasis on the working)	C. Researching the person (Emphasis on the worker)
Craftsman practicing his *artisanry*	Craftsman participating in societal *activity*
Technician working in a craft tradition	*Citizen/consumer*-involved communal life
Research by historians of technology/folkways	Research by political/economic/social historians
Henry Chapman Mercer	Thomas Jefferson Wertenbaker
Technology and Culture	*William and Mary Quarterly*
Craft demonstration/exhibition catalogues and film	Monograph/biography
Smithsonian/Hagley programs	Institute of Early American History and Culture
Society for History of Technology	Organization of American Historians
Hindle, *Technology in Early America* (1966)	Rock, *Artisans of the New Republic* (1979)
Four Tradesmen, ca. 1825	Seal, New York Mechanicks Society, 1791

suggest a *pattern* of a historiography that is far more detailed than this simple outline

serial publications because it rightly should be listed under all three divisions. As a hardbound annual from 1964 to 1979, *Winterthur Porfolio* printed articles with strong emphasis on the type of work identified in categories A and B. Now as a triannual journal, the serial publishes excellent scholarship in all three types of craftsman history.

Hence the reader should remember throughout the following analysis that historiographical reality is never as compartmentalized as the table might suggest. I have resorted to three categories solely for heuristic purposes. The divisions are only typologies of emphases, not taxonomies of dogmas. Like any typologies, they were fashioned to serve the objectives of their creator. In this case, that purpose was simply to analyze the major ways in which researchers have conceptualized their approaches to the study of the American craftsman over the past 100 years. A survey of the popular and professional literature suggested that there have been three such major emphases.

THE CRAFTSMAN AND HIS PRODUCTS

The first historians to pay serious attention to the early American craftsman were those who collected his products. A zealous cadre of antiquarians, preservationists, librarians, and private collectors—avocational historians I have called them—sought to identify who had made what, when, and where. They believed, as Scripture testifies, that "by their works you shall know them." Much like their counterparts of a century earlier who, during the first phase of the American natural-history movement, collected every new species for their cabinets of curiosities, these object-oriented gentlemen-scholars focused their energies on the discovery, description, and classification of the artifacts of early American craftsman history. Richard Saunders and William Dulaney have begun to document this late nineteenth- and early twentieth-century interest in the antique and the collectible which nurtured works such as Irving W. Lyon's *Colonial Furniture of New England* (1892), Wallace Nutting's *Furniture of the Pilgrim Century* (1921) and *Furniture Treasury* (1928–33), Luke Vincent Lockwood's *Colonial Furniture in America* (1913), E. Alfred Jones's *The Old Silver of American Churches* (1913), J. B. Kerfoot's *American Pewter* (1924), and Fiske Kimball's *Domestic Architecture of the American Colonies and of the Early Republic* (1922). This generation of patrician proponents of American art found in American objects an inspiring chronicle that stirred their pride. "These things," wrote Wendell and Jane Garrett, "buttressed the structure of the [nineteenth- and early twentieth-century] culture of liberty, progress and nationality." Sociologists Cesar Grana and C. Wright Mills suggested a parallel rationale when arguing that "the destruction of local traditions and the assault upon the past perpetuated by industrialization and world-wide modernization seems to make large numbers of people susceptible to an appetite for relics of pre-industrial life."[16] In addition

[16]Richard H. Saunders, "Collecting American Decorative Arts in New England," *Antiques*, pt. 1, "1793–1876," 109, no. 5 (May 1976): 996–1003; pt. 2, "1876–1910," 110, no. 4 (October 1976): 754–63; William L. Dulaney, "Wallace Nutting: Collector and Entrepreneur," in *American Furniture and Its Makers: Winterthur Portfolio 13*, ed. Ian M. G. Quimby (Chicago: University of Chicago Press, 1979), pp. 47–60; Wendell D. Garrett and Jane N. Garrett, "A Bibliography of the Arts in Early American History," in Walter Muir Whitehill, *The Arts in Early American History* (Chapel Hill: University of North Carolina Press, 1965), p. 37; Cesar Grana, *Fact and Symbol* (New York: Oxford University Press, 1971), p. 98; C. Wright Mills, *White Collar* (New York: Oxford University Press, 1951), pp. 220–24.

to an expanded, if often filiopietistic, interest in colonial craft products, fin de siècle America also witnessed cultural developments such as the colonial revival in architecture and the decorative arts, an unprecedented proliferation of local historical societies, an expansion of historic preservation activities, and, of course, the spread of the arts and crafts movement.[17] Although the research has yet to be done, it seems plausible that the manifestos and manufacts of, say, William L. Price, Isaac Scott, Elbert Hubbard, and Gustav Stickley may have had some indirect influence on the pioneering collecting and writing of the avocational historians on the colonial craftsman and his works.[18]

Be that as it may, these early researchers gathered an enormous amount of data on the "things" of early American life. With certain exceptions, however, their effort was primarily an aesthetic evaluation of the porringer, the highboy, or the decanter. The object of craft became the objet d'art. Such studies, ranging from erudite, highly disciplined evaluations by connoisseurs and museum curators to loosely arranged catalogues by antique enthusiasts with little knowledge of the history of craft technology, flourished from 1876 to 1924—from the opening of the United States Centennial Exposition in Philadelphia to the opening of the Metropolitan Museum of Art's American Wing in New York. As the Garretts suggest, the fault of that period "was the fault of insularity, of separation from the main currents of American historiography. It was a fault, begun not in carelessness or haste, but in a quest for 'some good old golden age.' "[19] Thus historical associationism, romantic nationalism, and a celebration of craft products almost solely as the artistic achievements of gifted individuals rather than the artifacts of a particular society tended to characterize this early trend in artisan research.

The best work in this historiographical tradition usually dealt with those products (silver, furniture, glass, ceramics) that have had the highest monetary value with American collectors. Such research began to appear

[17] For this background, see William Rhoads, *The Colonial Revival* (New York: Garland Publishing Co., 1977); Charles Hosmer, *Presence of the Past: A History of the Preservation Movement in the United States before Williamsburg* (New York: G. P. Putnam's Sons, 1965); and Robert Judson Clark, ed., *The Arts and Crafts Movement in America, 1876–1916* (Princeton: Princeton University Press, 1972).

[18] Walter Muir Whitehill, "Boston Artists and Craftsmen at the Opening of the Twentieth Century," *New England Quarterly* 50, no. 3 (September 1977): 387–408; Charles F. Montgomery, "Classics and Collectibles: American Antiques as History and Art," *Art News* 76, no. 9 (November 1977): 126–36.

[19] Garrett and Garrett, "Bibliography," p. 36.

in Homer Eaton Keyes's influential journal, the *Magazine Antiques*, founded in 1922 and my nominee for the most representative (and most carefully edited) serial publication of the craftsman "product" school. The school gained further impetus by the opening of the two major historical reconstructions of the 1920s, Colonial Williamsburg and Greenfield Village, and by the "flowering of American folk art" collecting in the 1930s. Holger Cahill's *American Folk Sculpture: The Work of Eighteenth- and Nineteenth-Century Craftsmen*, an exhibition catalogue published by Newark Museum in 1931, might be cited as the opening manifesto in a decade that concluded with the work of the Federal Art Project's Index of American Design. Cahill's early work betrays the tendency of so many subsequent folk art scholars to celebrate folk *art* rather than the folk *artist*, a tendency thoroughly exposed and analyzed by Kenneth Ames in *Beyond Necessity*.[20] A similar tendency underlay the Index of American Design in that it recruited unemployed contemporary artists to record over 15,000 examples of the work (furniture, textiles, ceramics, glassware) of earlier "artists." In 1950, Erwin Christensen published a selection of the index's most vivid color renderings in a lavishly illustrated book, *A Treasury of American Design*, a coffee-table volume depicting American crafts but no American craftsmen. In our own decade, Clarence Hornung has similarly "treasured" the work of the index and other American "popular folk arts and crafts." The recently published ten-volume microfiche edition of the entire index, along with multiple finding aids, attests to the continued viability of the *artiste* tradition of artisan historiography.[21]

In the past thirty years, however, the scholarship in this mode has become increasingly sophisticated in methodology, in the scrupulous use of evidence, and in greater receptivity to the techniques of other disciplines besides art history and its progeny, the history of the decorative arts. Work by Charles van Ravenswaay, Walter Muir Whitehill, Anthony Garvan, and Charles Montgomery exemplifies what might be

---

[20] Beatrice T. Rumford, "Uncommon Art of the Common People: A Review of Trends in the Collecting and Exhibiting of American Folk Art," in *Perspectives on American Folk Art*, ed. Ian M. G. Quimby and Scott T. Swank (New York: W. W. Norton, 1980), pp. 13–53; Kenneth L. Ames, *Beyond Necessity: Art in the Folk Tradition* (New York: W. W. Norton, 1977).

[21] Erwin O. Christensen, *The Index of American Design* (New York: Macmillan Publishing Co., 1950); Clarence Hornung, *A Treasury of American Design* (New York: Harry N. Abrams, 1972); Sandra Shaffer Tinkham, *The Consolidated Catalog to the Index of American Design* (Teaneck: Somerset House, 1979).

the origins of a "new" decorative arts history. Such researchers recognize, as Whitehill so poignantly put it, that "no amount of aesthetic incest of sitting and gazing at a chair or a piece of silver will tell one anything of great value about the object beyond its existence."[22]

Younger historians—Arlene Palmer Schwind, Charles Brownell, and Barbara Ward—and their recent scholarship (on glass, architecture, and silver respectively) have continued this revisionist critique. Increasingly cognizant that much of the data with which material cultural historians must work is only the most elite or the most expensive of the past craftwork, they have been as interested in the technical role of the craftsman as they have been in his artistic work and its provenance, influences, and imitators.[23]

THE CRAFTSMAN AND HIS PROCESSES

Such scholarship, emphasizing as it has the processes of past craftsmanship, takes particular interest in the tools, skills, methods of production, and working conditions of housewrights and potters, ironmasters and pewterers, cabinetmakers and cordwainers. Understandably such research has often been seen as a branch of economic history, folk-life or ethnographic studies, or the history of technology. The earliest work in this second tradition of craftsman historiography was done by avoca-

[22]Whitehill, *Arts in History*, p. 22; Charles van Ravenswaay, *The Arts and Architecture of German Settlements in Missouri: A Survey of a Vanishing Culture* (Columbia: University of Missouri Press, 1977); Walter Muir Whitehill, *Dumbarton Oaks: The History of a Georgetown House and Garden, 1800–1866* (Cambridge, Mass.: Harvard University Press, Belknap Press, 1967); Anthony Garvan, *Architecture and Town Planning in Colonial Connecticut* (New Haven: Yale University Press, 1951); George B. Tatum, *Philadelphia Georgian: The City House of Samuel Powel and Some of Its Eighteenth-Century Neighbors* (Middletown, Conn.: Wesleyan University Press, 1976); Charles F. Montgomery, *American Furniture: The Federal Period* (New York: Viking Press, 1966).

[23]In addition to their essays below, one should also consult Arlene Palmer, "Glass Production in Eighteenth-Century America: The Wistarburgh Enterprise," in *Winterthur Portfolio 11*, ed. Ian M. G. Quimby (Charlottesville: University Press of Virginia, 1975), pp. 75–101; Dwight P. Lanmon and Arlene M. Palmer, "Jack Frederick Amelung and the New Bremen Glassmanufactory," *Journal of Glass Studies* 18 (1976): 9–136; and Barbara McLean Ward and Gerald W. R. Ward, *Silver in American Life* (New York: American Federation of the Arts, 1979). See also Ian M. G. Quimby, "Apprenticeship in Colonial Philadelphia" (M.A. thesis, University of Delaware, 1963); and Martha Gandy Fales, *Joseph Richardson and Family, Philadelphia Silversmiths* (Middletown, Conn.: Wesleyan University Press, 1974).

tional historians such as Henry Mercer. His *Ancient Carpenters' Tools* (first published by Bucks County Historical Society in 1929), for example, continues to be a major reference work on woodworkers' tools. From Mercer (the subject of an important study by Donna Rosenstein) a line of historiographical lineage and methodological proclivity extends forward to popular books by Scott Graham Williamson, Edwin Tunis, and Eric Sloane and to detailed scholarship by modern historians such as Frank H. Wildrung, Robert Woodbury, Brooke Hindle, Merritt Roe Smith, and Charles Hummel. *Tools of the Woodworker* by Ralph Hodgkinson further demonstrates the thriving contemporary interest in this segment of craftsman research.[24]

Along with a fascination with American tools—particularly woodworking tools and tools made of wood—craftsmanship historians have become increasingly interested in artisan technical skills and modes of production.[25] In addition to careful examination of the extant workmanship, one way to explore the possible levels of competence and efficiency of early American craftsmen is to analyze trade primers and craft handbooks as did Benno Forman and Charles Montgomery in the reprint edition of Joseph Moxon's 1703 *Mechanick Exercises*. Another type of data gathered by researchers, particularly from the 1920s through the 1940s, would be what I call sourcebooks in regional arts and crafts. Beginning in 1927 with Henry Wyckoff Belknap's and George Francis Dow's works on New England craftsmen,[26] numerous researchers in

[24] Donna G. Rosenstein, "Historic Human Tools: Henry Chapman Mercer and His Collection, 1897–1930" (M.A. thesis, University of Delaware, 1977); Scott Graham Williamson, *The American Craftsman* (New York: Crown Publishers, 1940); Tunis, *Colonial Craftsmen*; Eric Sloane, *A Museum of Early American Tools* (New York: Funk and Wagnalls, 1962); Frank H. Wildrung, *Woodworking Tools of Shelburne Museum* (Shelburne, Vt.: By the museum, 1957); Robert S. Woodbury, *History of the Milling Machine* (Cambridge, Mass.: MIT Press, 1960); Brooke Hindle, *The Pursuit of Science in Revolutionary America* (Chapel Hill: University of North Carolina Press, 1956); Merritt Roe Smith, *Harpers Ferry Armory and the New Technology: The Challenge of Change* (Ithaca: Cornell University Press, 1977); Hummel, *With Hammer in Hand*; Ralph Hodgkinson, *Tools of the Woodworker: Tools to Be Pushed*, American Association for State and Local History technical leaflet no. 119 (Nashville, Tenn., 1979).

[25] Brooke Hindle, ed., *America's Wooden Age: Aspects of Its Early Technology* (Tarrytown: Sleepy Hollow Restorations, 1975); Paul Kebabian and Dudley Witney, *American Woodworking Tools* (New York: New York Graphic Society, 1978).

[26] Benno M. Forman and Charles F. Montgomery, eds., *Joseph Moxon's Mechanick Exercises; or, The Doctrine of Handy-Works Applied to the Arts of Smithing, Joinery, Carpentry, Turning, Bricklaying* (New York: Praeger Publishers, 1970). In this context, see also Charles C. Gillespie, ed., *A Diderot Pictorial Encyclopedia of Trades and Industry* (New York: Dover Books, 1959); and Charles Tomlinson, *Illustrations of Trades*

various regions went on to collect and publish elaborate compendiums containing detailed information about artisans extracted from probate and vital records as well as from advertising and news items in colonial newspapers.[27] Such documentary data was and continues to be of considerable use to scholars working on the craftsman as an agent in either technological or economic history.

In the quest for accurate documentation of what the craftsman actually did or made in the shop or factory, two organizations—Early American Industries Association (EAIA) (founded 1932) and Society for the History of Technology (SHOT) (founded 1954)—gave a popular and a professional focus and parallel publishing forums *(Chronicle of the Early American Industries Association* and *Technology and Culture)* to individual research efforts. The EAIA tended to be composed mostly of avocational and museum historians, whereas SHOT, at least in its early years, involved mostly academic historians—from universities (for example, Massachusetts Institute of Technology, Case Institute of Technology) with growing programs in the history of technology or from museums (for example, Hagley Museum or Smithsonian Institution) with extensive technological collections.

In addition to communicating past craftsmanship via the usual modes of scholarly discourse (for example, monographs and articles), early American work processes have been explained by the craft demonstration, a museum interpretive technique borrowed from European outdoor folk museums, and by the motion picture, a largely American technological innovation. While few historic activities are as widely illustrated to the general public as craft demonstrations and there is

---

(Ambridge, Pa.: Early American Industries Association, 1972). Henry Wyckoff Belknap, *Artists and Craftsmen of Essex County, Massachusetts* (Salem, Mass.: Essex Institute, 1927); Henry Wyckoff Belknap, *Trades and Tradesmen of Essex County, Massachusetts, Chiefly of the Seventeenth Century* (Salem, Mass.: Essex Institute, 1929); George F. Dow, *The Arts and Crafts in New England, 1704–1775: Gleanings from Boston Newspapers* (1927; reprint ed., New York: Da Capo Press, 1967).

[27] Other regional examples of such biographical directories of craftsmen include Rita Susswein Gottesman, comp., *The Arts and Crafts in New York: Advertisemenets and News Items from New York City Newspapers*, 3 vols. (New York: New-York Historical Society, 1938–65); Walter Hamilton Van Hoesen, *Craftsmen of New Jersey* (Rutherford, N.J.: Fairleigh Dickinson Press, 1973); James H. Craig, *The Arts and Crafts in North Carolina, 1699–1840* (Winston-Salem: Museum of Early Southern Decorative Arts, 1965); Alfred Coxe Prime, *The Arts and Crafts in Philadelphia, Maryland, and South Carolina: Gleanings from Newspapers*, 2 vols. (Topsfield, Mass.: Walpole Society, 1929–32); and Dean F. Failey, *Long Island Is My Nation: The Decorative Arts and Craftsmen, 1640–1830* (Setauket, N.Y.: Society for the Preservation of Long Island Antiquities, 1976).

hardly an American outdoor living-history museum without its role-playing craftsmen or artisans-in-residence, to my knowledge, no systematic historiographical assessment of craft demonstrations currently exists as to their accuracy or as to the role they have played in shaping the average American's perception of the colonial craftsman. One thing, however, is certain: They are of mixed quality. In some museum contexts, craft demonstrations are presented with conscientious research informing practically every move the living craftsman makes; in other situations, uninformed interpreters-as-surrogate-craftsmen perpetuate innumerable myths about the colonial artisan—myths suggesting that the craftsman was always an individualistic, relatively prosperous, upwardly mobile, consistently ingenious, white, Anglo-Saxon democrat who, independent of his European counterpart and largely by preferring hand tools over more efficient labor-saving machinery, developed an impressive range of aesthetically pleasing, indigenous American artifacts. [28]

Film, a medium seemingly perfectly suited to capturing the turner at his lathe or the ironworker at his tilt hammer, has been employed by the historians at Colonial Williamsburg to depict eighteenth-century work processes ranging from those of the apothecary to those of the wigmaker. Since World War II, folkways scholars and rural sociologists working in the South and Southwest have also been particularly taken with the use of film, both as a research tool and as a medium of communicating research. The New School of Social Research each year sponsors the International Craft Film Festival, screening a wide range of new 16-mm films dealing with all aspects of traditional and contemporary crafts. [29]

Many films on craft processes, like many books on the subject, often fail to delineate artisan intra- and intershop competition and

---

[28] Thomas J. Schlereth, "It Wasn't That Simple," *Museum News* 56, no. 3 (February 1978): 36–44. See also Ian M. G. Quimby and Polly Anne Earl, eds., *Technological Innovation and the Decorative Arts* (Charlottesville: University Press of Virginia, 1974), pp. vii–xiv.

[29] To secure the current listing of available films on craft activities, write Colonial Williamsburg Foundation, Film Section, Box C, Williamsburg, Va. 23185. For further information, contact International Craft Film Festival, New York State Craftsmen, Inc., 37 W. 53rd St., New York, N.Y. 10019. One of the best directories to filmed craft demonstrations is Don Tippman, comp., *Film Etc.: Historical Preservation and Related Subjects* (Washington, D.C.: Preservation Press, 1979), esp. "Buildings Crafts," "Handicrafts," and "Vanishing Trades."

cooperation. We need to know, for example, much more about the role of the journeyman in all craft shops and about his working arrangements with the master craftsman, other journeymen in the shop, and apprentices. On a related point, as the recent scholarship of Brock Jobe has demonstrated, the division of labor in many craft operations was much more commonplace than earlier research had suggested. Thus, for example, in the furniture trades a considerable degree of specialization took place with what almost amounted to the mass production of certain decorative parts (for example, finials, hand terminals) distributed by local jobbers. Revisionist scholars, however, have not entirely demolished one generalization propounded by the first generation of craftsmanship historians. In studies of both individual artisans and multigenerational craft families such as the Dominys of East Hampton, Long Island, ample evidence suggests that, despite specialization of work within the shop, most colonial craftsmen were jacks-of-all-trades. For instance, the Dominys concurrently pursued several lines of craft activities, working as cabinetmakers, carpenters, clockmakers, watch repairers, wheelwrights, gun repairers, and metalworkers in order to support themselves and their families.[30]

Other important issues have intrigued craftsmanship historians. Issues such as: In what proportions are spontaneity and adaptation found in American artisanship? When and where do American craftsmen first develop the idea of the interchangeability of parts? What is "American" about early American work processes? None, however, has monopolized this historiographical tradition like the question of where and when to divide the period of hand production from that of machine technology in early American history. In Lewis Mumford's periodization schema, the technology that the colonists brought with them to America was paleotechnic, while the new machine technology they later developed he called technic.[31] Other scholars have used less esoteric terms in the ongoing effort to locate precisely the introduction of various power sources, the expanded use of the machine, or the advent of true mass production.

As is evident from the growing scholarly literature on the shift from

---

[30] Brock Jobe, "The Boston Furniture Industry, 1720–1740," in *Boston Furniture of the Eighteenth Century*, ed. Walter Muir Whitehill (Boston: Colonial Society of Massachusetts, 1974), pp. 12–26; Hummel, *With Hammer in Hand*, pp. 3–26.

[31] Lewis Mumford, *Technics and Civilization* (New York: Harcourt, Brace, 1934), pp. 151–267.

"craft to national industry" or from "the manual arts to the machine arts," by the nineteenth century some type of division is inescapable in most American crafts.[32] Such a division is, however, by no means a sharp one. The difficulty in the history of each of the early American crafts is to state precisely what separates the earlier technology from the later. The earliest gristmills and iron plantations of the 1720s represented powered, machine operations; while in the 1850s, individual handicraft continued to be a part of much production in the shop and on the farm. Steam power was used as early as 1750, but as late as 1860 waterpower still dominated much industrial production and was even advancing in technological efficiency. Nevertheless, as Brooke Hindle and others have argued, "certainly between those two dates [1750 and 1850] the great technological divide was crossed, not only in America but in Britain and Europe as well."[33]

THE CRAFTSMAN AS A PERSON

Parallel with the scholarly investigation of the craftsman as a participant in a technological tradition has been a third line of inquiry that primarily studies the artisan as an important actor on the historical stage. It is an examination of, in the words of Alfred Young, "the craftsman as citizen."[34] In this endeavor, the focus is not so much on work or on working as it is on the worker, on the craftsman as an economic and political person, playing a significant role in society at large.

Biographies of individual craftsmen have always been popular in early American artisan study. Beginning with Walter Alden Dyer's 1915

[32] Lucius F. Ellsworth, *Craft to National Industry in the Nineteenth Century: A Case Study of the Transformation of the New York State Tanning Industry* (New York: Arno Press, 1977); Deborah Dependahl Waters, "From Pure Coin: The Manufacture of American Silver Flatware, 1800–1860," in *Winterthur Portfolio 12*, ed. Ian M. G. Quimby (Charlottesville: University Press of Virginia, 1977), pp. 19–33; William H. Mulligan, Jr., "The Family and Technological Change: The Shoemakers of Lynn, Massachusetts, during the Transition from Hand to Machine Production, 1850–1880" (Ph.D. diss., Clark University, 1982); Alan Dawley, *Class and Community: The Industrial Revolution in Lynn* (Cambridge, Mass.: Harvard University Press, 1976).

[33] Brooke Hindle, *Technology in Early America: Needs and Opportunities for Study* (Chapel Hill: University of North Carolina Press, 1966), p. 17.

[34] Alfred F. Young, *The Craftsman as Citizen: Mechanics in the Shaping of the Nation, 1760–1820* (forthcoming); see also Alfred F. Young, *The Democratic Republicans of New York: The Origins, 1763–1797* (Chapel Hill: University of North Carolina Press, 1967); and Young, *American Revolution.*

survey, *Early American Craftsmen*, through a myriad of studies on prominent cabinetmakers and architects (for example, Duncan Phyfe, Samuel McIntire), silversmiths and glassmakers (Jeremiah Dummer and Baron Stiegel), the individual American artisan has been repeatedly studied. Unfortunately, he has often been portrayed by writers prone to hagiography and historicism. Nonetheless, several excellent artisan lives have been written. Among them I would include Eric Foner's *Thomas Paine and Revolutionary America* (New York: Oxford University Press, 1976), Carl Van Doren's *Benjamin Franklin* (New York: Viking Press, 1938), Esther Forbes's *Paul Revere and the World He Lived In* (Boston: Houghton Mifflin, 1942), and Brooke Hindle's *David Rittenhouse* (Princeton, N.J.: Princeton University Press, 1964).

The collective biography of colonial artisans has been an equally durable mode of inquiry in craftsman research. Among academic historians, I am persuaded that this approach begins with Thomas Jefferson Wertenbaker in the 1920s. In his 1927 study, *The First Americans*, Wertenbaker was among the first historians to use inventories of craftsmen. His trilogy, *The Founding of the American Civilization* (1938–47), demonstrated an impressive knowledge of Anglo-American seventeenth- and eighteenth-century artifacts and artisans. To document his research, Wertenbaker made extensive use of the records of the Historic American Buildings Survey, the Pictorial Archives of Early American Art and Architecture at the Library of Congress, and research reports then in preparation at Colonial Williamsburg.[35]

Wertenbaker's work deserves mention because he was practically alone among early academic historians in recognizing the value of material culture as a resource for American artisan history. This state of affairs began to change after the Second World War when, in 1946, Richard Morris published *Government and Labor in Early America* and when, four years later, Carl Bridenbaugh brought out his Anson G. Phelps lectures under the title *The Colonial Craftsman*. Bridenbaugh sought to focus on the "artisan and his place in the colonial community" because in 1950 "no such treatment existed." It was the contributions of early American craftsmen as social, political, and economic groups that primarily interested Bridenbaugh, "rather than the anti-

[35]See, for instance, Thomas Jefferson Wertenbaker, *The Founding of American Civilization: The Old South* (New York: Charles Scribner's, 1942), pp. 220–70; and Thomas J. Schlereth, "Material Culture Studies in America: Notes toward Historical Perspective," *Material History Bulletin* 8 (1979): 89–98.

quarian quaintness of a Betty lamp or the exclusiveness attached to the possession of a unique Revere creamer or a block-front desk by Goddard."[36]

Bridenbaugh, like the social, labor, and political historians who followed his lead over the next three decades, aspired to focus colonial history on the study of large nonelite groups such as artisans and craftsmen. Researchers with this particular interest in the American artisan have been almost exclusively academic scholars. Many began their careers as straight political historians and, predictably, retained an absorbing preoccupation with the artisan's role in the Revolution. Some started out as labor historians with an obvious interest in the role the colonial craftsman played in American economic history.

No matter where they began, almost all have been influenced by at least one of two important methodological schools of historical interpretation: the work of British labor historians such as E. P. Thompson and E. J. Hobsbawm on the English working class and the pioneering studies of French social historians such as Marc Bloch, Georges LeFebvre, Georges Duby, Pierre Goubert, Emmanuel LeRoy Ladurie, and Fernand Braudel. The social science techniques of these European historians, promulgated in monographs and in two historical serials (*Annales, Economies, Societes, Civilisations* and *Past and Present*), have influenced American scholars.[37] They have, in turn, established a network of new journals where artisan research by the so-called new social historians is to be found. These include *Comparative Studies in Society and History, Journal of Interdisciplinary History, Journal of Social History, Historical Methods Newsletter,* and *William and Mary Quarterly.* Stephanie Wolf, in the introduction to *Urban Village,* also reminded us that this expanded focus by American scholars on the social roles and the social institutions of colonial America was also nurtured at home.

---

[36] It should be noted that Samuel McKee's early work, *Labor in Colonial New York, 1664–1776* (New York: Columbia University Press, 1935), preceded Morris's study and that Jackson T. Main, *The Social Structure in Revolutionary America* (Princeton: Princeton University Press, 1965), followed (and expanded) Bridenbaugh's initial foray into craftsman history. Bridenbaugh, *Colonial Craftsman,* p. 1.

[37] Eric J. Hobsbawm, "From Social History to the History of Society," *Daedalus* 100, no. 1 (Winter 1971): 20–45; see also Lawrence Stone, "History and the Social Sciences in the Twentieth Century," in *The Future of History,* ed. Charles F. Deltzell (Nashville, Tenn.: Vanderbilt University Press, 1977), pp. 3–42. The semiannual, and appropriately named, *History Workshop: A Journal of Social Historians,* published by the Labor History Group at Ruskin College, Oxford, has also begun to have a significant influence on craftsman scholarship in the United States.

In 1954 a group of American scholars comprising the Committee on Historiography issued a provocative report for the Social Science Research Council. Bulletin 64, as it is often known, began by defining history as one of the social sciences. The report then suggested that the historians' agenda for the latter half of the twentieth century should include ample use of the other social sciences—anthropology, sociology, demography, and social psychology as well as the more familiar (to historians) disciplines of economics and political science.[38]

This contemporary scholarship on artisans as functional social aggregates or political-interest groups has evolved along several different but obviously related lines of inquiry. Demography, for example, has informed analyses of local craftsmen by Wolf in Germantown, Pennsylvania, by Paul Faler in Lynn, Massachusetts, and by Robert St. George throughout southeastern New England.[39] Taking clues from Wertenbaker, some later historians of the craftsman as a community participant have tended to restrict their investigations to separate regions (for example, rural south, rural north), homogenous, religious, ethnic, or racial communities (for example, Paula Welshimer Locklair on Moravians), single urban areas (for example, Howard Rock's study of the tradesmen of New York City), or comparative cities (for example, Gary Nash's study of the artisans in seaports of Boston, New York, and Philadelphia.[40]

[38] Richard M. Beeman, "The New Social History and the Search for Community in Colonial America," *American Quarterly* 29, no. 4 (1977): 422–43; Lawrence Vesey, "The 'New' Social History in the Context of American History," *Reviews in American History* 7, no. 1 (March 1979): 1–12; Herbert Gutman and Gregory Realey, *Many Pasts: Readings in American Social History,* vol. 1 (Englewood Cliffs, N.J.: Prentice Hall, 1973), pp. 1–6; Beringer, *Historical Analysis,* pp. 203–306; Stephanie G. Wolf, *Urban Village: Population, Community, and Family Structure in Germantown, Pennsylvania, 1683–1800* (Princeton: Princeton University Press, 1980), pp. 3–7; *The Social Sciences in Historical Study: A Report of the Committee on Historiography,* Bulletin 64 (New York: Social Science Research Council, 1954).

[39] Wolf, *Urban Village,* chaps. 2–5; Paul Faler, "Cultural Aspects of the Industrial Revolution: Lynn, Massachusetts, Shoemakers and Industrial Morality, 1826–1860," *Labor History* 15 (Summer 1974): 367–94; St. George, *Wrought Covenant,* and his contribution to this volume.

[40] For separate regions, see, for example, Richard Pares, *Yankees and Creoles: The Trade between North America and the West Indies before the American Revolution* (Cambridge, Mass.: Harvard University Press, 1956); Alfred F. Young, "The Mechanics and the Jeffersonians: New York, 1784–1801," *Labor History* 5, no. 3 (Fall 1964): 247–76; and Gary J. Kornblith, "From Artisans to Businessmen: Master Mechanics in New England, 1789–1850" (Paper presented at the Seventy-first Annual Meeting of the Organization of American Historians, New York, April 14, 1978). For communities, see Locklair's essay

Ever since Bridenbaugh followed up his influential social history of the colonial craftsman with his equally pioneering studies, *Cities in the Wilderness* (1938) and *Cities in Revolt* (1955), urban history has given a distinctive cast to craftsman studies. Thus, for many scholars, the urban context, be it pre- or postindustrial, has been the geographical lodestone around which to wrap their research.[41] In chronological terms, however, the Revolution has usually been the historiographical watershed. Not surprisingly, some monographs examine the role of those whom Bryan Palmer has called the "most uncommon common men" in the most extraordinary event in the life of their generation. Other historians, such as Gary Nash, have concentrated their energies on the pre-Revolutionary period, studying craftsmen by combining analyses of social/economic history with narrative histories of local urban politics. In *The Urban Crucible*, Nash traces the periodic political mobilizations of urban craftsmen, for example, in Philadelphia in the 1720s and 1760s. He sees much more class identity and radical ideology within artisan ranks (using explanatory concepts such as deference or cultural hegemony) than previous historians thought existed in the pre-Revolutionary craftsman community.[42]

A third cadre of scholars pushes the socio-political-economic story into nineteenth-century America in works such as Rock's previously

---

in this volume as well as June Sprigg, *By Shaker Hands* (New York: Alfred A. Knopf, 1975); and Delores Hayden, *Seven American Utopias: The Architecture of Communitarian Socialism, 1790–1975* (Cambridge, Mass.: MIT Press, 1976). For urban areas, in addition to Rock, *Artisans of the New Republic*, see Dirk Hoerden, "Boston Leaders and Boston Crowds, 1765–1776," in Young, *American Revolution*, pp. 335–71; Gary B. Nash, "Up from the Bottom in Franklin's Philadelphia," *Past & Present*, no. 77 (November 1977): 57–83; and Ian M. G. Quimby, "The Cordwainers Protest: A Crisis in Labor Relations," in *Winterthur Portfolio* 3, ed. Milo M. Naeve (Winterthur, Del.: Winterthur Museum, 1967), pp. 83–101. For comparative cities, see Gary B. Nash, "Wealth and Poverty in Pre-Revolutionary America," *Journal of Interdisciplinary History* 6, no. 4 (Spring 1976): 545–84; and Joseph Ernst, "Ideology and an Economic Interpretation of the Revolution," in Young, *American Revolution*, pp. 161–85.

[41] David Montgomery, "The Working Classes of the Pre-Industrial City," *Labor History* 9, no. 1 (Winter 1968): 13–16; see also Charles Steffen, "Between Revolutions: The Pre-Factory Urban Worker in Baltimore, 1780–1820" (Ph.D. diss., Northwestern University, 1972).

[42] Richard Walsh, *Charleston's Sons of Liberty: A Study of the Artisan, 1763–1789* (Columbia: University of South Carolina Press, 1959); Young, *Democratic Republicans*; Olton, *Artisans for Independence*; Bryan D. Palmer, "Most Uncommon Common Men: Craft and Culture in Historical Perspective," *Labour* [Canada] 1, no. 1 (1976): 5–31; Gary B. Nash, *The Urban Crucible: Social Change, Political Consciousness, and the Origins of the American Revolution* (Cambridge, Mass.: Harvard University Press, 1979).

cited *Artisans of the New Republic,* Bruce Laurie's " 'Nothing on Impulse,' " Young's *Craftsman as Citizen,* and Herbert Gutman's *Work, Culture, and Society in Industrializing America.* Mention of Gutman's research suggests a final focus which I see emerging within my third historiographical movement, a methodological approach that scholars are now often calling working class culture studies.[43] These historians tend to be interested in sorting out several strains of what Gutman has labeled "craft cultural consciousness," what Joseph Ernst designates as "craft ideology," and what Nash terms "the artisans' constellation of values."[44]

Historiography as a branch of intellectual history does not lend itself easily to the use of artifacts as evidence. In this essay discussing colonial crafts, craftsmanship, and craftsmen, I have not offered a single visual illustration. If I were to do so, however, I think I could reduce my interpretation of the topic to three images which would symbolize the three major ways in which artisans, mechanics, and craftsmen have been viewed by the last several generations of American academic, museum, and avocational historians.

To symbolize the craftsman and his product, for instance, I would propose John Singleton Copley's 1770 portrait of Paul Revere holding the famous teapot he has made, perhaps pondering the final artistic design before taking up an engraving tool to finish the masterpiece (fig. 1). Of course, visual conceits of the craftsman at work (for example, his leather, sand-filled pad, his burin and needle) and of the craftsman as worker (for example Revere in simple linen body shirt and unpowdered hair) are in the painting. But I think it can be argued that both the viewer's and Revere's eyes are drawn to the teapot, the object, the craftsman's product.

A less well known group portrait, *Four Tradesmen* by an unknown German folk painter of the first quarter of the nineteenth century (fig.

---

[43] Bruce Laurie, " 'Nothing on Impulse': Life-Styles of Philadelphia Artisans, 1820–1860," *Labor History* 15, no. 3 (Summer 1974): 343–44; Herbert Gutman, *Work, Culture and Society in Industrializing America: Essays in American Working-Class and Social History* (New York: Alfred A. Knopf, 1976). See also Milton Cantor, ed., *American Working Class Culture: Explorations in American Labor and Social History* (Westport, Conn.: Greenwood Press, 1979).

[44] Gutman, "Work, Culture and Society," pp. 542–43; Ernst, "Ideology and the Revolution," pp. 161–85; Gary B. Nash, "The Transformation of Urban Politics, 1700–1765," *Journal of American History* 60, no. 3 (December 1973): 626–32.

Figure 1.   John Singleton Copley, *Paul Revere*. Boston, ca. 1770. Oil on canvas; H. 35″, W. 28½″. (Museum of Fine Arts, Boston, gift of Joseph W., William B., and Edward H. R. Revere.)

2), conveys the craftsman as active participant in his craft tradition. In the painting, a blacksmith, a cobbler, a baker, and an innkeeper are depicted with the tools of their trades. In Copley's painting, Revere contemplated his finished art, whereas in the folk portrait the focus is on the unknown artisans and how they are equipped to practice their crafts.

A third image that I think symbolizes the colonial craftsman as a

Figure 2. *The Four Tradesmen*. Southeastern Pennsylvania, ca. 1815. Watercolor on paper; H. 7½", W. 12½". (Courtesy Sotheby Parke Bernet, New York.)

legal, economic, and political person is the seal and motto of the New York Mechanick Society (fig. 3) as found on the society's membership certificates. The engraving depicts a muscular mechanic's arm, bared to the bicep and holding a hammer upright. Above the arm is lettered "By Hammer & Hand, all Arts do stand," a logo and epigram used by numerous colonial craftsmen's organizations.[45]

Unlike the first two graphics, where specific craftsmen are identified, the artisan on the society's certificate remains anonymous. We neither see his face nor know his name. I think he might serve, therefore, as an emblem for my third historiographical trend, indebted as it is to the "new" social history and its interest in "history from the bottom up." The iconography of this craft membership certificate serves at least two twentieth-century scholars as an appropriate colophon for their publications. In addition to its use by Hummel, Nash prefaces his essay in Young's *American Revolution* with this graphic.[46]

[45] Hummel, *With Hammer in Hand*, p. vii.
[46] Palmer, "Uncommon Common Men," pp. 5–9; Staughton C. Lynd, "The Revolution and the Common Man: Farm Tenants and Artisans in New York Politics, 1777–1788" (Ph.D. diss., Columbia University, 1962); Nash, "Up from the Bottom," pp. 57–

Figure 3.   Detail of 1791 membership certificate of the New York Mechanick Society. (Winterthur Museum.)

The three historiographical traditions also have their own historiographers. Whitehill's *The Arts in Early American History* surveys the scholarship done on the colonial craftsman and his products, whereas Hindle's *Technology in Early America* documents the literature on the colonial craftsman and his work processes. To date there is no single bibliographical compendium that collects "new" political and social history of the craftsman as citizen and consumer, but the bibliography in Rock's *Artisans of the New Republic* might serve as a reference point for anyone seeking a listing of the basic sources.[47]

Despite the impressive scholarship that has been done to date by academic historians, museum historians, and avocational historians, one must report that craftsman history is only slowly becoming an integral part of American history. In Abraham Eisenstadt's selected essays on the craft of American history, for example, there is hardly a mention

64; Gary B. Nash, "Social Change and the Growth of Prerevolutionary Urban Radicalism," in Young, *American Revolution*, pp. 3–36.

[47] Rock, *Artisans of the New Republic*, pp. 328–31.

of American craftsmen and their role in the American past.[48] The 1979 Winterthur conference, focusing as it did on three major perspectives that historians have taken when studying the craftsman in early America, sought to overcome this myopia as well as to stimulate a cross-disciplinary dialogue among decorative arts scholars and social historians, private collectors and historians of technology, art and architectural historians, as well as political and economic historians. The essays that follow, in addition to testifying to the conference's success in achieving that dialogue, are a superb documentary record of the current state of historical scholarship on crafts, craftsmanship, and craftsmen in early America.

[48] Abraham Eisenstadt, *The Craft of American History: Selected Essays* (New York: Harper & Row, 1966).

Artisans and Politics in Eighteenth-Century Philadelphia
Gary B. Nash

The political history of colonial America has only recently begun to take account of the crucial role played by urban artisans in the forging of a revolutionary mentality and a revolutionary movement. Yet the Revolution began in the seaboard towns and then spread outward to the countryside; and within these commercial centers artisans possessed great political potential, composing about half the taxable inhabitants and about the same proportion of the voters. In Philadelphia, the port to which this study of artisan political consciousness is devoted, 1,682 of the 3,350 taxable males in 1772 were artisans. Their political weight was critical in any contested election in the first two-thirds of the eighteenth century. And in the wake of the Seven Years' War, as the imperial crisis unfolded, they played a dynamic role in the formation of a revolutionary movement in the largest city of British North America. This essay examines the shaping of a highly politicized artisan community in Philadelphia during the eighteenth century and assesses the ambivalent nature of its political stance.

"Artisan community," of course, is only a phrase of convenience. At no time were artisans a unified body, identifying themselves as a class or a united interest group. They were divided by occupation, wealth, religion, status, and ideological position. They ranged from impecunious apprentice shoemakers to wealthy master builders. At the lower end of the scale were tailors, shoemakers, and coopers who had much in common with merchant seamen and porters; both groups shared low wages, uncertain prospects of advancement, and exclusion from the ranks of property holders. At the upper end were brewers, tanners, bakers, sugar boilers, and some construction tradesmen who blended into the ranks of shopkeepers, proprietors, and even real estate developers. In spite of these differences, artisans had much in common, most importantly their craft skills and a life defined by productive labor. In the broadest view we can see two seemingly contrary trends at work among eighteenth-century Philadelphia artisans. On the one hand, the spectacular growth of the city—from about 5,000 in 1720 to 25,000 on the eve of the Revolution—caused greater occupation specialization and greater differentiation of wealth within the body of artisans. On the other hand, a greater feeling of common interest, extending across craft lines, occurred in the late colonial period as many artisans reshaped their views of their relations to other parts of their community and transformed their understanding of their political roles, rights, and responsibilities. Nonetheless, no homogeneous artisan political community emerged, and the radical potential of the mechanics was severely limited because of the wide range of roles occupied by these tradesmen within the eighteenth-century urban economy.

Any inquiry into the political consciousness of the eighteenth-century artisan requires some definition of the mechanics' values and goals, for politics was not an end in itself for laboring men, but the accomplishment, through laws and public policy, of privately held notions of how society should function. No Philadelphia artisan at the beginning of the eighteenth century imagined that he should stand for election to the assembly, shape governmental policy, or challenge the prevailing wisdom that those with social status, education, and wealth were best equipped to manage civil affairs. But artisans did understand their own interests, had deeply held values, and possessed a keen sense of whether social equity and justice prevailed in their community. This was so notwithstanding a long history of upper-class attempts to define them as a part of the "unthinking multitude," the "base herd," and, when they took to the streets, the "vile mob."[1]

In discussing the artisan's mentality it is best to begin with the con-

---

[1] For contemporary definitions of mechanic and upper-class attitudes toward artisans, see Carl Bridenbaugh, *The Colonial Craftsman* (1950; reprint ed., Chicago: University of Chicago Press, Phoenix Books, 1966), p. 155; and Howard B. Rock, *Artisans of the New Republic: The Tradesmen of New York City in the Age of Jefferson* (New York: New York University Press, 1979), pp. 4–8.

cept of opportunity because that concept, central to the "economic man," is deeply embedded in almost all discussions of early American society. It is of primary importance in understanding the obstacles that stood in the way of artisan political unity. For most urban artisans at the beginning of the eighteenth century opportunity did not mean the chance to accumulate great material wealth or to achieve high social status. Philadelphia's laboring men grew up in societies where intergenerational mobility was, with some exceptions, extremely slow, where sons unquestioningly followed their father's trade, where the Protestant work ethic did not beat resoundingly in every breast, and where warding off dire need rather than acquiring riches was the primary goal. It was economic security rather than rapid mobility that was uppermost in their minds.

The urban laboring man's constraint about what was possible was shaped by the distinctly preindustrial nature of economic life in the ports of early eighteenth-century America. Work patterns were irregular, dictated by weather, hours of daylight, erratic delivery of raw materials, and vacillating consumer demand. When the cost of fuel for artificial light was greater than the extra income that could be derived from laboring before or after sunlight hours, who would not shorten his day during winter? When winter desended on the Delaware River seaport, business often ground to a halt, for even in the southernmost of the northern harbors ice often blocked maritime traffic. This meant slack time for mariners and dockworkers, just as laborers engaged in digging wells, building roads, and excavating cellars for house construction were idled by frozen ground. The hurricane season in the West Indies also forced slowdowns because few shipowners were willing to place their ships and cargoes before the killer winds that prevailed in the Caribbean from August to October.[2] Other urban artisans were also at the mercy of the weather. If prolonged rain delayed the slaughter of cows in the country or made impassable the rutted roads into the city, then the tanner laid

[2] Joseph J. Kelley, Jr., *Life and Times in Colonial Philadelphia* (Harrisburg, Pa.: Stackpole Books, 1973), p. 48. Richard Pares analyzed the effects of weather on the North American–West Indies trade in *Yankees and Creoles: The Trade between North America and the West Indies before the American Revolution* (Cambridge, Mass.: Harvard University Press, 1956), p. 18. Two excellent accounts of the irregular pace of northern mercantile life are W. T. Baxter, *The House of Hancock: Business in Boston, 1724–1775* (Cambridge, Mass.: Harvard University Press, 1945), pp. 184–220; and Virginia D. Harrington, *The New York Merchant on the Eve of the Revolution* (New York: Columbia University Press, 1935), pp. 76–125.

his tools aside, and, for lack of his deliveries, the cordwainer was also idle. The hatter was dependent upon the supply of beaver skins which could stop abruptly if disease struck an Indian tribe or war disrupted the fur trade. Weather, disease, and equinoctial cycles all contributed to the fitful pace of urban labor—and therefore to the difficulty of producing steady income. Every urban artisan knew "broken days," slack spells, and dull seasons.[3]

While moving to America could not change the discontinuous work patterns of preindustrial European life, it did bring about an adjustment in perception about what was achievable. Fernand Braudel tells us that in Europe "the frontier zone between possibility and impossibility barely moved in any significant way, from the fifteenth to the eighteenth century." But it moved in America. Philadelphia's artisans could anticipate more favorable conditions than prevailed in the homelands that they, or their parents, had left. Unemployment was virtually unknown in the early decades of settlement, labor commanded a better price relative to the cost of household necessities, and urban land was purchased reasonably.[4]

This did not mean that artisans and laborers worked feverishly to ascend the ladder of success. Craftsmen who commanded 5s. a day and laborers who garnered 3s. knew that weather, sickness, and the inconstancy of supplies (and sometimes demand) made it impossible to work more than 250 days a year. This would bring an income of about £35 to £60, hardly enough to send aspirations spiraling upward. Even if the margin between subsistence and savings was greater than in Europe, it was still thin enough that years of hard work and frugal living usually preceded the purchase of even a small house. Hence, laboring people

---

[3] "The grand complaint with laborers among us," wrote Benjamin Rush in 1769, "is that we do not pay them sufficient prices for their work. A plain reason may be assigned for this; we consume too little of their manufactures to keep them employed the whole year around" (*The Letters of Benjamin Rush*, ed. Lyman H. Butterfield, vol. 1 [Princeton, N.J.: Princeton University Press, 1951], pp. 74–75). The irregularity of work for Philadelphia's artisans lasted into the nineteenth century, as Bruce Laurie explained in " 'Nothing on Impulse': Life-Styles of Philadelphia Artisans, 1820–1850," *Labor History* 15, no. 3 (Summer 1974): 343–44. Much can be learned on the subject from Keith Thomas, "Work and Leisure in Pre-Industrial Society," *Past and Present*, no: 29 (December 1964): 50–66; and E. P. Thompson, "Time, Work-Discipline, and Industrial Capitalism," *Past & Present*, no. 38 (December 1967): 56–97.

[4] Fernand Braudel, *Capitalism and Material Life, 1400–1800*, trans. George Weidenfeld (New York: Harper Torchbooks, 1973), p. ix. On wage-price relatives in England and the colonies, see Victor S. Clark, *History of Manufacturers in the United States*, vol. 1, 1607–1860 (Washington, D.C.: McGraw-Hill Book Co., 1929), pp. 155–58.

were far from the day when the failure to acquire property or to accumulate a minor fortune produced guilt or aroused anger against those
above them. Most artisans did not wish to become lawyers, doctors, or
merchants.[5] Their desire was not to reach the top, but to get off the
bottom. Yet they expected to earn a "decent competency" and did not
anticipate the grinding poverty of the laboring poor everywhere in Europe.

Philadelphia, for three-quarters of a century after its founding, richly
nurtured this expectation of economic security and limited mobility.
Not everyone succeeded in the early years, but, with the exception of a
depression in the mid 1720s, the city experienced steady growth and
general prosperity from 1681 to the late 1750s. From 1685 to 1753, 55
percent of the artisans whose estate inventories have survived left personal property worth between £51 and £200 sterling, and another 25
percent left in excess of £200, an amount that signifies a very comfortable standard of living.[6] The city to which Benjamin Franklin came as
a printer's apprentice in 1725 was filled with young artisans who ascended
steadily, if not quite so spectacularly and stylishly as Poor Richard.[7]
Success for so many in the first eight decades of Philadelphia's history
must have affected the aspirations of other new arrivals. No wonder that
Franklin became the hero of the city's "leather apron men" and that his
little booklet, variously entitled *Father Abraham's Speech, The Way to
Wealth*, and *The Art of Making Money Plenty in Every Man's Pocket*
became a best seller in Philadelphia. It was not, however, a formula for
"unlimited acquisition," but rather a comfortable existence "which was
the midpoint between the ruin of extravagance and the want of poverty."[8]

A degree of economic ambition, then, was nourished by actual

[5] Bridenbaugh argued that among artisans the "driving desire" was "to raise themselves and their families above their present level" and "to get into the 'white-collar class' "
(*Colonial Craftsman*, p. 165). It is the second part of this statement to which I take
exception.
[6] Gary B. Nash, *The Urban Crucible: Social Change, Political Consciousness, and
the Origins of the American Revolution* (Cambridge, Mass.: Harvard University Press,
1979), table 5, pp. 397–98.
[7] James G. Lydon, "Philadelphia's Commercial Expansion, 1730–1739," *Pennsylvania Magazine of History and Biography* 91, no. 4 (October 1967): 401–18. The occupational careers of these artisans can be followed in part through the deed books, which
can be used to chart property acquisition and occupational change. For this period, see
Deed Books E-5/7, E-6/7, and E-7/8, City Archives, City Hall Annex, Philadelphia.
[8] J. E. Crowley, *This Sheba, Self: The Conceptualization of Economic Life in Eighteenth-Century America* (Baltimore: Johns Hopkins University Press, 1974), p. 84.

experience with what was possible. By the same token, ambition varied with occupation and to an extent with the particular era we are considering. It must be kept in mind that mechanics varied considerably in terms of income, wealth, and property ownership and that this affected their aspirations and, ultimately, the cast of their political thinking. Thus, those at the bottom of the hierarchy of artificers—coopers, tailors, shoemakers, stocking weavers, and ship caulkers—had more limited goals than silversmiths, house carpenters, brickmakers, and instrumentmakers. This modesty of aspiration at the lower levels of the artisan hierarchy was expressed clearly in 1779 by the shoemakers and tanners of Philadelphia. "For many years," they wrote, "the prices of skins, leather, and shoes were so proportioned to each other as to leave the tradesmen a bare living profit; this is evidently proved by this circumstance well known to everybody, that no person of either of these trades, however industrious and attentive to his business, however frugal in his manner of living, has been able to raise a fortune rapidly, and the far greater part of us have been contented to live decently without acquiring wealth; nor are the few among us who rank as men of property, possessed of more than moderate estates. Our professions rendered us useful and necessary members of our community; proud of that rank, we aspired to no higher."[9]

The last phrase of the shoemakers' petition—"our professions rendered us useful and necessary members of our community"—spoke directly to a second important part of the artisans' constellation of values—respectability. Craft pride and a desire to be recognized for contributing to the community were of great importance to them and functioned, as an English historian said, as "an alternative to wealth as a criterion for social judgement."[10] One of the keys to Franklin's success as an urban organizer was his skill in appealing to this dignity that artisans felt as members of the producing class. For example, in 1747, with the threat of a French attack looming and the assembly dragging its feet on military mobilization, Franklin exhorted the artisans of Philadelphia to organize a voluntary militia. Writing as A Tradesman, he argued that the "plain truth" of the matter was that the artisans had always been

[9]*To the Inhabitants of Pennsylvania in General, and Particularly Those of the City and Neighbourhood of Philadelphia* ([Philadelphia, 1779]), Library Company of Philadelphia.

[10]Geoffrey Crossick, *An Artisan Elite in Victorian Society: Kentish London, 1840–1880* (Totowa, N.J.: Rowman and Littlefield, 1978), p. 135.

at the heart of civic improvements and now must solve for themselves a problem that their upper-class leaders were cravenly evading.[11] The result was the formation of the Associators, who became a symbol of artisan strength and respectability. Called into being by the artisan par excellence among them, acting where upper-class leaders had failed, and electing their own officers, they never engaged the enemy, but nonetheless conferred upon themselves a collective strength and a confirmation of their value to the community.

Throughout the preindustrial period this artisan self-esteem and desire for community recognition jostled with the upper-class view of artisans as "mean," "base," and "vulgar," to invoke the contemporary definitions of *mechanic*. When wealthy urban dwellers referred to skilled craftsmen as "meer mechanics" or made generalized statements about laboring people as inferior, ignorant, and morally suspect, they ran squarely athwart the self-image of artisans, "the meanest" of whom, as one Philadelphian noted in 1756, "thinks he has a Right of Civility from the greatest" person in the city.[12]

In their attempts to gain respectability in the eyes of the community and maintain self-respect, artisans placed a premium on achieving "independence," or, to put it the other way around, on escaping dependency. At the most primary level, economic independence meant the capacity to fend off the need for charity and poor relief. "The ability to maintain oneself by one's labour without recourse to such things as charity" was "a crucial material and psychological dividing-line," wrote I. J. Prothero of the preindustrial London artisan, and the same may be said of his Philadelphia counterpart. In Philadelphia this self-maintenance proved attainable for almost every artisan for three generations after Penn's colony was founded. At a higher level, economic independence meant making the transition from apprentice to journeyman to master craftsman—the three-step climb from servitude to self-employment. This transition was of critical importance to eighteenth-century

---

[11] *The Papers of Benjamin Franklin*, ed. Leonard W. Labaree, vol. 3, *January 1, 1745–June 30, 1750* (New Haven, Conn.: Yale University Press, 1959), pp. 200–201.

[12] Jacob Duche, *Pennsylvania Journal* (March 25, 1756). Sixteen years later the same author would rephrase the notion, writing that "the poorest labourer upon the shore of *Delaware* thinks himself entitled to deliver his sentiments in matters of religion or politics with as much freedom as the gentleman or scholar. . . . For every man expects one day or another to be upon a footing with his wealthiest neighbour;—and in this hope shews him no cringing servility, but treats him with a plain, though respectful familiarity" (*Pennsylvania Packet* [March 30, 1772]).

artisans because it meant more than economic rewards and the freedom to control hours of work; it also meant respectability and an autonomous existence outside the workplace, something that often proved difficult when one's livelihood was dependent upon another man.[13]

Care must be taken in using words such as *autonomy* and *independence* to describe artisan values because these goals were framed by a broader corporate and communitarian outlook. The notion of belonging to a "trade" carried with it a sense of cooperative workshop labor where master craftsman, journeyman, and apprentice were bound together in service to themselves, each other, and the community. A man was not simply a carpenter or a cooper in Philadelphia, striving independently to make a living; he was also a member of a collective body, hierarchically structured but organized so that all mechanics, theoretically at least, would in time become masters. Men might aspire individually—Franklin could not brook the role of apprentice or journeyman and competed fiercely with his fellow printers in Philadelphia once he established his own shop—but this striving was reined by a collective trade identity and a commitment to the community in which he labored. "When I was a boy," wrote John Watson of the late eighteenth-century artisans, "there was no such thing as conducting their business in the present wholesale manner, and by efforts at monopoly. No masters were seen exempted from personal labor in any branch of business—living on the profits derived from many hired journeyman."[14]

This traditional outlook, stressing the mutuality of relations between craftsmen at different ranks within a trade and the community responsibilities of the trade itself, was challenged in the eighteenth century by the rise of the laissez-faire ethos which celebrated entrepreneurial, atomistic competition and the accumulative spirit. In the older view, labeled the "moral economy" by E. P. Thompson, all economic activity carried social responsibilities with it and was necessarily tied to the

---

[13] Iorwerth J. Prothero, *Artisans and Politics in Early Nineteenth-Century London: John Gast and His Times* (Hamden, Conn.: Dawson Publishing, 1978), p. 26. In those trades requiring greater organization and capital, the rise from journeyman to master proved impossible for many, if not most, men; nonetheless, the ideology of the independent craftsman figured importantly in the producer mentality of the eighteenth century.

[14] John F. Watson, *Annals of Philadelphia, and Pennsylvania, in the Olden Time*, vol. 1 (Philadelphia: Edwin S. Stuart, 1900), pp. 240–41. Watson completed his annals in 1842. For an exploration of the preindustrial artisan's collective trade identity, see Robert Sean Wilentz, "Class Conflict and the Rights of Man: Artisans and Radicalism in Antebellum New York" (Ph.D. diss., Yale University, 1979), chap. 2.

good of the community. This put limitations on what an artisan was entitled to charge for his product or his labor and even extended to hold "every man accountable to the community for such parts of his conduct by which the public welfare appears to be injured or dishonoured, and for which no legal remedies can be obtained."[15] But the newer outlook, "possessive individualism" which C. B. MacPherson has probed, legitimated unrestrained economic activity. The craftsman, like every member of the community, could charge as much as the market would bear for his goods and services, and his rights in holding property were inviolate. These jarring views surfaced dramatically at moments of economic crisis such as in Philadelphia in 1779 when food shortages and burgeoning inflation put severe pressure on many artisans and laborers. Bitterly opposed to the shipment of grain by the wealthy merchant Robert Morris at a time when bread was in short supply in the city, many artisans argued that Morris's property rights in the vessel were limited by the needs of the community. "We hold," they stated, "that though by the acceptance of wages [the shipbuilders] have not, and cannot have any claims in the property of the vessel, after she is built and paid for, we nevertheless hold, that they and the state in general have a right in the service of the vessel, because it constitutes a considerable part of the advantage they hoped to derive from their labours." This assertion that property was social in origin, carrying with it responsibilities to the commonweal, was the basis upon which they might concede that "the *property* of the vessel is the immediate right of the owner" but "the service of it is the right of the community collectively with the owners."[16]

It is impossible to chart precisely the advance of the new capitalistic mentality and the receding of the old corporate ethic. To some extent, in fact, the two were fused into a "collective individualism" where the values of community-oriented petty-commodity workshop production commingled with the new notions of economic rationality and pursuit

---

[15] Joyce Appleby, "The Social Origins of American Revolutionary Ideology," *Journal of American History* 64, no. 4 (March 1978): 935–58; E. P. Thompson, "The Moral Economy of the English Crowd in the Eighteenth Century," *Past & Present*, no. 50 (February 1971): 76–136; *Pennsylvania Packet* (June 29, 1779).

[16] C. B. MacPherson, *The Political Theory of Possessive Individualism: Hobbes to Locke* (Oxford: Clarendon Press, 1962); *Pennsylvania Packet* (September 10, 1779), as quoted in Steven Rosswurm, "Arms, Culture and Class: The Philadelphia Militia and the 'Lower Orders' in the American Revolution, 1765–1783" (Ph.D. diss., Northern Illinois University, 1979), p. 419.

of self-interest.[17] Very loosely one might argue that in times of prosperity the new bourgeois stance dominated the consciousness of artisans, particularly those in the more profitable trades, where opportunity for advancement was the greatest, and that in times of economic stress the moral economy compelled greater allegiance, especially among the lower artisans whose opportunities were far more circumscribed. Overarching this dialectic was the long-range tendency within many crafts for the bonds of mutuality to fray between masters and journeymen. Eventually the ties would be virtually severed as a class of capitalist entrepreneurs confronted rather than cooperated with a class of perpetually dependent wage laborers.

With these values of the workplace in mind we can turn to the political life of Philadelphia's mechanics. Here again the ideal was participation in the civic life of the community, with the public good the great end to be accomplished. Serving the commonweal, however, depended heavily on the independent exercise of political "will." As the Whig scientists of politics insisted in the eighteenth century, a republican form of government could only exist when its citizens were not cajoled, bribed, or dominated into making political decisions and choices, but freely exercised their independent judgment. This concept led directly back to economic independence because it was impossible for a man freely to assert his political will when he was beholden to another for his economic existence. Without economic self-sufficiency, the laboring citizen inevitably fell prey to the political desires of his patron, employer, landlord, or creditor. Economic dependency destroyed true political liberty—the essence of the "Independent Whig."[18]

Such an emphasis on the independent exercise of political will brings us face to face with the concept of deference. In the historical literature

[17] The phrase is from Yehoshua Arieli, *Individualism and Nationalism in American Ideology* (Baltimore: Penguin Books, 1964).
[18] [John Trenchard and Thomas Gordon], *Cato's Letters; or, Essays on Liberty, Civil and Religious*, 4 vols. (6th ed.; London, 1755), 2:16; 3:207–8. Another quite different way of surrendering one's political will to those with economic power was to accept election-time "bribes" in the form of liquor or other treats, as New York's *Independent Reflector* explained at length in an essay, "Elections and Election-Jobbers," in 1753 (see *The Independent Reflector; or, Weekly Essays on Sundry Important Subjects, More Particularly Adapted to the Province of New York, by William Livingston and others*, ed. Milton M. Klein [facsimile ed.; Cambridge, Mass.: Harvard University Press, 1963], pp. 278–84).

of the last generation this is the key concept for laying bare the dynamics of eighteenth-century politics because it provides the mediating device that seemingly reconciles two contrary tendencies in colonial politics: the conferring of the vote upon a broad group of property owners and the persistent management of politics by a small elite. *Deference* is the term employed to describe the unquestioning acceptance of an eighteenth-century moral order which consigned laboring people to economic, social, and political subordination. "Deference," wrote J. G. A. Pocock, "is the product of a conditioned freedom, and those who display it freely accept an inferior, nonelite, or follower role in a society hierarchically structured."[19]

From deference it is only a step to speaking of cultural hegemony, the notion that the ruling classes are able to obtain and maintain the consent of those subject to them because their rule gains legitimacy even in the eyes of the most oppressed members of society. "By diffusing its own concept of reality, morality, meaning, and common sense through the schools, press, religious bodies, the daily life of the streets, the workplace, and the family," the ruling class fosters the notion that they use their authority responsibly and for the good of the whole. Ultimately, this idea becomes a more powerful instrument in the hands of those in control than guns or clubs, for while class or racial conflict is not eliminated, it is largely muted by an acceptance of "the system" at the lower levels of society.[20]

The concepts of deference and cultural hegemony can be usefully employed in studying artisan politics in Philadelphia, but they must be used with care. For example, there is voluminous evidence that upperclass Philadelphians believed in and promoted as "natural" (or even ordained from on high) a system of social relations marked by gentle domination from above and willing dependency from below; but there

[19] J. G. A. Pocock, "The Classical Theory of Deference," *American Historical Review* 81, no. 3 (June 1976): 516. For theoretical considerations of deference, see Howard Newby, "The Deferential Dialectic," *Comparative Studies in Society and History* 17 (April 1975): 140–62; Edward Shils, "Deference," in *Social Stratification*, ed. J. A. Jackson (Cambridge: At the University Press, 1968), pp. 104–32; and Erving Goffman, "The Nature of Deference and Demeanor," in *Interaction Ritual: Essays in Face-to-Face Behavior* (Chicago: Aldine Publishing Co., 1967), pp. 47–95. John Alexander challenged the notion that deference was freely given in Philadelphia in "Deference in Colonial Pennsylvania and That Man from New Jersey," *Pennsylvania Magazine of History and Biography* 102, no. 4 (October 1978): 422–36.

[20] Alan Dawley, "E. P. Thompson and the Peculiarities of the Americans," *Radical History Review*, no. 19 (Winter 1978/79): 43.

is also evidence that laboring people did not always accept elite rule and cultural authority complaisantly. The key to making sense of the political activities of Philadelphia's artisans in the eighteenth century is to recognize that "a lived hegemony is always a process, . . . a realized complex of experiences, relationships, and activities, with specific and changing pressures and limits." As Raymond Williams has advised, cultural hegemony, as a form of dominance, "has continually to be renewed, recreated, defended, and modified" because in most historical circumstances it is "also continually resisted, limited, altered, challenged by pressures not at all its own." In other words, there is nothing static and immutable about a hegemonic condition; rather, it is "an institutionally negotiable *process* in which the social and political forces of contest, breakdown, and transformation are constantly in play."[21] It is therefore necessary to identify the changing conditions in eighteenth-century Philadelphia that altered class relations and political ties between artisans and those above them who functioned as the cultural standard-bearers and political magnates of their day.

Only twice in the long period from 1682 to 1776 were the basic goals of the artisans deeply threatened by severe economic adversity. On both occasions they quickly challenged the political dominance of Philadelphia's upper-class merchants and professionals. In the severe depression of the 1720s, when a steep decline of shipbuilding, trade, and house construction brought unemployment and harassment for debt to hundreds of artisans, the mechanics provided an opposing ideology that stressed the self-interest of the wealthy and, hence, the necessity for common people to organize in their own behalf. The immediate question around which artisans organized was the issuing of paper money, which they regarded as an antidote to the severe trade slump that affected almost every sector of the city's economy. But political contention soon leaped across this boundary, broadening to include debates on the accountability of representatives to their constituents, the organization of politics, and the nature of the body politic itself.[22]

It was in the early 1720s that Philadelphia's artisans first entered

[21] Raymond Williams, *Marxism and Literature* (Oxford: Oxford University Press, 1977), pp. 113–14; Geoff Elay and Keith Nield, "Why Does Social History Ignore Politics?" *Social History*, no. 5 (1980): 269.

[22] This is examined more closely in Nash, *Urban Crucible*, pp. 148–56; and Thomas Wendel, "The Keith-Lloyd Alliance: Factional and Coalition Politics in Colonial Pennsylvania," *Pennsylvania Magazine of History and Biography* 92, no. 3 (July 1968): 289–305.

into electoral politics in large numbers and thereby began to sense the power they commanded when they acted collectively. Instruments of a new form of popular politics appeared in the formation of party tickets through caucuses, the recruitment of immigrant German and Scots Irish voters, direct appeals to the electorate through broadside "advice" where positions on specific issues were announced and the wealthy denounced, outdoor political rallies that welcomed voters and nonvoters alike, political parades and demonstrations, and the formation of tavern-based artisan political clubs.

The cries of the wealthy gentry politicians under attack tell us how thoroughly alarmed they were at the sight and sound of artisans participating in politics on a mass basis. "Ye people head and foot run mad," wrote Isaac Norris, one of Philadelphia's wealthiest merchants. "All seems topside Turvey. Our publick Speeches tell ye Country & ye World that neither knowledge or riches are advantageous in a Country. . . . The Mobb is Hallood on to render obnoxious Every Man who has any proportion of those." Political power was no longer in the hands of "ye Wise, ye Rich or the learned," but had fallen to "Rabble Butchers, porters & Tagrags," and the political arena had shifted from gentlemen's parlors to "dramshops, tiff, & alehouses" where "a great number of modern statesmen & some patriots" could be found "settling affairs, cursing some, praising others, contriving lawes and swearing they will have them enacted cum multis aegis." The practical results were assembly elections in 1721 and 1722 that were "very mobbish and carried by a levelling spirit." They swept from office conservative men of wealth and replaced them with smaller traders and landowners.[23]

The opposition of the merchant-professional elite to paper money was a major factor in the growth of artisan-based politics in this era. Intensifying the hostility of laboring men to the wealthy were the attacks on artisan respectability led by merchant and proprietary officeholder James Logan. Always ready to take up the cudgels in defense of hierarchy, social order, and wealth, Logan argued in publicly distributed

[23] Isaac Norris to Stephen DeLancey, February 12, 1723, Norris to Jonathan Scarth, October 21, 1726, Norris Letter Book, Historical Society of Pennsylvania (hereafter cited as HSP); James Logan to John Penn, October 17, 1726, Penn Papers, Official Correspondence, vol. 1, pp. 237, 239, 247, HSP; Logan to Henry Gouldney, February 9, 1722/23, in *Pennsylvania Archives*, 2d ser., vol. 8 (Harrisburg, 1890), pp. 70–71. Five of Philadelphia's wealthiest merchants were swept from office in 1722, and two others lost their seats in the following year.

pamphlets that the depression of the 1720s was caused mainly by laboring-class perversity. It was idleness and fondness for drink that made
men poor and the charging of high wages by artisans that drove away
employment. Those who tried "new politics" and invented "new and
extraordinary Measures" such as paper money misunderstood the roots
of economic distress. The rich were rich because of their "Sobriety,
Industry and Frugality," the poor were poor because of their "Luxury,
Idleness and Folly." Logan paid a price for this personal attempt at
cultural hegemony. His house was attacked by an angry mob who tore
off the window shutters, bombarded his bedchamber with bricks, and
threatened to level one of Philadelphia's most gracious structures.[24] He
was publicly attacked in pamphlets for his contempt of the "poorer sort"
and for leading a group of Pennsylvanians who wished to recreate, it
was charged, "the Old English Vassalage."[25]

The political mobilization of artisans in the mid 1720s and the
distinctly undeferential behavior of laboring people shows how quickly
the sense of interclass partnership, the basis of hegemonic rule by Philadelphia's solons, could be shattered. Previously, the superior wisdom
of the elite, and, hence, the legitimacy of their rule, had been generally
accepted, although Philadelphia's early years had been so filled with
contention and its social ranks had been so fluid that no firm legacy of
merchant family political dynasties had been handed down to the 1720s.
Now the affective bonds between social ranks were shattered. Nothing
was more important in undermining the sense of partnership than the
published pronouncements by men such as Logan and Norris that the
mechanics themselves were responsible for Philadelphia's economic
difficulties because they demanded too much for their labor and squan-
dered their earnings at the taverns. Mercantile opulence was indispens-
able to the economic health of the community, argued Logan, in an
early form of the trickle-down theory, and only the "Sot, the Rambler,

[24] James Logan, *The Charge Delivered from the Bench to the Grand Jury* (Philadelphia, 1723), HSP; Logan to James Alexander, October 23, 1749, Logan Letter Book,
HSP. Logan was recalling an incident that occurred almost twenty-five years before,
which indicates how searing the experience must have been to a man who regarded
himself as one of Pennsylvania's chief assets.

[25] Among the many pamphlets published from 1723 to 1728 that indicted Logan as
arrogant, power hungry, and insensitive to the difficulties of laboring people, the fullest
is the forty-five page pamphlet attributed to William Keith, *The Observator's Trip to
America, in a Dialogue between the Observator and His Country-man Roger* ([Philadel-
phia], 1726), HSP.

the Spendthrift, and Slip Season" found themselves in economic straits.[26] Such comments struck at the artisans' self-respect, their search for independence, and their sense of belonging to an organic society where people of different statuses were mutually involved in a social partnership. It was plain that those who lived by the labor of their hands had suffered most in the depression. Thus aroused, what had been a politically passive, deferential laboring class at one moment became a politically conscious, highly active body of mechanics at the next.

Leadership of the artisans, however, remained in the hands of those near the top of the social hierarchy. The chief pamphleteer for paper money was Francis Rawle, a lesser merchant, and the leader of the political mobilization was none other than the ex-Jacobite Tory placeman, Sir William Keith, appointed by William Penn in 1717 as governor of Pennsylvania but by the early 1720s thoroughly alienated from Penn's widow and her proprietary officeholders led by Logan. It was Keith who not only endorsed the issuing of paper money in 1722 but also proposed legislation for reducing the interest rate, curbing lawyers' fees, and restricting the imprisonment of debtors. By the next year he had organized the first artisans' political group in Philadelphia's history—the Leather Apron Club—and for the next few years masterminded the artisan-based political campaigns.[27]

Politics *cum multis aegis* came to an end when prosperity returned to Philadelphia in the 1730s. Now artisans reassumed their former role of acting as a check on the exercise of power by those in the upper ranks through annual assembly and local elections but otherwise leaving public affairs to their betters. They had intervened only when those with more time (and presumably more learning) to apply to politics abused the trust placed in them by their constituents. But the 1720s left a legacy to succeeding generations. It included not only the necessity of laboring-class political mobilization in times of adversity but also residual distrust of the wealthy and a suspicion that they did not, as they claimed, always act for the public good because they were better educated and therefore, in theory, disinterested.

Finally, the 1720s shattered the belief that in Pennsylvania eco-

---

[26] Gary B. Nash, *Quakers and Politics: Pennsylvania, 1681–1726* (Princeton, N.J.: Princeton University Press, 1968); Logan, *Charge Delivered*; James Logan, A *Dialogue Shewing, What's Therein to Be Found* ([Philadelphia], 1725), HSP.
[27] Nash, *Urban Crucible*, pp. 148–55; Wendel, "Keith-Lloyd Alliance," pp. 289–305.

nomic opportunity was limitless and that therefore one man's rise to wealth was not accomplished at somebody else's cost. Pennsylvanians had been casting off the European conception of societies containing fixed quantities of wealth that must be distributed like a pie, so that when one man's piece was cut larger, others had to satisfy themselves with narrower slices. Now the artisan had learned that in Philadelphia too the aggrandizement of wealth and power by the few could be costly to the many. The point was driven home in a parable of class relations spread through the streets near the end of the depression. "A Mountebank," ran the story, "had drawn a huge assembly about him: Among the rest, a fat unwieldy Fellow, half stifled in the Press, would be every Fit crying out, Lord! what a filthy Crowd is here! Pray, good People, give Way a little! Bless me! what a De[vi]l has raked this Rabble together? What a plaguey squeezing is this? Honest Friend, remove your Elbow. At last, a Weaver that stood next him could hold no longer; A Plague confound you (said he) for an overgrown Sloven! and who in the De[vi]l's Name, I wonder, helps to make up the Crowd half so much as your self? Don't you consider (with a P–x) that you take up more Room with that Carcass than any Five here? Is not the Place as free for us as for you? Bring your own Guts to a reasonable Compass (and be B[un]ged) and then I'll engage we shall have Room for us all."[28]

During the postdepression generation, from 1730 to the early 1750s, Philadelphia's rapidly expanding economy offered most artisans the opportunity to achieve their goals of economic security, respectability, and independence. This is indicated in hundreds of deeds recording acquisitions of property by artisans and scores of estate inventories showing substantial artisan wealth. In such a climate the inflamed politics of the 1720s subsided and laboring men were content to leave the management of public affairs in the hands of those above them. This may be called deference, but we should employ that term only in the limited sense that artisans saw no need to intervene directly in politics, other than to cast their ballots, so long as those for whom they voted were responsive to their needs. Rapid urban growth and full employment after 1730 restored the atmosphere of interrank solidarity. The artisans, wrote Brother Chip some years later, for years had "tamely submitted" to the nomination of all candidates for office in Philadelphia by a

[28] [William Keith], *A Modest Reply to the Speech of Isaac Norris, Esq.* ([Philadelphia, 1727]).

"Company of leading Men" who did not permit "the affirmative or negative voice of a Mechanic to interfere."[29]

Yet, while the hegemonic control of the elite had been reestablished, it had constantly to contend with the ideal of the independent voter. Pamphleteers such as Constant Trueman kept artisan voters alert to the idea that the preservation of political "will" or "independence" required habits of mind that abhorred subservient behavior. "Let me tell you, Friends," wrote Trueman in 1735, "if you can once be frightened by the Threats or Frowns of great Men, from speaking your Minds freely, you will certainly be taught in a very little Time, that you have no liberty to act freely, but just as they shall think proper to Command or Direct; that is, that you are no longer Freemen, but Slaves, Beasts of Burden, and you must quietly submit your Necks to the Yoke, receive the Lash patiently let it be ever so Smart, and carry all the Loads they think proper to clap on your Backs, without kicking or wincing."[30]

Trueman's admonitions spoke directly to the fact that many artisans, especially those in the service and retail crafts, lived in a world of economic clientage where their economic security was bound up with an employer, landlord, or extender of credit. This, of course, was the antithesis of the ideal world where they would enjoy economic independence; and to the extent that artisans deferred politically to powerful men with economic leverage on them, they alienated their political selves because their independent exercise of judgment had been abridged. In Philadelphia, however, the ability of patrons to strong-arm their laboring clients was somewhat muted by the use of the secret ballot.[31]

In the depression that beset Philadelphia at the end of the Seven Years' War the interclass trust, which alone could sustain political deference that was based on affective bonds between different social strata, melted away. When the postwar commercial depression bottomed out early in 1765, hopes revived for better times. But within a year the

[29] A detailed account of the placid period of politics from the end of the depression of the 1720s until the beginning of the Seven Years' War is given in Alan Tully, *William Penn's Legacy: Politics and Social Structure in Provincial Pennsylvania, 1726–1755* (Baltimore: Johns Hopkins University Press, 1977); Brother Chip, *Pennsylvania Gazette* (September 27, 1770).

[30] Constant Trueman, *Advice to the Free-Holders and Electors of Pennsylvania* ([Philadelphia, 1739]), pp. 1–2.

[31] In the context of nineteenth-century England and Virginia, see the valuable discussion by Paul F. Bourke and Donald A. Debats, "Identifiable Voting in Nineteenth-Century America: Toward a Comparison of Britain and the United States before the Secret Ballot," *Perspectives in American History* 9 (1977/78): 259–88.

Philadelphia grand jury reported that many of "the labouring People, and others in low circumstances, who are willing to work, cannot obtain sufficient Employment to support themselves and their Families." Reports of unemployment continued for the next two years, and by the end of 1769 forced sales of property reached an all-time high. An economic revival occurred in 1770, but it was short-lived because within two years a severe contraction of British credit again brought widespread unemployment.[32]

Compounding the difficulties of laboring Philadelphians was the upward movement of food prices, which had risen sharply during the Seven Years' War. Although they fell modestly between 1765 and 1769, they then began a climactic five-year climb that elevated the cost of a weighted nineteen-item laboring man's diet 23 percent between 1769 and 1774. This punishing upswing caused no *crise de subsistance* in Philadelphia, but the situation was serious enough to put hundreds of artisans in difficult straits and for the Philadelphia overseers of the poor to begin distributing bread for the first time in the city's history.[33]

The severity of the post-1760 depression can be seen most clearly in the rapid growth of a large class of indigents in Philadelphia for the first time in its history. Urban poverty challenged the governing modes of thought in Philadelphia, shook artisans' confidence in the internal economic system, and intensified class feeling. "He that gets all he can honestly, and saves all he gets (necessary Expenses excepted)," printer Ben was fond of saying to his fellow mechanics, "will certainly become RICH."[34] Now, the inapplicability of this system of moral economics was made plain. Even for those who escaped poverty in the 1760s in Philadelphia, the impoverishment of so many below them was impossible to ignore because when indigency befell a large portion of the lowest laboring ranks, not simply the aged and infirm, it signified sickness in the entire economic body.

[32] *Votes and Proceedings of the House of Representatives of the Province of Pennsylvania*, ed. Gertrude MacKinney, in *Pennsylvania Archives*, 8th ser., vol. 7 (Harrisburg, 1935), p. 5830; Nash, *Urban Crucible*, pp. 319–20.

[33] Billy G. Smith, "The Material Lives of Laboring Philadelphians, 1750–1800," *William and Mary Quarterly*, 3d. ser., 38, no. 2 (April 1981): 172–75; Minutes of the Overseers of the Poor, 1768–74, City Archives, City Hall Annex, Philadelphia. See especially entries for January 27, 1772; March 9, November 1, December 13, 1773; February 28, October 17, 1774; February 1, March 1, April 5, 1775.

[34] Gary B. Nash, "Poverty and Poor Relief in Pre-Revolutionary Philadelphia," *William and Mary Quarterly*, 3d ser., 33, no. 1 (January 1976): 3–30; *Papers of Benjamin Franklin*, 3:308.

The response of the laboring poor to the new system of poor relief that was instituted in 1767 in Philadelphia indicates how the respectability as well as the economic security of the lower artisans was undermined and how strongly they resented this. Faced with ballooning poor-relief costs, which necessitated heavier taxes, the Assembly agreed to let a group of Quaker merchants dismantle the old out-relief system and replace it with a "bettering house" where the poor would be confined and, it was said, taught better work habits. The decision to end out-relief drew the Quaker merchants who managed the bettering house into a heated dispute with the overseers of the poor. The overseers, drawn mostly from the ranks of established artisans, were far closer to the needy in their neighborhoods and understood the resentment of the non-Quaker poor who were being driven into a Quaker-dominated institution. Underlying these upper-class Quaker attempts at moral management was the old notion that unemployment and poverty were attributable not to structural weakness in the economy, but to moral weakness within the laboring class. In effect, these indictments were attacks on laboring-class respectability. As such they were staunchly resisted, not only by the overseers of the poor but by the poor themselves. Many of them, the overseers reported, "declared in a Solemn manner that they would rather perish through want" than go to the bettering house, whose very name was an insult to their struggles for respect and a secure place in society. Charity was in itself distasteful to laboring Philadelphians, but charity that carried with it an accusation of moral failing was not to be endured.[35]

In the face of the economic ills of the 1760s and 1770s Philadelphia's artisans embarked on the most intense period of organizing in their history. The cordwainers organized a craft guild in 1760, journeymen carpenters established their own company and attempted to set wage rates a few years later, and tailors drew together in 1771 in order to fix prices at levels that would yield them a decent subsistence. All of this, of course, was taking place in the midst of the gathering storm between the colonies and England. And central to the response of the seaport cities to British attempts to extract greater economic advantages from the North American colonies were three nonimportation movements which drew artisans into the political arena as never before.

All of the instrumentalities of popular politics that had appeared in

[35] Nash, *Urban Crucible*, pp. 327–31; Minutes of the Overseers, June 15, 1769.

the 1720s reemerged in the turbulent 1760s. Outdoor political rallies, vitriolic political campaign literature, petition drives, club activity, and attacks on the wealthy as subverters of the community's welfare characterized the elections of 1764 and 1765 when the voter turnouts reached all-time highs in Philadelphia.[36] In the following decade, however, a transformation of mechanic consciousness ushered in a new era of politics. Most striking, artisans began to exert themselves as a separate political entity. This can be traced in the newspaper and pamphlet appeals, beginning about 1767, which were addressed specifically to the mechanic segment of the community as a separate interest. Popular politics gathered momentum in 1768 when artisans, attempting to spur foot-dragging merchants to adopt nonimportation, themselves called public meetings, published newspaper appeals, and organized secondary boycotts of importing merchants. Thereafter artisans began to transcend mere craft allegiances and build political strength which Franklin had anticipated twenty years before when he declaimed that within their separate crafts the mechanics "are like separate Filaments of Flax before the Thread is form'd, without Strength because without Connection, but UNION would make us strong and even formidable," even when opposed by "the *Great . . .* from some mean views of their Own."[37]

Moreover, the 1760s brought into the political arena the younger and poorer artisans, who, for lack of property, were not yet entitled to vote. Pamphlets and broadsides were read by the unenfranchised, outdoor political rallies and street demonstrations were open to all, organizers of petitions gathered signatures from voters and nonvoters alike.

---

[36] Gary B. Nash, "The Transformation of Urban Politics, 1700–1765," *Journal of American History* 60, no. 3 (December 1973): 626–32. By this time—and, in fact, for several decades before—the level of political literacy and popular participation in politics was far higher in Philadelphia than in English towns of equivalent size. In Birmingham, for example, which had a population of about 24,000 in 1750 and perhaps 30,000 on the eve of the American Revolution, the parliamentary election of 1774 drew a record 405 voters—the high-water mark of "popular articulacy" in this era. Philadelphia, by contrast, with about 15,000 inhabitants in 1765 (not including Southwark and Northern Liberties), drew 1,448 voters to the polls in 1764 and 1,798 in 1765. For Birmingham, see John Money, "Taverns, Coffee Houses and Clubs: Local Politics and Popular Articulacy in the Birmingham Area in the Age of the American Revolution," *Historical Journal* 14, no. 1 (March 1971): 33.

[37] Nash, *Urban Crucible*, pp. 305–9, 374–75; Charles S. Olton, *Artisans for Independence: Philadelphia Mechanics and the American Revolution* (Syracuse, N.Y.: Syracuse University Press, 1975), pp. 33–41. Franklin's statement about union is from *Plain Truth; or, Serious Considerations on the Present State of the City of Philadelphia, and Province of Pennsylvania* (Philadelphia, 1747) in *Papers of Benjamin Franklin*, 3:202.

By usage, if not by law, the lower artisan became politically conscious and politically active long before the electoral laws conferred the right of "citizen" upon him.

It took until March 1769 for popular pressure to bring Philadelphia's merchants into the nonimportation fold, and by that time the disillusionment with them in the artisan community was widespread. A year later the merchants tried to break free of the agreement, confirming the suspicions of leather-apron men that, whatever the situation in the past, a community of interest no longer existed between mechanic and merchant. Desiring to end nonimportation after drawing down their inventories, the merchants imperiously informed the artisans that they had "no *Right* to give their sentiments respecting an importation" and called the artificers a "Rabble."[38] Here was additional evidence to craftsmen that the partnership between men in different ranks was at an end and that they must work independently for their objectives, even assuming responsibility for defining and enforcing the community's goals.

Artisans were not able to halt the merchants from resuming importations in the spring of 1770. This contributed to the feeling that the organic connection between those who labored with their hands and those who did not was broken and hence accelerated the change of artisan consciousness. Deciding to jettison their reliance on upper-class leadership—this had not occurred in the 1720s—mechanics called a public meeting of their fellows and formed their own Mechanics Committee. They took another unprecedented step by deciding that they must not only use their votes to elect men above them who were responsive to their needs but must also now elect men from their own ranks. Their dominance under severe attack, the merchant elite attempted to invoke the old norms: "The Mechanics (though by far the most numerous especially in this County)" they sputtered, "have no Right to *Speak* or *Think* for themselves."[39]

In the fall of 1770, for the first time in many decades, an artisan proudly announced himself as a candidate for sheriff. Artisans soon began to fill elected positions as tax assessors and collectors, wardens, and street commissioners, and insisted on their right to participate equally with merchants and gentlemen in the nomination of assemblymen and other important officeholders. The day was past, announced Brother

[38] *To the Free and Patriotic Inhabitants of the City of Phila. and Province of Pennsylvania* (Philadelphia, 1779), as quoted in Olton, *Artisans for Independence*, p. 43.
[39] *Pennsylvania Gazette* (September 27, 1770).

Chip, taking a moniker with special meaning to ships carpenters, when laboring men would tamely endorse men nominated by the elite. Chip occupied still more radical ground by asserting that it was "absolutely necessary" that one or two artisans be elected to the Assembly from Philadelphia. Appalled at this crumbling of deference, merchants and other members of the elite hurled "Many Threats, Reflections, Sarcasms, and Burlesques" against the artisans. This did little to deter laboring men because secret balloting went far to keep them immune from economic retaliation by those they offended.[40]

Possessing many votes and inspirited by success in electing their own kind to important offices, the artisans began pressing the legislature in 1772 for laws that would benefit them. They vigorously opposed excise taxes on liquor, called for the weekly publication of full assembly debates and roll calls on important issues, and demanded the erection of public galleries to end forever "the absurd and Tyrannical custom of shutting the Assembly doors during debate." It was enough to leave some genteel Philadelphians muttering, "It is Time the Tradesmen were checked—they take too much upon them—they ought not to intermeddle in State Affairs—they will become too powerful."[41]

Intermeddling in state affairs was also taking another direction in the 1770s: the de facto assumption of governmental powers by committees called into being by the people at large, artisans most numerous among them. Tradesmen had first clothed themselves in such extralegal authority in policing the nonimportation agreement in 1769. In 1774, in the wake of the Boston Port Bill, they showed that they were far more unified and aggressive than in the past by putting forward a radical slate of candidates for enforcing the Continental Association that drubbed a slate offered to the electorate by the city's conservative merchants.[42]

This heightened artisan consciousness culminated in the final year before independence. A new surge of radicalism, led by middling men such as Thomas Young, James Cannon, Thomas Paine, and Timothy Matlack and centered in the thirty-one companies of the Philadelphia

[40] Olton, *Artisans for Independence*, pp. 50–52; Brother Chip, *Pennsylvania Gazette* (September 27, 1770). The elite are quoted in Olton, *Artisans for Independence*, p. 53.

[41] A *Trademan's Address to His Countrymen* ([Philadelphia, 1772]), Library Company of Philadelphia; *Pennsylvania Gazette* (September 22, 1773), as quoted in Olton, *Artisans for Independence*, p. 56.

[42] Richard Alan Ryerson, *The Revolution is Now Begun: The Radical Committees of Philadelphia, 1765–1776* (Philadelphia: University of Pennsylvania Press, 1978), pp. 79–86.

militia that had been organized in the spring of 1775, produced demands for the most radical reforms yet suggested by the colonists. Curbing the individual accumulation of wealth, opening up opportunity, divorcing the franchise from property ownership, and driving the mercantile elite from power became explicit objectives enunciated in a flood of polemic literature that swept over Philadelphia. "Our great merchants . . . [are] making immense fortunes at the expense of the people," charged a Tradesman in April 1775, just before a special Assembly election. Sounding the tocsin on economic inequality that English and European republican writers warned against but genteel American Whigs usually saw fit to ignore, Tradesman argued that the merchants "will soon have the whole wealth of the province in their hands, and then the people will be nearly in the condition that the East-India Company reduced the poor natives of Bengal to." Men of this kind must be stopped in "their present prospect of making enormous estates at our expense." Invoking the older notion of an organic community, Tradesman yearned for the day when their "golden harvests" were put to an end and "all ranks and conditions would come in for their just share of the wealth."[43]

This acerbic language, hurled across class lines, was delivered anonymously so the writer would need not fear retaliation from a land-lord, employer, or creditor. It reveals the alternative culture that some artisans sought to create through seizing control of the political process. Three days earlier in another newspaper an account appeared that takes us deeper into the hegemonic crisis that was occurring in Philadelphia. "A poor man," it was stated, "has rarely the honor of speaking to a gentleman on any terms, and never with familiarity, but for a few weeks before the election. How many poor men, common men, and mechanics have been made happy within this fortnight by a shake of a hand, a pleasing smile and a little familiar chat with a gentleman: who have not for the seven years past condescended to look at them. Blessed state which brings all so nearly on a level."[44] The account can be read as evidence that the poor man and the artisan had truly internalized the message promulgated from above—that society was best governed when the elite ruled and laboring men deferred. But the barbed tone of the statement and its thinly disguised disdain of the upper class also portray an urban society where interclass relations were no longer marked by

[43] Tradesman, *Pennsylvania Packet* (April 30, 1776).
[44] *Philadelphia Evening Post* (April 27, 1776).

trust, harmony, mutual respect, and a sense of partnership within hierarchy. When we consider such a description of veiled interclass hostility alongside a knowledge of what was actually happening in the streets of Philadelphia in the spring of 1776, where artisans and small traders were taking power from the hands of the old elite, it becomes clear that while a deferential pose may have still been maintained by the most vulnerable in the society, the old social equilibrium was now in disarray.[45] It could have survived only within an economy where laboring people were able to fulfill their goals of a "decent competency," dignity, and economic independence.

By autumn 1775 the Philadelphia militia had become a school of political education much in the manner of Oliver Cromwell's seventeenth-century New Model Army. The militia, wrote Eric Foner, "quickly developed a collective identity and consciousness, a sense of its own rights and grievances," and "became a center of intense political debate and discussion."[46] Organizing the Committee of Correspondence, which included men of no previous political experience, such as tailor Frederick Hagener and paperhanger Edward Ryves, the privates began exerting pressure on the Assembly to take a more assertive stand on independence. They also made three radical demands for internal change: first, that militiamen be given the right to elect all their officers, rather than only their junior officers, as the Assembly had specified in the militia law; second, that the franchise be conferred on all militiamen, regardless of age and economic condition; and, third, that the assembly impose a heavy financial penalty, proportionate to the size of his estate, on every man who refused militia service, using this money to support the families of poor militiamen.[47]

Although upper-class Whigs might call the militia privates "in general damn'd riff raff—dirty, mutinous, and disaffected," there was no denying the power of these men.[48] Generally from the lowest ranks of the laboring population, as opposed to the master craftsmen who from 1770 to 1774 had gradually gained control of the extralegal committees,

---

[45]The rapid disintegration of the old elite's political power is most fully analyzed in Ryerson, *Revolution*.

[46]Eric Foner, *Tom Paine and Revolutionary America* (New York: Oxford University Press, 1976), p. 64.

[47]Olton, *Artisans for Independence*, p. 74; Foner, *Tom Paine*, p. 65; Ryerson, *Revolution*, pp. 133–34, 138–45, 160–62.

[48]Quoted in Foner, *Tom Paine*, p. 63.

they played a major role in the creation of the radical Pennsylvania constitution of 1776. "An enormous proportion of property vested in a few individuals," they advised the convention, "is dangerous to the rights, and destructive to the common happiness of mankind, and therefore every free state hath a right by its laws to discourage the possession of such property." This distinctly uncomplaisant call for a ceiling on wealth was accompanied by the advice that in electing representatives the people should shun "great and overgrown rich men [who] will be improper to be trusted [for] they will be too apt to be framing distinctions in society, because they will reap the benefits of all such distinctions."[49]

The ability of Philadelphia's artisans to organize and assert their collective strength was best exemplified in the move to broaden the franchise. This required breaking through one of the foundations of elite domination—that only property ownership entitled one to political rights. In the other northern cities voices were raised occasionally for the political rights of the propertyless and the poor.[50] But only in Philadelphia, where a combination of artisans, shopkeepers, and small traders captured control of the political process and then were themselves pressured from below by a highly politicized militia composed mainly of lower artisans, was the franchise given to all taxpayers, regardless of whether they owned property. In a society where the proportion of those without property was growing among artisans, this was a break with the past of enormous significance. It swept away "the basic economic presupposition that the ownership of a specified amount of property was an essential guarantee of political competence."[51] Many avid patriots, such as Bostonian John Adams, were aghast at this, for "it tends to confound and destroy all distinctions, and prostrate all ranks to one common level."[52] That, of course, was what the radical architects of Pennsylvania's constitution had in mind.

[49] *An Essay on a Declaration of Rights* (Philadelphia, 1776); *To the Several Battalions of Military Associators in the Province of Pennsylvania* ([Philadelphia, 1776]). For a general discussion of the eruption of egalitarian sentiment, see Foner, *Tom Paine*, pp. 123–26.

[50] For example, in New York, see *New-York Journal* (August 18, 1774; June 20, 1776); and Merrill Jensen, *The American Revolution within America* (New York: New York University Press, 1974), pp. 72–74.

[51] J. R. Pole, *Political Representation in England and the Origins of the American Republic* (New York: St. Martin's Press, 1966), p. 273. The issue of broadening the franchise was first raised in April 1776 (Olton, *Artisans for Independence*, pp. 76–77; Foner, *Tom Paine*, pp. 125–26).

[52] Quoted in Pole, *Political Representation*, p. 273n.

There emerged in the revolutionary era no perfect crystallization of artisan consciousness or all-craft solidarity. Artisans were still bound in part by allegiance to particular crafts, and, more important, long-range changes in trades such as shoemaking, tailoring, and printing were increasingly separating journeymen from masters. But, most of all, the revolutionary potential of the Philadelphia artisanry was limited by the strong hold that the "liberal" economic outlook held on large numbers of property-owning, modestly prosperous mechanics in the more lucrative trades. Although these men figured powerfully in the nonimportation movements and in the swelling sentiment for independence after 1774, they did not share the radical social perspective that lay behind the insurgency of the lower artisans of the Philadelphia militia. It was here that a genuine counterideology, stressing egalitarianism and communitarianism, resonated with greatest force.

The tensions within the artisan population of the city that always lurked behind the appearance of unity on questions such as nonimportation and independence became tragically evident in the price control crisis of 1779. Lower artisans for the most part advocated strict regulation of prices as a way of reinstituting the moral economy at a time when inflation was pushing the cost of life's necessaries beyond the reach of ordinary families, many of whom had sacrificed the male head of household to military duty. The majority of upper artisans, however, hewed to the ideology of free trade and laissez-faire principles of political economy. They thereby demonstrated how resilient were the bourgeois values of the old leadership which had been swept from office in the final days before independence and had been overpowered in the struggle over the Pennsylvania constitution of 1776.[53] This, then, would be one of the legacies of the Revolution in its largest commercial center: a struggle within the artisanry between those who, while united by an ideology of productive labor, were divided on how far political rights should be extended, how far the powers of government should reach in regulating the economy for the public good, and how relations within the workplace should be structured. It was by no means evident at the time, in the midst of the greatest social and political upheavals ever experienced in the Pennsylvania capital, what the outcome of these

---

[53] The price-control crisis of 1779 and the civil strife that accompanied it are covered fully in Foner, *Tom Paine*, pp. 145–82; and John Alexander, "The Fort Wilson Incident of 1779: A Case Study of the Revolutionary Crowd," *William and Mary Quarterly*, 3d ser., 31, no. 4 (October 1974): 389–612.

internal tensions would be. But to virtually every Philadelphia artisan it became apparent that in the course of defining issues that were palpable in terms of their daily existence, and through the process of struggling around these issues, they had gained a new political self-awareness and a new understanding of their role vis-à-vis those who stood above them in the social order.

Fathers, Sons, and Identity: Woodworking Artisans in Southeastern New England, 1620–1700
Robert Blair St. George

William Bradford, governor of Plymouth Colony, walked the dusty streets of Plymouth slowly, restlessly. Worried by the number of "strangers" who had come to the town with hopes of gaining quick and lasting fortunes, he carefully noted any new faces in the village. And one day, early in 1631, he saw that a young carpenter had arrived from Massachusetts Bay, their new neighbor to the north. Bradford returned home and promptly penned a letter to his counterpart John Winthrop, complaining how "Richard Church came . . . as a sojourner to worke for the present, though he is still here resident longer then he proposed . . . and what he will doe, neither we nor I thinke he himselfe knows, because he came to us upon falling out with his partner."[1] Despite his concern for the wayward artisan's fate, Bradford's tone belies a distinct

The author is indebted to Richard Bushman and the late Benno M. Forman for their criticism of an earlier version of this essay which was presented at the 1979 Winterthur conference and received the Colonial History Essay Prize for 1980 from the Colonial Society of Pennsylvania.

[1] *The Mayflower Descendant*, 34 vols. (Boston: Society of Mayflower Descendants, 1899–1937), 9:8.

belief that Church was somewhat confused, drifting aimlessly in the wake of discovering that not every dream he had of life in New England would easily come true. Church, born in the small village of Ashton in Northamptonshire, had arrived in Boston at the age of twenty-two in 1630 and within six months had already moved twice due to difficulty in practicing his trade. His unsettled career suggests that woodworking artisans, as a distinct subset of settlers bound by both common technical knowledge and economic dependence on the same natural materials, warrant the attention of social historians and historically minded folklorists interested in what made people move at particular times to particular places.

For the time being, if we choose to read geographical mobility as one index of changing motivations and expectations, the difficulties that Church undoubtedly confronted seem to have followed him the rest of his days. He lived successively at Plymouth—where he first climbed onto the historical stage—Duxbury, Hingham, Eastham, and Sandwich before dying at the house of his son Caleb in Dedham in 1668 (fig. 1).[2] Yet beyond being merely interested in the frequency of his travels, we must also realize that along another axis of change moved the individual artisan's drive to manifest cultural continuities with England and construct the New World as a secure society. In general, the careful study of woodworking artisans in southeastern New England during the seventeenth century suggests at once that the stereotypical view of the first period of settlement as one of comfortable, bucolic stasis may prove largely false for certain economic sectors of the population. So much is apparent from the lives of Church's first-generation contemporaries— men like Dolar Davis, a joiner who moved five times, or Thomas Painter, a carpenter who moved no fewer than nine times in his life—and their sons and grandsons in the next two generations. More significantly, close study of woodworkers suggests that the process of guiding New

[2]For demographic data on Church, see Robert Blair St. George, "A Retreat from the Wilderness: Pattern in the Domestic Environments of Southeastern New England, 1630–1730" (Ph.D. diss., University of Pennsylvania, 1982), pp. 40–41, 50, 62, 383, n. 105. Biographical data on the 438 woodworkers and builders represented in the tables that accompany this essay are abstracted in the same volume, pp. 369–415. Each worker is listed alphabetically and indexed according to the trade(s) he practiced; his dates of birth, marriage, working lifetime, and death; the location(s) where he worked; his place of English regional origin (for first-generation workers); and his relations among other artisans listed. All members of trades dependent on wood for their livelihood are included (see table 11); all other artisans cited in this essay, except where noted, may be consulted in this list.

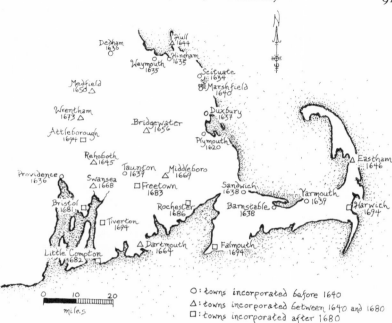

Figure 1.   Map of southeastern New England region: incorporated towns and the progress of seventeenth-century settlement. (Drawing, Robert Blair St. George.)

England through its first three generations of social and occupational life also framed a series of complex negotiations which effectively transformed the cultural identity of the artisan as an individual and redefined the shape of colonial society as a whole; it is this transformational process that serves as the focus of the present essay.

Before moving to analysis we should first address the issue of whether the artisans who underwent such a change in cultural identity actually formed a percentage of the colonial population significant enough to support claims that such a change could really have affected society at large. In examining the lives of sometimes illiterate and always obscure craftsmen whose actions typically lie beneath the level of historical scrutiny, we must pause to consider exactly how much of past reality we are including. In southeastern New England in the seventeenth century 438 artisans found either full- or part-time employment in the wood-

TABLE 1. Shop Generations, 1620–1700

Generation	Cohort (No.)	(%)
First	123	28.1
Second	225*	51.4
Third	46	10.5
Unaccountable	44	10.0
Total	438	100.0

* Of the 225 second-generation artisans, 33 (14.7%) were born in England and arrived in New England either before or during their training.

TABLE 2. Percentages of Adult Male Householders Working in the Woodworking/ Building Trades in the Plymouth Colony Area during the First Two Generations

Generation	Estimated population	Number of adult householders	Tradesmen (No.)	(%)
First	2,520 (1653 census)	420.7	87	20.7
Second	10,105 (1690 census)	1,686.9	174	10.3

working and building trades (table 1). Of these, 394 can be located in one of three shop generations. While this does not seem to be a very large number of workers in a region that extended more than 2,000 square miles into the wilderness, estimates indicate that the 87 first-generation workers within Plymouth Colony alone comprised fully one-fifth of the adult male householders, while their second-generation followers made up one-tenth (table 2).[3] At proportions of one-fifth and

[3] In defining shop generations in table 1 I have used the following distinctions based on the artisans' "fresh contact" with old English culture: First-generation workers include only those who received all of their training in England and were twenty-one years of age and working upon arrival. Artisans of the second generation include those who completed their training—having begun it here or not—in New England under first-generation masters. Third-generation artisans include those who both began and completed their training in New England under the second-generation master. This framework allows for the fact that some third-generation artisans may have had fellows of their own age who, having been trained by a grandfather, may have had craft knowledge comparable to second-generation workers. The estimated numbers of adult male householders presented in table 2 are derived from detailed research on militia lists for the years 1653 and 1690 published

one-tenth respectively, artisans of the first two generations formed a significant quantitative sector of their societies, and available evidence further suggests that the same high percentages held for most places in the English colonies in the seventeenth century and in certain locations until the close of the eighteenth.[4] Strictly in numerical terms, then, it would be a serious oversight to ignore them in any study of local social change during the period.

---

in Richard LeBaron Bowen, *Early Rehoboth: Historical Studies of Families and Events in This Plymouth Colony Township,* vol. 1 (Rehoboth, Mass.: Privately printed, 1945), p. 1–24. See also data presented in Joseph B. Feet, "Population of Plymouth Colony" *American Statistical Association Collections* 1, pt. 2 (1845): 143–44; and Herbert A. Whitney, "Estimating Precensus Populations: A Method Suggested and Applied to the Towns of Rhode Island and Plymouth Colony in 1689," *Annals of the Association of American Geographers* 55 (1965): 179–89. The total number of inhabitants projected by Bowen for 1653 and 1690 (2,520 and 10,105) indicate that for those years artisans must have comprised 3.4% and 1.7% of the respective Plymouth Colony populations. The reader is reminded that although table 1 records 123 first-generation and 225 second-generation workers, these include everyone working in the various political jurisdictions in the southeastern region: Massachusetts Bay Colony (Suffolk County), Plymouth Colony (after 1685 divided into Plymouth, Barnstable, and Bristol counties of the Province of Massachusetts Bay), and Rhode Island and Providence Plantations.

[4]Charles Henry Pope, *The Pioneers of Massachusetts* (1900; reprint ed., Baltimore: Genealogical Publishing Co., 1965), pp. 523–24, presents an overall occupational breakdown for 1,725 first-generation heads of households. Of this total, 348 (20.2%)—a percentage in agreement with my own findings—found employment in the woodworking and building trades as carpenters, joiners, housewrights, clapboard rivers, coopers, dish turners, ship carpenters, shipwrights, traymakers, turners, wheelwrights, masons, plasterers, millwrights, nailers, pipe-stave makers, plowwrights, and sawyers. Benno M. Forman, "Boston Furniture Craftsmen, 1630–1730," typescript, 1969, personal collection, p. I–4, indicates that 16% of the 853 taxable heads of Boston households in 1676 were woodworkers; this figure is slightly low in that his findings report only those artisans capable of making furniture. It should be noted that of the available town studies of local woodcrafting in seventeenth-century New England, none to date has been inclusive of all the trades connected by economic demands. For selective treatments, see Robert F. Trent, "The Joiners and Joinery of Middlesex County, Massachusetts" (M.A. thesis, University of Delaware, 1975), pp. 46–49, for detailed information on early Watertown and Concord; and Robert Blair St. George, "Style and Structure in the Joinery of Dedham and Medfield, Massachusetts, 1635–1685," in *American Furniture and Its Makers: Winterthur Portfolio 13,* ed. Ian M. G. Quimby (Chicago: University of Chicago Press, 1979), pp. 3, 37–46. Alan Kulikoff, "The Progress of Inequality in Revolutionary Boston," *William and Mary Quarterly,* 3d ser., 28, no. 3 (July 1971): 377, indicates that 351 members of the woodworking and building trades in Boston in 1790 claimed the highest percentage of that city's 2,754 known artisans (12.8%), although this, too, is biased because it excludes a number of shipwrights who fall into Kulikoff's further category of "marine crafts." Carville V. Earle, *The Evolution of a Tidewater Settlement System: All Hallow's Parish, Maryland, 1650–1783,* Department of Geography Research Paper no. 170 (Chicago: University of Chicago, 1975), pp. 64–67, reports that between 1660 and 1790 woodworkers in this area of the Chesapeake accounted for 18% of all "occupational persons."

Any discussion of artisan life in seventeenth-century New England falls logically into two parts. First we must examine the general trends in English society in the decades immediately preceding the Great Migration and how specific considerations of geography and local economy may have contributed to a defined set of expectations for life in the New World. Second, we must monitor the progress of these expectations as they affected the delicate relationship between family power and occupational status in New England. In other words, our attention should focus on the related problems of cultural separation, accommodation, and development, where accommodation demands at the very least the psychological confrontation of inherited needs and environmental realities.[5]

In the years before the Great Migration England was in the throes of a long and often violent process of internal change, the course of which has been well charted by several modern historians.[6] The turmoil of the times is apparent to modern historians even as it had been to contemporary diarists, who saw that their country was in agony. One in their midst, Robert Cushman, a wealthy backer of the first *Mayflower* voyage, took the time in 1621 to set down some of the reasons why England was almost daily becoming a less and less attractive place to raise a family. The towns of England, he wrote, "abound with young tradesmen, and the hospitals are full of the ancient; the country is replenished with new farmers, and the almshouses are filled with old laborers. Many are there who get their living with leaving burdens; but more are fain to burden the land with their whole bodies. Multitudes get their means of life by prating, and so do numbers more by beg-

[5] David Sabean, "Aspects of Kinship Behavior and Property in Western Europe," in *Family and Inheritance: Rural Society in Western Europe, 1200–1800*, ed. Jack Goody, Joan Thirsk, and E. P. Thompson (Cambridge: At the University Press, 1976), p. 113.

[6] The key recent studies that should be consulted for background reading on the upheaval and turmoil of seventeenth-century England (in order of publication) are Christopher Hill, *The Century of Revolution, 1603–1714* (New York: W. W. Norton, 1966), esp. pp. 1–101; Lawrence Stone, *Social Change and Revolution in England, 1540–1640* (New York: Barnes & Noble, 1965); Peter Laslett, *The World We Have Lost: England before the Industrial Age* (1965; rev. ed., New York: Charles Scribner's Sons, 1971); and Christopher Hill, *The World Turned Upside Down* (London: Temple Smith, 1972). More specific topics are treated with balance and care in Paul S. Seaver, ed., *Seventeenth-Century England: Society in an Age of Revolution* (New York: New Viewpoints, 1976); and Alan Macfarlane, *The Origins of English Individualism* (New York: Cambridge University Press, 1979), pp. 34–61, 165–88.

ging."[7] Fortunately, Cushman was sensitive and sympathetic to the struggles of New England settlers, and his words summarize the historical issues that need exploration in depth: the effect that a rising class of landowners (called by historians alternately the yeomanry or the "English Bourgeoisie"[8]) had on the national economy, the influence of their sudden rise on the occupational opportunities of young and old and men and women, and the disciplinary problems posed by vagrants and unlanded migrant laborers. He touched also on two closely related points which bear directly on the position of the younger artisan in a changing society. First, chronic underemployment was brought on by unpredictable economic fluctuations in which men are reduced to misfits, but not deservedly, through their own failings: not "always through intemperance, ill husbandry, indiscretion, &C., as some think, but even the most wise, sober, and discreet men go often to the wall, when they have done their best."[9] Second, there followed from this an implied fear that economic and social demise might not be related directly to individual moral corruption, a fear that must have shaken the seventeenth-century artisan soundly, as it forced him to recognize that his own actions, no matter how rational and morally correct they seemed, could easily go awry. He feared, too, that God's reason may have turned to wrath aimed at punishing not merely the individual for his particular sins but all men for generations of earthly depravity and moral backsliding.

The problems related to the rise of the yeomanry may be grouped conceptually around two poles, one social and the other economic, which defined status in terms of genealogical longevity and material wealth. Without question, the single most important determinant of status in early seventeenth-century England was the firm ownership of land. Unlike most artisans in the woodworking and building trades, yeomen were freeholders of the lands they worked. As a result, they were blessed with a surplus of crops in years of good harvest, while in leaner years they could always manage to fend off utter starvation.

---

[7] Robert Cushman, "Reasons and Considerations Touching the Lawfulness of Removing out of England into the Parts of America," in *Chronicles of the Pilgrim Fathers of the Colony of Plymouth, from 1602–1625*, ed. Alexander Young (1844; reprint ed., Baltimore: Genealogical Publishing Co., 1974), p. 247.

[8] See C. F. George, "The Making of the English Bourgeoisie, 1500–1700," *Science and Society* 35, no. 4 (Winter 1971): 385–414.

[9] Cushman, "Reasons and Considerations," p. 247.

Whatever happened at the market, the yeoman could pride himself on his economic autonomy, and so deeply embedded in his world view was the need to feel self-sufficient that the resultant boom in "cottage industry" expanded beyond its origins in the East Anglian textile trade and threatened to put local artisans out of business. Instead of purchasing everything from farmyard implements to household furniture from the village joiner, for instance, farmers insisted on making them in their own cellar shops. Instantly, then, the English yeoman not only wiped out the artisan's hope of ever accumulating much freeheld land, but he also made direct inroads on the artisan's means of survival.

Perhaps the country artisan's fear of imminent bankruptcy was not too far from the truth. At least one commentator observed by the late sixteenth century that unlanded folk had almost no civil power, claiming that "all artificers, as tailors, shoemakers, carpenters, brick-makers, brick-layers, etc. . . . have no voice nor authority in our commonwealth and no account is made of them, but only to be ruled and not to rule others," while just three years into the seventeenth century John Stowe could state that "it is no marvaile that . . . Artificers . . . do leave the Countrie townes, where there is no vent, and do flie to London, where they can be sure to find quick and ready market."[10] Yet while the city offered more work and money to anxious artisans, it also left them entirely dependent on the success of the yeomanry for their foodstuffs and clothing. In years of poor harvest—and there were several in the two decades preceding the Great Migration[11]—yeomen picked up

---

[10]Thomas Smith, *The Commonwealth of England* (1583), as quoted in Laslett, *World We Have Lost*, p. 32; John Stowe, *Survey of London* (1603), as quoted in Benno M. Forman, "Continental Furniture Craftsmen in London, 1511–1625," *Furniture History* 7 (1971): 94. One of the most underresearched problems in the early economic history of England is determining the extent to which rural artisans owned land. I have followed the cautious lead of W. G. Hoskins, "The Leicestershire Farmer in the Seventeenth Century," in W. G. Hoskins, *Provincial England: Essays in Social and Economic History* (London: Macmillan, 1963), pp. 159–60, in assuming that while a few artisans may have had small holdings, the great majority were either tenants on larger estates or unlanded migrants. Additional information on the lucrative opportunities London offered to rural artisans should be consulted in F. J. Fisher, "The Development of London as a Center of Conspicuous Consumption in the Sixteenth and Seventeenth Centuries," in *Essays in Economic History*, ed. E. M. Carus-Wilson, vol. 2 (London: Edward Arnold, 1954), pp. 197–207.

[11]W. G. Hoskins, "Harvest Fluctuations and English Economic History," *Agricultural History Review* 16 (1968): 15–17, 19, 24, 28–29. Mildred Campbell, *The English Yeoman under Elizabeth and the Early Stuarts* (New Haven: Yale University Press, 1942), p. 159, adds that the combined effects of a depression in the East Anglian cloth trades

the slack by turning again to their cottage crafts, leaving mechanics destitute through no fault of their own. As Cushman himself intimated, the artisan's existence had by the 1620s become little more than a sad game, a wheel of fortune which would spin out years of prosperity only to follow them ruthlessly with the wreck of famine.

By the time emigration to New England began, the apparent irrationality of artisan life had been further aggravated by the fact that while commodity prices had continued to soar, wages had not exceeded ten pence per diem since reaching that rate in the late 1580s. This combined with the other problems to prevent young artisans just reaching their majority between 1620 and 1635 from opening new shops. The evils of crowdedness, chronic underemployment, and fierce competition for what little business there was led the younger woodworker "to pluck his meanes as it were out of his neighbor's throat, there is such pressing and oppressing in town and country . . . so as a man can hardly set up a trade, but he shall pull down one or two of his neighbors."[12]

Competition within the woodworking and building trades took on a more terrifying aspect when one's neighbor and embittered rival for local support was also one's father, grandfather, or brother. On one hand, perhaps the most honored customs of "traditional" English culture urged sons to defer to parental discretion, remain at home, and toil in the shops of their fathers. Yet on the other hand, economic conditions were such that if sons did take up the family trade, they would risk challenging patriarchal authority by usurping part of the elder craftsman's local clientele. Indeed, to stay in one's ancestral village in the face of such sobering circumstances would have meant social and economic demise for both father and son and would have all but guaranteed the brand of foreseeable collapse so lamented by Cushman. One solution offered a way to alleviate generational tensions and avoid fam-

---

beginning in the late 1620s and a particularly poor corn crop in Norfolk in 1632 resulted in an unusually high percentage of yeomen who "crossed over" into the occupational domain of woodworkers and builders in order to augment sagging incomes. This coincidence of events may have been a direct cause of the migration of many artisans from East Anglia to New England in the mid 1630s (see table 4). See also "Depression in the English Cloth Industry, 1629" and "The Essex Cloth Industry in Depression, 1629," in *Seventeenth-Century Economic Documents*, ed. Joan Thirsk and J. P. Cooper (Oxford: Clarendon Press, 1972), pp. 32–33, 224–32.

[12] E. Phelps Brown and Sheila V. Hoskins, "Seven Centuries of Building Wages," *Economica*, n.s. 22, no. 87 (August 1955): 198; A. C. Edwards, "Sir John Petre and Some Elizabethan London Tradesmen," *London Topographical Record* 23, no. 115 (1972): 75; Cushman, "Reasons and Considerations," pp. 246–48.

ily conflict: migration to New England.

For young artisans especially, migration provided a means of venting hostility toward a competing family member without causing a real breakdown in the family unit. In short, New England offered hope to English artisans that at least their children might be raised in a less unsteady context. As their numbers indicate (table 2), the decision to emigrate resulted, ironically, in a density of woodworkers in New England higher than that which prevailed in most parts of England at the time. [13] The extent to which the first-generation artisan's family served as a stabilizing force in settlement may be explored in terms of two overarching patterns: *generational continuity*, as outlined by inheritance customs in wills of estates; and *territorial continuity*, as measured by the frequency and distance of migration within the region. In turn, each of these was further conditioned by a third pattern—*vocational continuity*, assessed by the trade(s) chosen by succeeding generations. Pertinent and detailed questions appear on every front: Why did the early New England artisan bequeath the tools of his trade with such caution? Why did the early artisan move? Was it in most cases, as in that of Richard Church, caused by disagreements between business partners? Or did they regard frequent migration as normative behavior for an artisan? More broadly speaking, did families in the woodworking trades in southeastern New England recover the strength that in old England had been sapped by generational tensions and tightened purse strings?

In the woodworking trades in the seventeenth century the influential links between generations (our first pattern of family stability) were related in part to the length of their members' lives and the frequency

---

[13] For example, while first-generation artisans in the woodworking and building trades accounted for one in every five first-generation heads of households in Plymouth Colony, their counterparts in seventeenth-century Gloucestershire totaled far fewer. In a 1608 muster role of that western county, only 6% of those reporting an occupation were woodworkers or builders (A. J. Tawney and R. H. Tawney, "An Occupational Census of the Seventeenth Century," *Economic History Review* 5, no. 1 [October 1934]: 36, table 1). Probably more typical of the first-generation artisan's native village was Goodnestown-next-Wigham in Kent, which had only two carpenters among its 62 households in 1676, or the rural deanery of South Malling in Sussex, which had but three woodworkers to sustain its 242 households between 1580 and 1640 (Laslett, *World We Have Lost*, pp. 68–69; Julian Cornwall, "Evidence of Population Mobility in the Seventeenth Century," *Bulletin of the Institute of Historical Research* 40, no. 2 [November 1969]: 143–44). Additional information on Kent may be consulted in Peter Clark, "The Migrant in Kentish Towns, 1580–1640," in *Crisis and Order in English Towns*, ed. Peter Clark and Paul Slack (London: Routledge & Kegan Paul, 1972), p. 121.

with which the aged held onto their possessions. For example, first-generation workers in the southeastern region lived almost as long as did the elders of seventeenth-century Andover—a mean of 69.8 years as compared with 71.8 years—while their offspring of the second generation lived nearly as long (table 3).[14] Their long tenancy in shops and on the land had both positive and negative effects on the shape of early New England artisan culture.

Without doubt, the long lives of the first generations—who often lasted well into the 1680s—insured that members of the succeeding generations learned well the proper rules for upholding established standards of workmanship and the "artificial" environment, or as one first-generation Charlestown shipwright phrased it in 1672, "the rules of art and the Custum of building amongst the English."[15] Ideally, members of the first generation would "retire" slowly, beginning with the marriage of the first son, who often inherited not only his father's farm but also the tools of his trade—powerful and recognized symbols of parental sanction and occupational status. In return, he cared for his aging parents until their deaths. In one instance, Francis Smalley of Truro on Cape Cod explicitly stated in his will: "my Carpenters Tools I give to my *Elder* son Francis," while in Providence Henry Brown, a well-equipped turner and joiner, specified that although he was bequeathing tools to both his sons, only the *eldest* was privileged to receive a complete set with which to continue running the family shop. Brown wrote that "all manner and sorts of my Working Tooles (only Excepting my Coopers tools), shall be Equally given to my two sons Richard & Joseph," but added the clause that his "Coopers tooles shall be all & wholy given to Richard."[16] Clearly, the fact that obedient eldest sons of the second

[14] Philip J. Greven, Jr., *Four Generations: Population, Land, and Family in Colonial Andover, Massachusetts* (Ithaca, N.Y.: Cornell University Press, 1970), pp. 21–40, 73–99.

[15] Records of the Quarterly Courts of Middlesex County, Massachusetts, Middlesex County Court House, East Cambridge, 3:59. The social significance of transferals in material culture is an aspect of New England's seventeenth-century settlement which historians repeatedly overlook or to which they assign a secondary value. The importance of making connections between material forms and social relations is discussed in Robert Blair St. George, *The Wrought Covenant: Source Materials for the Study of Craftsmen and Community in Southeastern New England, 1620–1700* (Brockton, Mass: Brockton Art Center, Fuller Memorial, 1979), p. 16; and Abbott Lowell Cummings, *The Framed Houses of Massachusetts Bay, 1625–1725* (Cambridge, Mass.: Harvard University Press, Belknap Press, 1979), pp. 95–117.

[16] Barnstable County Wills and Inventories (photostatic copies of original manuscripts), Barnstable County Court House, Barnstable, Mass., 3:338–39; *Early Records of*

TABLE 3. Ages at Death of First- and Second-Generation Artisans

Age	First generation (No.)	(%)	Second generation (No.)	(%)
22–29	1	2.6	4	4.0
30–39	1	2.6	5	5.0
40–49	3	7.9	10	10.0
50–59	4	10.5	16	16.0
60–69	8	21.1	26	26.0
70–79	6	15.8	29	29.0
80–89	12	31.6	9	9.0
90–99	3	7.9	1	1.0
100+	0	0.0	0	0.0
Total	38	100.0	100	100.0
	(Years)		(Years)	
Mean	69.8		62.0	
Median	71.0		65.0	

generation dutifully obeyed their fathers and remained in town rein-
forces our image of the seventeenth century as an era of family strength.

There is little reason to doubt that both Smalley and Brown would
have wholeheartedly agreed with the general themes sketched by one
Puritan divine, who felt that "Children should be very willing and ready,
to Support and Maintain their Indigent Parents. If our Parents are Poor,
Aged, Weak, Sickly, and not able to maintain themselves; we are bound
in duty and conscience to do what we can, to provide for them, nour-
ish, support, and comfort them." Some children seem to have taken
these thoughts seriously, too. Children like those of Hingham joiner
Stephen Lincoln did help their parents—and not just after the patriarch
had quit the daily grind of shop and fields. In fact, an artisan's offspring

the Town of Providence, 23 vols. (Providence: Snow & Farnham, 1892–1915), 6:210–11
(emphasis added). The most detailed study of aging and retirement for the period is John
Demos, "Old Age in Early New England," in *Turning Points: Historical and Sociological
Essays on the Family*, ed. John Demos and Sarane Spence Boocock, supplement to *The
American Journal of Sociology* 84 (Chicago: University of Chicago Press, 1978), pp. S248–
87; see esp. pp. S271–72. Additional information should be consulted in Gene W. Boy-
ett, "Aging in Seventeenth-Century New England," *New England Historical and
Genealogical Register* 134 (July 1980): 181–93.

were expected—perhaps were even planned—to serve as an invaluable source of free labor. This is a long-ignored aspect of *preindustrial* family structure, which recently has led R. M. Hartwell to include a well-wrought chapter titled "Children as Slaves" in *The Industrial Revolution and Economic Growth.*[17] In 1684 Lincoln used the labor of his sons, Stephen, Daniel, and David, all of whom were then in their teens, to gain credit in the account book of James Hawke, Hingham's town constable. Recording the payments with scrupulous attention, Hawke compiled Lincoln's credit for the single month of March 1684, showing the degree to which the latter relied on the strong backs of his sons to remain financially solvent:

	£. s. d.
due for 3 dais of daniel	00.03.00
due for 1 day of david	00.01.00
due for 1 day of steven	00.01.06
due to you for david two dais	00.02.00
due for 1 day of David	00.01.03
due to you for: three dais of David	00.03.09
two dais of David	00.02.00
two dais of David	00.02.00
four dais of David	00.05.00 [18]

Because most woodworking artisans in seventeenth-century New England were skilled with the plow as well as with the plane, the need for additional hands dramatically increased, especially at harvest. In some instances householders could find enough laborers for seasonal hire to gather crops with little delay; but for other less wealthy workers, children provided a means of keeping pace with the exigencies of year-round work in two occupations (fig. 2).[19] The demand for children on

[17]Benjamin Wadsworth, *The Well-Ordered Family; or, Relative Duties* (1712), reprinted in David T. Rothman and Sheila M. Rothman, eds., *The Colonial American Family* (New York: Arno Press and New York Times, 1972), pp. 99–102. In preindustrial England "the supply of children was determined by parents as investment decisions, decisions arrived at by balancing the gains and costs of rearing children" (R. M. Hartwell, *The Industrial Revolution and Economic Growth* [London: Methuen, 1971], p. 401).

[18]Account book of James Hawke, Constable of Hingham, Mass. (1677–85), on deposit at Massachusetts Historical Society, Boston, [19–20]. For additional information on children as a labor resource, see Lawrence Stone, *The Family, Sex, and Marriage in England, 1500–1800* (New York: Harper Colophon, 1979), pp. 295–96.

[19]The monthly division of farm work presented in figure 2 is drawn from Campbell, *English Yeoman*, pp. 209–11, and from a late sixteenth-century husbandry calendar

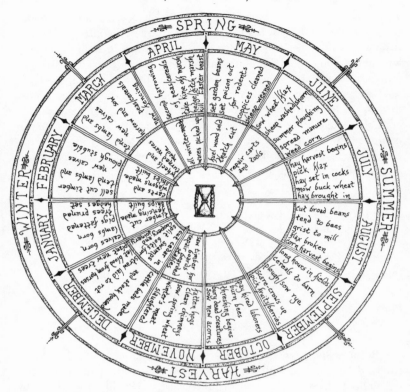

Figure 2.   The farmer-craftsman's annual work cycle: inner circle describes artisan work; outer circle represents farm work. (Drawing, Robert Blair St. George.)

the seventeenth-century New England farmstead was realized very soon after settlement. By 1652, the mean size of artisans' families in Medfield, for example, had stabilized at a little over 6.0 members, a sizable

reprinted in Dorothy Hartley and Margaret M. Eliot, *Life and Work of the People of England*, vol. 2 (London: B. T. Batsford, 1925), pp. 24–27. The difficulties the farmer-craftsman had in scheduling work were typified in 1634 when sawyers William Hammond and Nicholas Prestland told their employer, Edward Winslow, that although they would be faithful workers, they reserved the right to quit his service when it came time to bring home the harvest (Nathaniel B. Shurtleff, ed., *Records of the Colony of New Plymouth in New England*, vol. 1 [1855; reprint ed., New York: AMS Press, 1968], p. 30).

increase over the average of 3.6 members in at least one comparable English village in the period.[20]

In return for the assistance of sons on the farm and in the shop, fathers who had moved into a state of gradual retirement would sometimes help the sons they had blessed with name, trade, and property. Not unexpectedly, a patriarch would help his son in matters related to the craft(s) that they had both mastered; in this way, too, a parent could continue to assert his seniority in a real and a symbolic sense. Nathaniel Winslow, a shipwright working along the busy banks of the North River at Marshfield, noted in his daybook an indebtedness to his father for both cash and labor:

> What I have reseived of father
>> mony [£]3.00.00
>> drawing spruse plank
>> drawing plank from Leftenant Thomas Sawmill
>> mony [£]4.10.00
> The account of what Father hath don for me
>> 1 day going to bie plank
>> 7 tun of timber and drawing of it in the yard
>> drawing plank 2 days
>> more timber one tun and 22 fet
>> 33 fet of bord
>> 1 day drawing the keel.[21]

With sons helping fathers make the transition into old age and fathers helping sons when labor ran short, life in the woodworking and building trades in southeastern New England rested squarely on the continuity defined by work roles unchanged over several generations.

Such intergeneration trust, with its implications for role stability and status maintenance, fostered the development of local craft "dynas-

---

[20] The mean size of Medfield artisans' families in 1652 is derived from the relevant entries in a nearly complete transcription of a town rate listing (now lost) for that year reprinted in William S. Tilden, *History of the Town of Medfield, Massachusetts, 1650–1886* (Boston: George H. Ellis, 1887), pp. 51–56. The mean size of artisans' families in Medfield conforms to the general findings for other New England towns during the period, which are summarized in John Demos, "Demography and Psychology in the Historical Study of the Family," in *Household and Family in Past Time*, ed. Peter Laslett and Richard Wall (Cambridge: At the University Press, 1972), p. 561, n. 2. See also Laslett, *World We Have Lost*, pp. 66–67.

[21] Daybook of Nathaniel Winslow of Marshfield, Mass., entry of November 28, 1728, Joseph Downs Manuscript and Microfilm Collection, Winterthur Museum Library.

TABLE 4. Migration Distances during Working Lifetime

Generation	Nonmigrant (No.)	(%)	Less than 15 miles (No.)	(%)	15–30 miles (No.)	(%)	Over 30 miles (No.)	(%)	Total (No.)	(%)
First	44	35.8	12	9.7	39	31.7	28	22.8	123	100.0
Second	157	69.8	18	8.0	35	15.6	15	6.6	225	100.0
Third	34	73.9	6	13.0	5	10.9	1	2.2	46	100.0
Total	235		36		79		44		394	
	(59.6%)		(9.1%)		(20.1%)		(11.2%)		(100.0%)*	

* This represents the total number (N = 394) of those workers who can be placed in a working generation; it does not include the 44 who remain unaccountable (see table 1).

ties" or strong families whose active participation in a specific trade or group of trades grew to extend over many decades. When migration distances—one measure of territorial continuity—are compared for each of the first generations of woodworking artisans (table 4), we see that the foundations of kinship set by first-generation workers held firm despite an apparently high rate of movement. Two of every three first-generation artisans migrated to some degree, and almost all of those who did moved more than fifteen miles away from their home village.[22] Through the succeeding two generations overall migration decreased noticeably and, while localized migration within a fifteen-mile radius in the second and third generations increased by as much as one-half, long-distance migration decreased dramatically from its peak in the first generation (remember artisans like Dolar Davis, who moved five times, or Thomas Painter, who moved nine times). This pattern indicates perhaps that once local kinship had developed to a point where migration between nearby towns caused little or no occupational or family stress, population stabilized spatially. In addition, because the pattern suggests the emergence of more highly localized social groups, it confirms the findings of other scholars who have noted that the declining ability of towns to regulate social movement during the second generation was countered by a rise in the power of families.[23]

[22] A fifteen-mile radius is used here as a standard of significant migration because it was the average distance between adjacent towns in the region and the average limit of a day's return ride by horse and cart during the period.

[23] James A. Henretta, "The Morphology of New England Society in the Colonial Period," *Journal of Interdisciplinary History* 2, no. 2 (Autumn 1971): 397. Thomas R.

Part of the variations in first-generation migration may be related logically to the English regional origins of the immigrant artisans themselves (table 5 and fig. 3). The origins of a little over half of the documented first-generation woodworkers and builders in southeastern New England can be traced. Fully one-third of this group came from the eastern English counties of Norfolk, Suffolk, and Essex, where a high percentage of yeomen engaged in cottage crafting, where there was early enclosure of open fields, and where the predominance of primo- and ultimogeniture had made life for trained artisans especially difficult. When these craftsmen arrived in the New World, they labored to recreate the small nucleated village of the East Anglian countryside. Thus it is no surprise to find that almost all of the East Anglian artisans in southeastern New England settled and worked in the two towns of Dedham and Hingham (table 6), both of which were characterized throughout the period by extremely high percentages of sons remaining in the shops of their fathers.

TABLE 5. **English Regional Origins of First-Generation Artisans in Southeastern New England**

Region	Artisans (No.)	(%)
East Anglia	22	33.8
London/Southeast	16	24.6
Midlands	8	12.4
West Country	16	24.6
Northern Counties	2	3.1
Foreign (Holland)	1	1.5
Total identified	65	100.0

Cole, "Family, Settlement, and Migration in Southeastern Massachusetts, 1650–1805," *New England Historical and Genealogical Register* 132 (1978): 174–75, presents migration distances for the inhabitants of Sandwich, Mass., which are in fundamental agreement with those in table 4. For general theoretical concepts concerning the relation of social structure and occupational stress, see Eugene Litwak, "Occupational Mobility and Extended Family Cohesion," *American Sociological Review* 25, no. 1 (February 1960): 9–21; and Eugene Litwak, "Geographical Mobility and Family Cohesion," *American Sociological Review* 25, no. 3 (June 1960): 385–94. Julian Wolpert, "Migration as an Adjustment to Environmental Stress," *Journal of Social Issues* 22, no. 4 (October 1966): 92–102, proposes an ecological model for mobility stimulus which is in fact relevant to the plight of some seventeenth-century woodworkers who were forced to migrate because of depletions in materials necessary to their trades; for instance, some carpenters were forced to quit towns where wealthy tanners refused to limit their practice of bark stripping, which resulted in the retarded growth and premature death of timber trees.

Figure 3. Map of English regional origins of woodworking artisans who migrated to southeastern New England (see table 5). (Drawing, Robert Blair St. George.)

In a similar effort, the Kentish artisans working along the eastern coast of Plymouth Colony—with their highest concentration at Scituate—attempted to duplicate the demographic profile and social structure of their home county. Kentish carpenters and joiners like Dolar Davis, who was born near East Farleigh, moved frequently in New England between contiguous towns. Arriving in Boston in 1634, he was at Cambridge the following year and by 1634 had spent time at Duxbury, Scituate, and Barnstable. In 1655 he moved up to Concord in Middlesex, where some of his fellow emigrés from the marshy lowlands of Kent had settled. After twelve years there he returned to Barnstable, where he remained until his death in 1673. Along the way he had left some sons settled in Concord and some in Barnstable.

This pattern, chaotic as it may seem to those used to stories of Puritan utopian closed communities, closely relates to migration patterns found by recent scholars in the southeastern English counties of Kent, Sussex, and nearby Surrey, three areas characterized less by demographically insular villages than by settlement unified by an extensive kinship system which spread over a fairly wide expanse of the local landscape. In other words, a kind of overarching kin structure—what Alan Everitt has termed a "county community" in Kent—connected families in small villages into a cohesive and systemic totality. Thus Kentish society, for example, was typified more by clanlike kin groups than by the independent nuclear families so readily associated with East Anglia. The strength of the Kentish structure was fostered inevitably by the local prevalence of gavelkind, which urged children to marry within the general area and settle on local family lands. As a result, children in the southeastern counties rarely strayed more than fifteen to thirty miles from their home villages, despite the high frequency of their travels. Kentish woodworkers, one of them probably Davis's father, while moving almost continually, seldom roamed beyond immediate adjacent villages.[24]

[24] Joan Thirsk, "Industries in the Countryside," in *Essays in the Economic and Social History of Tudor and Stuart England in Honour of R. H. Tawney*, ed. F. J. Fisher (Cambridge: At the University Press, 1961), p. 70, discusses the ramifications of gavelkind for the rural inhabitants of the north downs of Kent. A more elaborate picture of the custom as it developed in the Weald is available in Joan Thirsk, ed., *The Agrarian History of England*, vol. 4, 1500–1600 (Cambridge: At the University Press, 1967), pp. 57–59. For the local migration habits of woodworkers in Kent, see Clark, "Migrant in Kentish Towns," pp. 126–29; and W. K. Jordan, "Social Institutions in Kent, 1480–1660," in *Essays in Kentish History*, ed. Margaret Roake and John Whyman (London: Frank Cass,

TABLE 6. English Regional Origins of First-Generation Immigrants to

Region	Dedham (No.)	(%)	Hingham (No.)	(%)
East Anglia	43	79.6	63	73.3
London/Southeast	2	3.7	3	3.5
Midlands	4	7.4	9	10.5
West Country	1	1.9	9	10.5
Northern Counties	4	7.4	2	2.2
Total identified	54	100.0	86	100.0

By contrast, East Anglian villages seem to have been more insular. Families came and went less often and land passed from father to son more often as an undivided unit of blessing. We should be careful, however, not to confuse insularity with complexity and stability. The towns of Norfolk, Suffolk, and Essex, from which came a great many of the townsmen of Dedham and Hingham, were comprised of a high percentage of relative newcomers to the area who had been lured from remote locations in the north and west by the promise of an economy bolstered by the prosperity of the textile trade.[25] As a result, these rural villages—the prototypes for New England's introspective, reflexive towns—had not yet had sufficient time to develop the extensive and deeply embedded kinship structures of their Kentish counterparts. In

---

1973), pp. 87–89. The concepts of county community and clan are well explained in Alan Everitt, "Social Mobility in Early Modern England," *Past & Present*, no. 33 (April 1966): 57–60. Evidence that similar patterns of intense local migration along kinship lines also pervaded nearby Sussex and Surrey shows that an overwhelming percentage of migrants in these southeastern counties moved more than twice during their lifetimes—as did many of the artisans from these counties who later moved to the southeastern New England region. The English artisans rarely died more than three parishes away from their place of birth (Cornwall, "Evidence of Population Mobility," p. 150; E. E. Rich, "The Population of Elizabethan England," *Economic History Review*, 2d ser., 2, no. 3 [1950]: 258).

[25] A notable example occurred when John Thurston, a master joiner trained in Thornebury, Gloucestershire, moved to Wrentham, Suffolk, before eventually migrating to Massachusetts (Frank Thurston, Thurston family genealogist, to St. George, December 15, 1977). Another instance of a young woodworker migrating eastward in England (although not specifically to take advantage of East Anglia's prosperity) occurred when Jenkyn Davis traveled from Haverfordwest in Wales to Sandwich in Kent prior to setting sail for Lynn, Mass., in 1638; see Benno M. Forman, "The Seventeenth-Century Case Furniture of Essex County, Massachusetts, and Its Makers" (M.A. thesis, University of Delaware, 1968), p. 58.

Four Towns in Southeastern New England

Scituate		Taunton		Total for region	
(No.)	(%)	(No.)	(%)	(No.)	(%)
3	3.9	—	—	139	27.7
50	65.8	1	5.0	132	26.4
9	11.8	5	25.0	88	17.5
9	11.8	14	70.0	103	20.6
5	6.7	—	—	39	7.8
76	100.0	20	100.0	501	100.0

effect, the assumed insularity of East Anglian villages in the period may have been little more than a reflex to their own youth. In Kent, where years of undisturbed settlement were less subject to rapid economic change, mobility among rural artisans was indicative of a different kind of social structure.

Keeping these regional variations in mind, we must be careful when attempting to claim that the more migratory of the first-generation artisans were also the more unstable and insecure. For, in fact, geographical mobility alone does not prove an adequate measure of all patterns underlying past behavior. Clearly, the problem of evaluating family cohesion on the basis of first-generation migration alone must be viewed in relation to the demographic continuities manifest by the individual worker. Different artisans from different places in England possessed different regional models or timetables for the correct recreation of optimum cultural order. And although these regional habits may have endured only for a short time in the New World, they may account for certain kinds of spatial behavior which reappear frequently in studies of seventeenth-century New England society.

The general trend through the first three generations of artisan life in the southeastern region shows that the frequency of craftsman migration—our second measure of territorial continuity—was greatest in the first generation and then steadily declined as families gained local prominence. For instance, Richard Church, our original protagonist, lived in no fewer than seven towns in thirty-six years. His sons Nathaniel, Joseph, Caleb, and Benjamin were all woodworkers—although Benjamin is more famous for having killed "King Philip," the Wampanoag sachem Metacom. Three of these four sons moved only twice, while Church's grandson Thomas never moved from the town of his upbringing, Little Compton. The powerful Carpenter family of Rehoboth also exemplifies the pattern well. While the family patriarch, William Carpenter, a native of Horwell in Hampshire, had migrated from Weymouth to Rehoboth in the late 1640s, his sons remained in the area. William and Samuel, both carpenters and joiners, remained in Rehoboth proper; Joseph, wheelwright and turner, set up shop in Swansea just a few miles down the road. Even the grandson remained in town as wheelwright, joiner, and turner. (Note that here late generations were known to practice secondary and tertiary crafts—more of this later.) And in other towns other families became no less firmly entrenched. In Scituate the Stetsons and Stockbridges were dominant; Barnstable had the Davises and Crockers. By far the most dramatically kinship-bound was early Hingham, where the Lincolns, Hobarts, and Beals accounted for all but a few of the town's woodworkers throughout the century. And miraculously, by 1680 these three families formed almost one-fourth of the town's population.[26]

Both generational and territorial continuity were reinforced by the frequent location of woodworking shops in domestic contexts. As sons grew into apprentices, the boundaries between home life and work were never clear, and the family gained additional meaning as an agent of vocational continuity—our third pattern of stability. The well-equipped shop of Jonathan Fairbanks, wheelwright of Dedham, for example, was spread throughout the family dwelling. His inventory of 1668 records that tools and stock were found in the "Roome called the New House," the "working Celler," and the "Hall Chamber."[27] If an artisan's shop was not actually in his house—although most often the shop *was* there— it was never far away. Usually it stood next to the house, still within reach of growing children and nearby kin, as did the small weaver's

[26] John Coolidge, "Hingham Builds a Meetinghouse," *New England Quarterly* 34 (1961): 442. The remarkable consolidation of dominant Norfolk kin groups in seventeenth-century Hingham is charted in John J. Waters, "Hingham, Massachusetts, 1630–1661: An East Anglian Oligarchy in the New World," *Journal of Social History* 1, no. 4 (Summer 1968): 351–70.

[27] Suffolk County Probate Records, Suffolk County Court House, Boston, 5:112–14. Fairbanks's house, built ca. 1637, survives on its original site in Dedham, Mass., and is described in detail in Cummings, *Framed Houses*; and Abbott L. Cummings, "Appendix I: Summary Abstracts of the Structural Histories of a Significant Sampling of First Period Houses at Massachusetts Bay," in *Architecture in Colonial Massachusetts*, ed. Abbott L. Cummings, Publications of the Colonial Society of Massachusetts, vol. 51 (Boston: By the society, 1979), pp. 135–37.

Figure 4. Peak House, Medfield, Mass., late seventeenth century, with later shop structure. From Joseph Warner Barber, *Historical Collections of Massachusetts* (Worcester, Mass.: Dorr, Howland, 1839).

shop which survived alongside the so-called Peak House in Medfield (fig. 4). When younger artisans went into business, they often built adjacent to their father's property. In 1677 Barnstable "Granted to John Davis, Junr. Leiberty to Set up a Shop on a Knoll of Ground over against his house adjoyning to his fathers fence." In Providence almost thirty years later the impulse to keep house and shop adjacent was so strong that the town selectmen, "Upon the request of [carpenter] Joseph Whipple . . . Granted unto him that he may have Liberty to remoove his little house which he calleth his old shopp & to set it on the west side of the highway . . . over ag[ainst] his new dwelling house."[28]

[28] Barnstable Town Records, manuscript transcriptions by Mary R. Lovell and Gustavus Hinckley (1895), Office of the Town Clerk, Hyannis, Mass., 1:115; *Early Records of Providence*, 11:95. A similar instance of a son's being located by town mandate next to his father occurred when carpenter Thomas Thurston, son of joiner John Thurston of Medfield, petitioned that town for his own land in 1653. After due consideration the selectmen permitted him "six acres for his House lot of upland Adjoyning unto His fathers

The close proximity of a father's labor to his sons' upbringing made it inevitable that a crafting family could reinforce its current status in the community and provide for its future economic security by training its own members to take over the shop when the patriarch wearied. The pervasive trend toward "in-family" training held firm and even strengthened between the second and third generations. While the total number of legal apprenticeships recorded in the region dropped to zero, the number of artisans trained by family members (fathers, uncles, or grandfathers) almost tripled, and the number trained by non–family members fell by more than half of what it had been between the first and second generations (table 7). Logically, as families tightened their networks of local power, they consolidated their craft knowledge and chose to channel it through their own youth. Overall, this trend suggests that the extensive practice of nonfamily apprenticeship, which characterized the training of the second generation, may have become less customary a means of social control as the emergence of strong kin groups guaranteed the occupational security of the next generation. Seen in this light, the "tribalism" of the first generation, rather than having been a practice by which indulgent adults could minimize spoiling their own children, may have functioned as a social mechanism designed to hold children steady in the shaky first years of settlement before relations could supervise the growth and calling of the child on their own. [29]

Beyond question, however, a large majority of second-generation woodworkers were not trained by members of their own families, while those of the third generation clearly were, although some second-generation artisans did risk punishment by law in order to train their own sons. So important was the idea of family training to Benjamin Hearndon, carpenter of Providence, that he tried to keep his son at home despite the youth's legal obligation to another worker. In short order the selectmen of Providence responded, "In Answer to a Letter from the

---

House loote on the North este" (Medfield Town Records as quoted in Tilden, *History of Medfield*, p. 59).

[29] Edmund S. Morgan, *The Puritan Family: Religion and Domestic Relations in Seventeenth-Century New England* (New York: Harper & Row, 1966), pp. 77, 168–86, first put forward the concept of "tribalism"; see also John Demos, *A Little Commonwealth: Family Life in the Plymouth Colony* (New York: Oxford University Press, 1970), pp. 73–74. Another explanation might be that when older couples took on young servants after their natural children had already left home, tribalism may have functioned as a means by which disoriented parents could preserve a quasi-normative family structure rather than confront life alone. See pp. 117–19 of this essay.

TABLE 7. Training the Second and Third Generations

Generation	Legal apprenticeship recorded (No.)	(%)	Trained in family (No.)	(%)	Trained outside family (No.)	(%)	Total (No.)	(%)
Second	10	4.4	59	26.2	156	69.4	225	100.0
Third	—	—	33	71.7	13	28.3	46	100.0

Massachusetts Colony touching the returning of an Apprentice of his Master in the Bay: It is Ordered, that if the said Apprentice his father Benjamin Hearndon, in whose keeping, the said Apprentice is, do not returne the said Apprentice speedily unto the Bay, that the Constable shall forthwith apprehend him, & convey him to his Master."[30] In turn, the migration patterns of those second-generation woodworkers who *were* trained by family members confirm that increasingly strong kin ties fostered geographical stability (table 8). Here again long-distance migration dropped by 100 percent, while local migration increased. A general pattern emerged through the second and third generations of either complete nonmigration or limited migration within a fifteen-mile radius, both of which attest to the rise in importance of the association between kinship structure and place of habitation.

This relationship between family and location was supported as well by the ties linking artisans' families. The two most influential networks were those created by the bonds of marriage and by business partnership, each of which functioned differently. Marriage to the daughter of an elder woodworker or to the widow of a deceased contemporary artisan insured the selection of a mate used to the seasonal nature of the farmer-craftsman's life and meant a chance to acquire the decedent's tools. It guaranteed as well a hand in the shop. Indeed, some women in the region seem to have been skilled at handiwork, although documentary references are only suggestive. The presence of "Joyners tooles with other things" in the 1633 inventory of Martha Harding of Duxbury deserves consideration, as does the 1666 will of Francis Godfrey. A joiner and carpenter who had built the first Bridgewater meetinghouse just four years earlier, Godfrey specified that while a few of his tools were to go to a grandson, he wished to reserve for "my Wife

[30] *Early Records of Providence,* 2:78.

TABLE 8. Migration Distances of Family-Trained Second- and Third-Generation Artisans from Their Place of Training

Generation	Nonmigrant (No.)	(%)	Less than 15 miles (No.)	(%)	15–30 miles (No.)	(%)	Over 30 miles (No.)	(%)	Total (No.)	(%)
Second	35	59.3	7	11.9	8	13.6	9	15.2	59	100.0
Third	20	60.6	9	27.2	2	6.1	2	6.1	33	100.0

Elizabeth Godfrey one broad and one narrow axe, one hand saw, one hatchett, one square, one Drawing knife, one adds, one hammer, one pair of Chisells, two augurs (one mortising auger and one smaller augur), and three planes (one smoothing plane, one rabbeting plane, and one Joynter), all of the best I have."[31] A well-planned marriage could function in at least three additional ways for the seventeenth-century artisan: it could affect upward social and economic mobility if one's bride were born of wealth; it could gain a migrant artisan acceptance in a new community if he married one of its residents; and it could link together for economic protection all of the artisans who practiced a particular trade in a town.

An artisan's relationship to other workers in his family, particularly as manifest in business partnerships, also affected the texture of family cohesion in the woodworking trades. Almost without exception, partnerships in the southeastern region fell along family lines and consisted of either brothers or brothers-in-law working side by side in the same shop. Typically, tools were owned in common, as were those of Joseph and Anthony Waterman of Marshfield. Joseph's inventory of 1715 listed among their common possessions "the Tools in partner between his

[31] Plymouth Colony Wills and Inventories, Plymouth County Court House, Plymouth, Mass., 1:19–20. Circumstantial evidence that Martha Harding may have been a working artisan is offered by the complete absence of historical references to her husband, suggesting that he may have died either in England or on an early Atlantic crossing; see *Mayflower Descendant*, 17:156. Impetus to marry and remarry artisans' widows, like the incentive for having children, might be attributed to the need for free labor as well as to emotional demands. The economic functions of marriage are summarized in K. H. Connell, "Peasant Marriage in Ireland: Its Structure and Development since the Famine," *Economic History Review*, 2d ser., 14, no. 3 (1962): 503ff. See also Lois Green Carr and Lorena S. Walsh, "The Planter's Wife: The Experience of White Women in Seventeenth-Century Maryland," *William and Mary Quarterly*, 3d ser., 34, no. 4 (October 1977): 561–62.

brother Anthony Waterman & him" at £3.12.06. In no instances did
artisans working in the same town go into partnership with other than
a kinsman and in only one case did an artisan team up with workers in
another town—that being when Charles Stockbridge of Scituate was
retained by the town of Hingham to mastermind the construction of its
second meetinghouse (Old Ship) in 1680. When Stockbridge acknowledged payment for the job in the spring of 1682, he signed his name
after writing "Received by me . . . and my partners Stephen & Joshua
Lincoln of Hingham."[32] But surely this was an exception due to the
elaborate construction and special nature of the project.

Decreased migration, increased power of the family, sons trained
by fathers in domestic settings, marriage, and partnership: the list reads
like a survey of social unity. Yet underneath such a calm surface not all
the currents of family cohesion and generational stability flowed so
smoothly. While the nearness of one's kin was significant in channeling
the growth of the woodworking trades, the very qualities that promoted
strength at times also provoked uncertainty. The resulting instability—
and it must have been in large part a psychological one—seems to have
resulted from the reluctance with which some older artisans passed tools,
shops, and lands to their eager offspring. In their conservative attitudes,
many first-generation workers placed their sons in a position essentially
identical to that in which they had found themselves before leaving
England, suggesting that their deep need to prove their independence
to strict parents resulted not only in migration but, later, also in the
overbearing treatment of their own children. Intent on maintaining their
established brand of patriarchal order, first-generation artisans held on
to the firm ownership of land and trade—often until death—and thereby
forced their sons to remain in town with less than full economic status
in one trade, remain in town and take up alternate trades, or leave town
entirely in order to prove their status as independent householders. We
will see that second- and third-generation woodworkers increasingly chose
the second of these options.

The manner in which this New World generational crisis found
resolution differed from its antecedent in England due to the wide-

[32] Plymouth County Wills and Inventories, Plymouth County Court House, Plymouth, Mass., 3:390–91; quoted from the Selectmen's Records of the Town of Hingham
in Arthur Marble, "The Old Ship, the Ancient Meeting House of the First Parish of
Hingham," unpaginated typescript in the Office of the First Parish (Unitarian) Church,
Hingham, Mass.

spread availability of land for artisans. In one sense, the presence of land made elder farmer-craftsmen closefisted. Their fields were cleared, well manured, and in a good year brought a decent profit at the local market. Because land insured them secure balance between agriculture and craft which they had so envied in the English yeomanry, they were sorely hesitant to relinquish its control too quickly. For once they had, they risked becoming ancillary social creatures dependent on others. Carpenter John Paine of Eastham was likely not the only younger artisan to conceive of the elder worker as "some older infirm person whose life is Even a burden to them Selves and they them Selves a burden & a trouble to all about them." First-generation craftsmen, therefore, were often very specific about the restrictive transfer of both land and tools. Frequently they would permit their sons to use their property as if it were their own while still retaining legal ownership. Artisans in the southeastern region did this with their land almost as often as did the husbandmen of Andover. Thus John Gorham, joiner and turner of Yarmouth on Cape Cod, ordained that his eldest son should "have the Dwelling house that hee now lives in, with the barne and halfe the upland belonging to the said farme."[33] By retaining titles to lots already being worked by their sons, parents may have continued to wield disciplinary power and insure that their old age would be spent comfortably. Other artisans treated the tools of their trade with similar caution. In 1663 Thomas Lumbert of Barnstable willed to his son Caleb "the three yeare old mare that was alwaies accounted him, and his Carpenters tooles." In nearby Sandwich John Chipman declared, "I will and

[33] "Deacon John Paine's Journal," in *Mayflower Descendant*, 9:99; Plymouth Colony Wills and Inventories, 3, pt. 1, bk. 2:164. Greven, *Four Generations*, pp. 80–84, discusses the implications of land transfer by will rather than by deed and maintains that Andover parents used property as a kind of leverage for their future security. Demos, *Little Commonwealth*, pp. 164–70, states that in Plymouth Colony as a whole parents do not seem to have used land in such a manner. While I have found that many artisans in Plymouth Colony did—suggesting perhaps that rules of inheritance and attitudes toward land varied due to vocation or an emerging sense of class distinction—we must remember that artisans represented only one specific sector of colonial society. The notion that parents could prolong their children's dependence on them and alter the timing of the family life cycle must be treated with caution, for, depending on age, vocational choice, and order of birth, a child's expectations of substantive inheritance could have ranged from high to nil. In the latter case an attempt at control on the part of parents would have caused no discontinuities. See also Robert V. Wells, "Family History and Demographic Transition," *Journal of Social History* 9, no. 1 (Fall 1975): 11; and R. A. Schofield, "Age-Specific Mobility in an Eighteenth-Century Rural English Parish," *Annales de Demographie Historique* (1970): 265–68.

bequeath to my son Sam[uel] . . . all my Carpinters Tools & Husbandry Implements which are now in his possession and occupation in Barnstable."[34]

Presumably these arrangements usually worked smoothly and proved an effective and efficient way to restore the sharp swaths cut by the Grim Reaper. At the very least, they urge us not to forget that the family is a unit with both social and temporal meaning. Yet in some instances the timing and technique of inheritance may have caused a few problems for younger artisans of the second and third generations, subject as they sometimes were to parental discretion well into middle age. An occasional artisan, lacking a sizable landed inheritance, also found himself blessed with too few of his father's tools with which to start a shop of his own. While it was not very serious when John Crocker of Barnstable directed that his "Carpenters tools be equally Divided between . . . sons Jonathan and John," this kind of partible inheritance could be very damaging in cases where too many brothers competed for their father's attention. John Thomson of Middleboro died in 1696, having decreed, "my four sons shall Have All my Tooles of all Sorts for Carpentry," while William Nickerson of Harwich willed that his carpenter's and cooper's tools worth only two pounds, ten shillings be split five ways— each share worth a meager ten shillings—among five sons. Worse still, a father could always use the bequethal of tools to motivate his sons to follow in his footsteps. In some trades the value of tools alone warranted compliance with parental pressure. While not a woodworker, William Bassett, a Duxbury blacksmith, willed over twelve pounds' worth of tools to his son Jonathan with the caveat that he could have "all the tooles Conditionally that he shall use them in my trade or else they shalbe Devided to my fouer [other] Children." Gorham limited his son in both land and career when he inserted into his will a clause giving the youth "the use of . . . the land that lyeth between the said dwelling house and the tanyard, during all the time he shall keep tanning in that place and no longer."[35]

To a limited degree the delay of adult status affected all generations, implicit as it was in a predominantly agrarian society. As long as

[34] Plymouth Colony Wills and Inventories, 2, pt. 2:24; Barnstable County Wills and Inventories, 3:228–29.

[35] Barnstable County Wills and Inventories, 3:130–31, 618–19, 4:3; Plymouth County Wills and Inventories, 1:241–42; Plymouth Colony Wills and Inventories, 1:128, and 3, pt. 1, bk. 2:164.

TABLE 9. Migration and Aging of First- and Second-Generation Artisans *

Age	Move to New England		First move in New England				Second move in New England			
	First generation (No.)	(%)	First generation (No.)	(%)	Second generation (No.)	(%)	First generation (No.)	(%)	Second generation (No.)	(%)
20–29	17	60.7	6	24.0	12	70.6	6	46.1	5	41.7
30–49	11	39.3	14	56.0	5	29.4	3	23.1	6	50.0
50+	0	0.0	5	20.0	0	0.0	4	30.8	1	8.3
Sample	28	100.0	25	100.0	17	100.0	13	100.0	12	100.0

* See note 36 for key to age categories.

farming served as the mainstay of economic security and tools continued to function as symbols of occupational responsibility, parents were
cautious about passing property to the next generation. Throughout the
seventeenth century the effects of inheritance were felt most acutely by
artisans in their twenties—the same years that witnessed the termination
of apprenticeships, marriage and parenthood, and the highest frequency
of migration. Indeed these intersecting patterns suggest that one function of migration may have been to intensify a shift in social status by
accentuating a change in social milieu (table 9). In some instances artisans in their twenties moved more than once; perhaps for them social
adjustment came less easily, for over 70 percent of the second-generation artisans whose ages at the time of their first move are known moved
while in their twenties and over 40 percent of those known to have
moved a second time did so while in the same age group. Migration
remained fairly frequent throughout the middle years, when wealth was
rising and full economic status was developing, indicating a relationship
between economic change and geographical mobility. Notably, more
than half of the first-generation artisans whose ages at the time of their
first move within New England are known moved between the ages of
thirty and fifty, a period in the life cycle that for two reasons may have
been characterized by a kind of midlife crisis. The first was the departure of children from the family circle. Here again parents threatened
by the dissolution of the nuclear family may have moved as a way of
marking the inevitable restructuring of their social world. For the sev-

enteenth-century family was, after all, more than a series of blood relations; it was a way of categorizing experience.

The second factor which may have contributed to a high rate of migration during midlife was the death of one's aged parents, an event that frequently leaves children painfully aware that they themselves are entering the last phase of life. In some cases parental death stimulated a new interest in the passage of time and a feeling of having been deserted by society. For example, carpenter John Paine of Eastham began to note his birthdays in his diary shortly before the death of his mother in April 1704, writing: "I am just now entering the fourty Sixth year of my pilgrimage." Three years later, when his father died, a more shaken Paine grieved: "On the Sixteenth day of august 1707 My aged father Thomas Paine departed his life: I am now left fatherless and motherless as to my natural parents but my God is a father of the fatherless upon whose providence I cast my Self o thou god of my father do not cast me off though my father and my mother have forsaken me." The additional fact that almost a third of the first-generation artisans for whom data exist moved a second time after the age of fifty may indicate that in a good many instances the stabilization of wealth did not guarantee a sedentary existence. This was no doubt due to the occasional artisan who kept working well into "'old age'" and therefore had little or no reason to alter established habits of geographic mobility.[36] So long as he possessed knowledge (the "rules of art") valued by other men in town and region, the willing craftsman could quite literally work his way to the grave.

Implicit in the fundamental relations described—those of generation, territory, vocation, and, as we have seen, maturation—was a key transformation, a key shift in the identity of the artisan and the organization of his world. Specifically, this change came about as the delicate balance of family structure and individual aspiration was upset. As outlined, the progress of the seventeenth-century artisan was typically measured in increments of family strength and decreasing frequency and

---

[36] "Deacon Paine's Journal," pp. 49–50; Demos, "Old Age," p. S261. Table 9 structures the aging process in groups of 20 to 29 years, 30 to 49 years, and 50 and more years in keeping with Demos's suggestion that these divisions are most revealing of overall trends in wealth accumulation ("Old Age," p. S266). Forman, "Boston Furniture Craftsmen," p. IX–1, refers to Henry Fane, turner of Boston, who was still engaged in "bottoming chairs" at age eighty-three.

distance of migration—both of which are distinctly social-scientific trends. Yet rising from between these two processes came something whose importance far exceeded them, something that may just help answer the prodding question, Why should social historians study the role of artisans in the past life? For upon peering into the preindustrial culture of southeastern New England, we learn that more was happening than just the slow, clocklike mutation of a cool, agrarian society. We must dig deeper than the statistical surface if we are to discover how people felt about their own lives.

If, like some recent social scientists, we interpret "identity" as a reference to degrees of unity or fragmentation existing within the personality of the individual as he relates his image of himself to his image of the surrounding society,[37] the evidence presented by the careful analysis of the behavior of southeastern New England's early woodworking artisans indicates that two types of personal fragmentation took place. And behind both stood not the breakdown of the family unit—as modern social critics would have us believe—but rather the tenacity and ultimate vindication of the family in local culture. Most noticeable is a trend suggesting that as families became more geographically rooted and more kindship-bound over the course of the first three generations, their heads became less identified with one calling and instead divided their time not only between farming and a craft (as they had always done) but also between farming and two, three, four, and even five crafts (table 10). The inventories of many artisans show this to have been the case. Thomas Tingley of Attleborough owned "Carpenters and Masons tools" at his death in 1724; William Blanton died in Rehoboth later that same year with "augers and chisels and other tools belonging to the Trade of a housewright and all Husbandry tools" in his estate, along with "Lombs, slays, and other tools belonging to the weaver's trade"; Thomas Paine of Truro died in 1721 possessed of tools for carpentry, coopery, surveying, and smithing; and Robert Millerd of Rehoboth, although calling himself a tanner in his will, died in 1709 the owner of tools for tanning, blacksmithing, and shoemaking worth a total of fourteen pounds, ten shillings.[38]

[37] See Tamara Hareven, "The Search for Generational Memory: Tribal Rites in Industrial Society," *Daedalus* 107, no. 4 (Fall 1978): 137–38; and Eric Erikson, *Life History and the Historical Moment* (New York: W. W. Norton, 1975).

[38] Bristol County Wills and Inventories, Bristol County Court House, Taunton, Mass., 2:265; 5:8, 31; Barnstable County Wills and Inventories, 4:10.

TABLE 10. Number of Trades Practiced: Occupational Identity Trends, 1620–1700

Generation	One trade (No.)	(%)	Two trades (No.)	(%)	Three or more trades (No.)	(%)	Total (No.)	(%)
First	102	82.9	18	14.6	3	2.5	123	100.0
Second	162	72.0	54	24.0	9	4.0	225	100.0
Third	31	67.4	12	26.1	3	6.5	46	100.0
Total	295	(74.8%)	84	(21.3%)	15	(3.9%)	394	(100.0%)

In effect, a man's occupational identity—his image of his own work and his conception of how his work functions in local society—at the close of the seventeenth century no longer rested on a single calling. Men who had been trained for one task branched out into several others, changing their self-image and reputation and, in so doing, changing the relations of production in their community as well. Many of the secondary trades practiced by second- and third-generation artisans would in the first generation have commanded the skill of an individual trained specifically *for that task and no other.* For example, in a 1671 court case that found a first-generation shipwright named William Carr guilty of breach of contract, another shipbuilder named Abell Osuff testified that Carr had caused grave problems by letting a worker perform a task which clearly fell out of his defined occupational domain, his niche in the local hierarchy of task distribution. Osuff's words attest to the first generation's sense of discrete roles for individuals: "He the said Carr had a man named Isaac Sheffield, that was unskilled in that kind of labor . . . for caulking the vessell; and the said Sheffield spent a considerable time about Caulking as his master appointed him, but it plainly appeared that as he had no experience, so the most that he did was ineffectual, and some sort was worse than if he had never meddled therewith, especially considering the danger thereby occuring (the place where he wrought being neer the Keel)."[39]

Perhaps the younger mechanics picked up these added skills strictly to keep down prices by eliminating needless middlemen. Yet, in a deeper vein, the reluctance of the first generation to grant the second generation the tools of their trade forced that younger generation to diversify

[39] Records of the Quarterly Courts of Middlesex County, 3:59.

TABLE 11. Breakdown of Woodworking/Building Trades by Generation

Trade	First generation (No.)	(%)	Second generation (No.)	(%)	Third generation (No.)	(%)	Total per trade (No.)	(%)
Carpenter	45	36.7	114	50.8	17	37.0	176	44.6
House carpenter	2	1.6	7	3.1	2	4.3	11	2.8
Joiner	14	11.4	14	6.2	3	6.5	31	7.9
Turner	1	0.8	4	1.8	3	6.5	8	2.0
Dish turner	2	1.6	—	—	—	—	2	0.5
Wheelwright	1	0.8	4	1.8	3	6.5	8	2.0
Cooper	14	11.4	15	6.7	—	—	29	7.4
Setwork cooper	—	—	—	—	1	2.2	1	0.3
Pumpmaker	—	—	1	0.4	—	—	1	0.3
Shipwright	11	8.9	5	2.2	3	6.5	19	4.8
Blockmaker	1	0.8	—	—	—	—	1	0.3
Millwright	2	1.6	—	—	—	—	2	0.5
Sawyer	5	4.1	1	0.4	—	—	6	1.5
Clapboard river	1	0.8	—	—	—	—	1	0.3
Plasterer	1	0.8	—	—	—	—	1	0.3
Nailer	2	1.6	1	0.4	—	—	3	0.8
Combined two of above trades	13	10.6	40	17.8	9	19.6	62	15.6
Combined three or more of above trades	2	1.6	5	2.2	1	2.2	8	2.0
Combined above trade(s) with other trade(s)	6	4.9	14	6.2	4	8.7	24	6.1
Total	123	100.0	225	100.0	46	100.0	394	100.0

if it did not leave town. As we have already noticed, more artisans chose to diversify rather than leave, and in the end this pattern transformed the well-structured society of the first decades of settlement—replete with specialized artisans like dish turners, set-work coopers, clapboard rivers, and plasterers—into a world where the roles of everyday life were more complex, more overlapping, more interdependent, and more tightly integrated (table 11). In this new order the distinctions between one artisan's work domain and that of his neighbor were less clear. In turn, when the second generation was faced with training their offspring, they sometimes deliberately specified that the youngster should learn two (often related) trades. Although it does not involve a woodworker, one case is particularly instructive. In Providence in 1676 Zachariah Mathewson and his wife promised John Taylor that they would take his son Benjamin and not only "learn him to Read & to Write" but also "to Tann leather & to make shoes."[40] Once on his own, Benjamin would be fully able to practice two legitimate trades: tanning (the curing and preparation of hides) and shoemaking (the transformation of the leather into costume). And because this meant that his future customers would have only one stop to make when in need of a pair of shoes, the diversification of occupational skill seems to have resulted in less social interaction among *all* townsmen but more intense and frequent interaction with a few select individuals. Writ large, this pattern could easily have been an underlying force for the early emergence of self-regulating neighborhoods, so-called self-sufficient households, or the gradual evolution of social class distinctions based on moral preference.

If we view the urban-rural continuum in terms of specialized versus integrated occupational identities or concentrated versus diffused roles, the changing profile of task distribution among southeastern New England artisans shows a general emergence of social class distinctions over the course of the seventeenth century. The trend troward seeing "rural" as different from "urban" is further evident when we check the migration into and out of the Boston–Charlestown area from and to the hinterlands (table 12). The migration activity shows that about one in every five first-generation woodworkers at least attempted to live in a setting

[40]*Early Records of Providence*, 15:76. The continuum from simple to complex (or single to multiple) roles is a more useful model for the analysis of relative ruralism than that derived from vague notions of geographical isolation or "folk versus elite" oppositions. See Gwyn Evan Jones, *Rural Life: Patterns and Processes* (London: Longmans, 1973); and Louis Wirth, "Urbanism as a Way of Life," *American Journal of Sociology* 44, no. 1 (July 1938): 1–24. The effects that occupational diversification has had on modern industrial society are summarized in E. A. Wrigley, "The Process of Modernization and the Industrial Revolution," *Journal of Interdisciplinary History* 3 (1972): 223ff.; the more subtle changes brought about by such diversification are discussed in Margaret Mead, "The Implications of Culture Change for Personality Development," *American Journal of Orthopsychiatry* 17 (1947): 641; Michael Zuckerman, "The Fabrication of Identity in Early America," *William and Mary Quarterly*, 3d ser., 34, no. 2 (April 1977): 192–93; and Richard Bushman, *From Puritan to Yankee* (New York: W. W. Norton, 1970), pp. 267–88.

TABLE 12. Urban-Rural Migration of Artisans

Migration pattern	First generation (No.)	(%)	Second generation (No.)	(%)	Third generation (No.)	(%)
Boston–Charlestown to hinterlands	11	8.9	1	0.4	—	—
Hinterlands to Boston–Charlestown	9	7.3	1	0.4	1	2.2
Boston–Charlestown to hinterlands and returned	—	—	—	—	—	—
Hinterlands to Boston–Charlestown and returned	4	3.3	11	4.9	—	—
Total urban-rural migrants	24	19.5	13	5.7	1	2.2
Total rural nonmigrants	99	80.5	212	94.3	45	97.8
Total	123	100.0	225	100.0	46	100.0

that was distinctly urban by the late 1640s,[41] but the percentage fell to one in every twenty second-generation artisans, and fell still further to include only one in every fifty workers in the third generation. A steady movement toward a self-conscious rural stasis pervaded the period, again suggesting that while first-generation artisans, secure in their more narrowly defined economic roles, migrated easily from city to country, their offspring somehow felt less confident in areas outside those described by the tight circle of relations. And despite our modern tendency to assume that artisans will inevitably seek a market that, like seventeenth-century Boston, could afford the highly specialized crafts of upholsterer, carver, pailmaker, wine cooper, and pipe-stave maker, the artisans of the second and third generation clearly *preferred* their rural world, where family matters were of increasingly central concern. Watching the medieval universe recede behind them, these artisans rejected a firm occupational identity and opted instead to keep family and household together.

Insofar as both a newly arrived consciousness of rural society and its foundation in moral economy came as by-products of increasing family cohesion, we can see that the growth of seventeenth-century New England society as a whole cannot be explained as a process of

[41] Darrett B. Rutman, *Winthrop's Boston: A Portrait of a Puritan Town, 1630–1649* (Chapel Hill: University of North Carolina Press for the Institute of Early American Culture, 1965), pp. 164–201.

preservation and extension alone.[42] Built solidly into the *mentalité* of this agrarian culture was a mechanism that pushed families together but broke the individual apart, leaving him to contemplate a relentless dialectic between his obligation to local society and the larger world of upward material mobility.

The first three generations of artisan existence in early New England tell us much about moments in the transition from medieval to modern society which would be difficult to approach if we assumed that an agrarian economy meant a kind of occupational sameness. In summary, the four essential qualities of artisan life in southeastern New England during the period included an overall stabilization of demographic movement, which saw the concept of family more closely identified with the concept of place than it had been in medieval society; a rise in the power of families—not society as a whole—in educating and influencing the occupational direction of their own offspring; a steady rate of role diffusion, which meant that more and more people were becoming more and more alike in vocational skills and social status; and, finally, a constant movement by families toward isolated farmsteads within town boundaries as lots at the town center grew scarce and unaffordable.[43] This made similar people live farther and farther apart. Joined to a steadily decreasing level of lay piety in the church, these processes are at the root of modern individualism. And while we have focused specifically on the changes in the artisan's world, these patterns grew from the same vital issues that affected a widespread segment of colonial American society. Working from obscure carpenters like Richard Church, we can spin webs in which to catch for analysis later moments in time. For if the ground rules of modern American individualism were adumbrated by the close of the seventeenth century, they would not be codified until the Industrial Revolution.

[42]James A. Henretta, "Farms and Families: *Mentalité* in Pre-Industrial America," *William and Mary Quarterly*, 3d ser., 35, no. 1 (January 1978): 7–8.

[43]Kenneth A. Lockridge, *A New England Town: The First Hundred Years* (New York: W. W. Norton, 1970), pp. 93–118.

Boston Goldsmiths, 1690–1730
Barbara McLean Ward

Between 1690 and 1730 Boston was the undisputed colonial leader in the production of gold and silver objects, and some of the finest American silver ever produced was made in Boston at this time. The goldsmithing craft thrived in Boston during the last decade of the seventeenth century and the first decade of the eighteenth century. The influx of English officials into Boston following the establishment of the Dominion of New England and the proclamation of the Royal Charter in 1691 jarred the traditional preferences of the town's social elite and stimulated a demand for stylish objects on a par with those made in London.[1] With the end of Queen Anne's War in 1714, however, inflation and recession slowed economic growth in Boston, and by the 1730s many goldsmiths were unable to make more than a subsistence-level wage. Fewer native craftsmen entered the trade, and the influx of fully trained immigrant craftsmen slowed considerably as opportunities diminished.

Details of the lives of the craftsmen who worked in Boston during this period not only reveal the inner workings of a particular craft but also shed light on the role of the artisan in pre-Revolutionary urban society. Examination of correlations between wealth, occupational mobility, family background, and social status for one craft group allows for a better understanding of the diversity of the artisan class and the widening gap separating laboring artisans from merchant-producer

[1] For the changing political status of the colony and its social consequences, see Bernard Bailyn, *The New England Merchants in the Seventeenth Century* (1955; reprint ed., New York: Harper & Row, 1964), pp. 192–97; and Richard S. Dunn, *Puritans and Yankees: The Winthrop Dynasty of New England, 1630–1717* (1962; reprint ed., New York: W. W. Norton, 1971), pp. iii–vi, 219–20.

craftsmen during the colonial period. The inner dynamics of the gold-smithing craft, as revealed through the exploration of the hierarchy within the trade, relationships between masters, journeymen, and apprentices, and the variety of business practices common among goldsmiths of this period, provide data for further study of the work culture of the urban craftsman.

Goldsmiths are a particularly fruitful group for study because we know who they were, what they made, and who were their patrons. They marked the objects they produced with distinctive hallmarks and often engraved the initials and coats-of-arms of the purchasers/owners. Thus, we can both discover the forms and techniques of a particular craftsman and learn the identity of his clients. Within the last fifty years much biographical work has been done on Boston goldsmiths by scholars in the field of American decorative arts. This essay seeks to bring together the points of view of the social historian and the art historian, to present new information, and to analyze the biographical data compiled by Kathryn C. Buhler, John Marshall Phillips, Francis Hill Bigelow, Martha Gandy Fales, and others on the members of the craft who worked in Boston during the period 1690–1730.[2]

[2] Extensive biographical work on Boston goldsmiths by Kathryn Buhler has been extremely helpful in the preparation of this essay. Much of this work has been published in Kathryn C. Buhler, *American Silver, 1655–1825, in the Museum of Fine Arts, Boston*, 2 vols. (Greenwich, Conn.: New York Graphic Society, 1972); Kathryn C. Buhler, *Massachusetts Silver in the Frank L. and Louise C. Harrington Collection* (Worcester, Mass.: Barre Publishers, 1965); and Kathryn C. Buhler, *Colonial Silversmiths, Masters and Apprentices* (Boston: Museum of Fine Arts, 1956). The principal primary sources consulted include Boston vital records printed in *Record Commissioners Reports of the City of Boston*, vols. 9 (1883), 24 (1894), and 28 (1898); *Suffolk County Probate Records*, (Waltham, Mass.: Graphic Microfilm of New England, 1957); Records of the Inferior Court of Common Pleas for Suffolk County, Social Law Library, Suffolk County Court House, Boston; and Suffolk County Court Files, Office of the Clerk of the Supreme Judicial Court of Suffolk County, Suffolk County Court House (hereafter cited as SCCF). Published works consulted include Henry N. Flynt and Martha Gandy Fales, *The Heritage Foundation Collection of Silver with Biographical Sketches of New England Silversmiths, 1625–1825* (Old Deerfield, Mass.: Heritage Foundation, 1968); Oliver A. Roberts, *History of the Military Company of Massachusetts Now Called the Ancient and Honorable Artillery Company of Massachusetts, 1637–1888*, vol. 1 (Boston: Alfred Mudge & Son, Printers, 1895); Hermann Frederick Clarke, *John Coney, Silversmith, 1655–1722* (1932; reprint ed., New York: Da Capo Press, 1971); and Hollis French, *Jacob Hurd and His Sons Nathaniel and Benjamin, Silversmiths, 1702–1781* (1939, addenda printed 1941; reprint ed., New York: Da Capo Press, 1972). Francis Hill Bigelow and John Marshall Phillips manuscript notes at Yale University Art Gallery (hereafter cited as Bigelow-Phillips notes) have also been a valuable source of information. The full results of my work to date appear in Barbara M. Ward, "The Craftsman in a Changing Society: Boston Goldsmiths, 1690–1730" (Ph.D. diss., Boston University, 1983).

In contrast to traditional studies which have singled out exceptional craftsmen as the basis for broad generalizations, this paper attempts to analyze the available data from documentary evidence and surviving objects for all of the eighty-two goldsmiths so far identified. It is hoped that this method will provide new insights into (1) the hierarchy that developed within the craft; (2) the distribution of wealth among goldsmiths and how it related to wealth distribution in the community as a whole; (3) the apparent decline in the social mobility of goldsmiths toward the end of the period; (4) the working relationship between master craftsmen and between master craftsmen and their journeymen and apprentices; and (5) the range of work performed by men working within the same craft.

Much of the literature on the craft of the goldsmith has focused on the special respect accorded to the members of the trade because they understood the mysteries of working with precious metals. In medieval times goldsmiths were innovators in the arts, and they enjoyed important royal and church patronage. By the seventeenth century, however, the goldsmith was principally an imitator of the stylistic innovations in the other arts and was regarded by his contemporaries as merely a mechanical artist. When Jaspar Danckaerts visited Boston in 1680, he took it as a symbol of declining piety and incipient materialism that the sons of four clergymen were apprenticed to goldsmiths, but this may also suggest that Bostonians considered the craft of the goldsmith to be an honorable and lucrative calling.[3]

Although there was generally a high level of prosperity among Boston goldsmiths of the seventeenth century, there was by no means an equality of either status or interests among craftsmen. Goldsmiths, like all craftsmen, "could be found in every rank from that of the privileged urban gentry all the way down to that of the white indentured servants and Negro slaves. They constituted a vertical, not a horizontal, section of the colonial population." One's position within the craft was determined by birth and family position and enhanced by financial success and prudent marriage alliances. Because the goldsmith worked in pre-

---

[3] Eva M. Link, *The Book of Silver*, trans. Francisca Garvie (New York: Praeger Publishers, 1973), p. 47; R. Campbell, *The London Tradesman* (1747; reprint ed., Newton Abbot, Devonshire: David and Charles, 1969), pp. 141–42; Bartlett Burleigh James and J. Franklin Jameson, eds., *Journal of Jaspar Danckaerts, 1679–1680* (New York: Charles Scribner's Sons, 1913), pp. 274–75.

cious metals, his business required that he make a substantial capital investment in order to become an independent master craftsman. This usually required that he have either family resources or sufficient personal contacts with local and foreign merchants to command substantial amounts of credit. Such personal connections might come as a result of the skill that he had shown as a journeyman or the good will of his former master. Brock Jobe noted the latter circumstance in his study of Boston furniture craftsmen of the early eighteenth century. As James Henretta has said, for Bostonians of the late seventeenth century, "the best opportunities for advancement rested with those who could draw upon long standing connections, upon the credit facilities of friends and neighbors and upon political influence."[4]

It is little wonder, then, that a man like Jeremiah Dummer, whose father, Richard, was one of the largest landowners in Massachusetts and a leading political figure in the colony, had no trouble setting himself up as an independent goldsmith and attracting the most distinguished patrons. Not only did he produce fine silver for many homes, but he also received commissions from churches, some as far away as Connecticut. It is clear that his neighbors respected him for his leadership qualities as well as for his skill in the craft. During most of his life Dummer served in positions of responsibility in both town and colony governments. Because of his father's extensive connections he was readily accepted by the Boston elite. In addition, he was resourceful and industrious enough to turn the profits of his goldsmithing business into wise investments in shipping and other enterprises.[5]

Not all goldsmiths had Dummer's ready access to the upper classes, but their trade potentially gave them several advantages over other craftsmen. In a money-scarce economy, which ran on a system of debits and credits "by book," the artisan often waited for long periods of time before he was paid for his labors. When he eventually received payment

[4]Carl Bridenbaugh, *Cities in the Wilderness: The First Century of Urban Life in America, 1625–1742* (1938; reprint ed., New York: Oxford University Press, 1971), p. 143; Brock Jobe, "The Boston Furniture Industry, 1720–1740," in *Boston Furniture of the Eighteenth Century*, ed. Walter Muir Whitehill (Boston: Colonial Society of Massachusetts, 1974), p. 11; James A. Henretta, "Economic Development and Social Structure in Colonial Boston," in *Colonial America: Essays in Politics and Social Development*, ed. Stanley N. Katz (Boston: Little, Brown, 1971), p. 452.

[5]Hermann Frederick Clarke and Henry Wilder Foote, *Jeremiah Dummer: Colonial Craftsman and Merchant, 1645–1718* (1935; reprint ed., New York: Da Capo Press, 1970), pp. 3–51.

it might well be in the form of inflated paper money and credits on other shops.[6] The goldsmith was one of the few craftsmen likely to have access to hard money on a fairly regular basis. Customers were encouraged to bring metal directly to the goldsmith as the raw material for the goods they ordered, and, in this way, the largest manufacturing goldsmiths received payment for the goods they made even before they began to fill the order. Most goldsmiths eagerly sought used objects, but only the wealthiest could pay cash for old silver and gold. The volume of the merchant-producer goldsmith's business demanded that he have a constant supply of precious metals on hand in his shop. Journeyman goldsmiths or any workman who lived by piecework received only enough silver from their employers to do the job, and they were required to account strictly for all the metal they used. These marginal craftsmen were not apt to have the credit resources of the most affluent members of the craft. The established merchant-producer goldsmith, on the other hand, enjoyed a favorable position within the local merchant community because his stock appreciated with the rate of inflation.

The most successful goldsmiths served a luxury market and constantly came into contact with the most affluent members of society. They could often boast of friendly relationships with the local clergy, justices and gentlemen, and the wealthiest merchants. These men trusted the goldsmith to produce wares of the latest fashion and of sterling quality. With no assay offices and guilds to certify the quality of the metal in a given piece, the maker's hallmark became the customer's only guarantee of quality. The goldsmith's success in business no doubt depended at least in part on his reputation for integrity and honest dealing. The craftsman who received the trust and respect of his social superiors also received the general notice of his fellow citizens. Many goldsmiths were elected to fill responsible positions in the town, militia, military company, and church.

Not all goldsmiths received the same measure of trust. The patterns of patronage revealed by the diary and ledger of Samuel Sewall help to illuminate the hierarchy among goldsmiths. For instance, when purchasing large or important objects—such as a beaker (1700), the half pike for the Artillery Company (1701), two tankards (1701, 1710), a cup for a prize (1702), or a salver and a spout cup for wedding presents

---

[6]Carl Bridenbaugh, *The Colonial Craftsman* (1950; reprint ed., Chicago: University of Chicago Press, Phoenix Books, 1966), pp. 153–54.

(1710)—Sewall usually patronized John Coney. Although he ordered a tankard from Edward Winslow in 1719, the ledger shows that Sewall was more likely to purchase from this goldsmith such lesser objects as spoons (1702, 1714), a gold necklace (1708), porringers (1709), gold buttons (1712), and rings (1722, 1726). It is surprising that from his close friend and cousin, Jeremiah Dummer, Sewall mentions ordering only a ring (1702), spoons (1706), several porringers (1710), and a whistle (1710). Other accounts with Dummer for unspecified services exist for the years 1694 to 1701, and it is possible that Sewall ordered plate from Dummer during those years. After 1710 Dummer's health failed, and it is evident that Sewall was more inclined to take his important orders to Coney after that date.[7]

On several occasions, particularly after 1710, Sewall also patronized John Edwards, buying gold rings from him in 1716, 1723, and 1724, spoons in 1711 and 1725, silver shoe buckles in 1719, and a porringer in 1724. A tankard with the Sewall arms, which was later given to the Old South Church, bears Edwards's mark and may be either the tankard Edwards mended for Sewall in 1724, which is listed in the ledger, or a separate commission which was never noted. For small work Sewall frequently went to the shop of William Cowell. In his accounts Sewall listed clasps for two Psalters (1711), a gold locket and gold beads (1719), silver spoons (1725), and a chain (1726) purchased from Cowell. At the time of his daughter's funeral in 1710, he recorded single orders to his former ward Samuel Haugh for six rings and to Peter Oliver for ten rings. In 1723 he ordered a ring from Nathaniel Morse, and in 1725 he purchased a spoon from Jacob Hurd.

These accounts show that Sewall considered John Coney to be the foremost producer of hollowware in Boston. He purchased lesser items from Edward Winslow on most occasions, but he must have considered Winslow to be a competent smith when he commissioned him to make a tankard in 1719. After 1710 Sewall patronized John Edwards frequently, and he seems to have been impressed with William Cowell's selection of jewelry. Sewall sometimes visited two or more goldsmiths' shops in the same week, which suggests that he matched the job to the craftsman rather carefully instead of habitually going to the same man. When he had an order too large to be filled by one firm alone, he

divided his order according to his regard for the abilities of the craftsmen. No doubt other customers followed similar patterns. Although
personal preference and family and business connections served to divide
the market among a number of goldsmiths, certain men achieved local
renown. Coney's important government, college, and church commissions show that Sewall's preference was shared by other influential Boston citizens. Although they produced much fine silver, Dummer and
Winslow were probably best known for their government service. Dummer served as selectman and justice of the peace for many years, Winslow was well known as the sheriff of Suffolk County (fig. 1), and both
were appointed justices of the Inferior Court of Common Pleas in their
later years.

Other goldsmiths, like Thomas Savage, David Jesse, and John Noyes,
produced work of high quality proving that they too were accomplished
craftsmen. However, they did not enjoy the same level of private and
church patronage as did Dummer, Coney, and Winslow. Although
probate records are not available for either Savage or Noyes, evidence
of property holding and office holding for these men, and for Jesse as
well, indicate that all of them belonged to the upper ranks of the middle
class. Productivity figures and documentary evidence suggest that all
three were independent craftsmen employing apprentices and an occasional journeyman.

Below Savage, Jesse, and Noyes in the hierarchy of the craft were
others who seem to have produced very few objects. These men probably relied for their income on small work, such as jewelry, and a steady
stream of repair work. Some may also have been jobbers or pieceworkers whose livelihood was based on making objects for the larger shops
on special order. No doubt many served as journeymen for at least a
part of their careers. Although we cannot know for sure how many men
actually worked as goldsmiths independently, the fact remains that of
the eighty-two men included in this study, only thirty-three are known
today by more than a handful of surviving objects, and at least twenty
men appear in the records for whom no objects have yet been discovered. Although the rate of survival may not be constant for all goldsmiths' work of this period, such figures indicate that hollowware
commissions, the most lucrative part of the market, were controlled by
a very few craftsmen. There can be little doubt that John Coney, from
whose shop more than 110 objects survive, produced more silver than

Figure 1. John Smibert, *Edward Winslow*. Boston, 1730. Oil on canvas; H. 32½", W. 27½". (Yale University Art Gallery, Mabel Brady Garvan Collection.)

did John Noyes or Thomas Savage, known by fewer than two dozen objects each.

The fortunes of the goldsmith rose and fell with the fortunes of his customers. During the 1690s most Bostonians were employed and wages were relatively high. Numerous merchants engaged in shipping and enjoyed a comfortable prosperity; a few of them amassed considerable wealth. When royal officials arrived in Boston in the late 1680s and 1690s, following the revocation of the old company charter, they brought with them the ostentatious life-style of Restoration England. The Boston mercantile elite sought to compete with these new officials for power and prestige, and one result was a growing demand for luxury goods. Boston goldsmiths prospered as a consequence.

During this decade the market in silver was dominated by Coney and Dummer, followed by John Allen and John Edwards, William Rouse, Edward Winslow, and Timothy Dwight. The remaining business was divided among such men as Noyes, Savage, Jesse, and immigrants Richard Conyers, Edward Webb, and William Cross. Other men working at the end of the seventeenth century, who may have been journeymen or jobbers, were James Barnes, Jr., Jonathan Belcher, Samuel Foster, René Grignon, Samuel Haugh, Eliezur Russell, Robert Sanderson, Jr., and Thomas Wyllys. In 1685 Samuel Sewall wrote in his diary that young Samuel Clark, a goldsmith trained with Hull and Sanderson, had chosen to go to sea for a short time because he had "no work in the shop." In spite of the fact that he had served his apprenticeship in a well-known firm and came from a good family, Clark apparently found that he could not make a living working as an independent goldsmith. Another craftsman who came to Boston toward the end of the seventeenth century, Henry Hurst, is documented as having worked as a journeyman until at least 1701.[8]

By the early years of the eighteenth century some Bostonians were reaping large profits from the production and shipping of war materials. Such men had more money to spend on luxury goods than previously, a fact that may account for the survival of so many superbly crafted silver objects in the early baroque style. Between 1700 and 1710 Coney and Dummer continued to be the leading goldsmiths in Boston. The bulk of Edward Winslow's finest work dates from this period and shows a skill and sophistication that attracted the notice of his contemporaries. John Allen and John Edwards made several outstanding individual pieces, and the many church commissions that they were called on to fill are a clear indication that the partners were widely respected. Records reveal that all of these men earned a very comfortable living from their craft.[9]

During the decade from 1710 to 1720, Boston experienced postwar

---

[8] Thomas, *Diary of Sewall*, 1:77; SCCF, no. 5565a.

[9] Gary B. Nash, *The Urban Crucible: Social Change, Political Consciousness, and the Origins of the American Revolution* (Cambridge, Mass.: Harvard University Press, 1979), pp. 54–58; Clarke, *John Coney*, inventory printed between pp. 12 and 13; Clarke and Foote, *Jeremiah Dummer*, pp. 42–43; *Suffolk County Probate Records*, nos. 8478, 10609, 12211.

recession coupled with a rapid depreciation of the provincial currency. The economic instability of the period suggests that there was less opportunity for the young goldsmith just starting his career than had been the case in the previous two decades. With Dummer forced to retire because of ill health, Coney, Winslow, and Edwards continued as the leading goldsmiths in Boston. John Dixwell and William Cowell, two other craftsmen who had begun to receive attention before 1710, were established enough to make quite a good living during this period. Others such as Benjamin Hiller, Nathaniel Morse, John Noyes, and Thomas Savage (who returned to Boston from Bermuda in 1714) were also factors in the market. Morse was probably best known then, as now, for his exceptional abilities as an engraver. John Noyes also made beautiful silver and is now particularly well known for a pair of candlesticks in the Museum of Fine Arts, Boston (fig. 2). Edward Webb and William Cross continued to practice the craft until the midteens, and Webb died with a considerable estate. Thomas Milner, whom Webb names in his will as his "kind friend," may well have worked alongside him in his shop. Peter Oliver made some exceptional pieces of plate shortly before he died at the age of thirty in 1712. Other goldsmiths who are known only by name probably worked as journeymen or had their primary business in repair work. Among these are Abraham Barnes and Daniel Gibbs who arrived in Boston aboard the *Globe* from Ireland in 1716. The pathetic example of Daniel Legaré of Braintree, son of a Huguenot goldsmith, emphasizes the competitiveness that characterized the Boston market. Although Legaré inherited his father's business and enjoyed some success in the craft while he was working in his hometown, when he set up shop in Boston in 1714 he found it difficult to obtain customers where so many accomplished goldsmiths already were established. In 1722 he was imprisoned for debt but was released when he was able to prove solvency.[10]

During the 1720s a whole new generation of native goldsmiths came into prominence. They entered the business at a time when Boston's economic future was becoming increasingly bleak, and it is not surprising that many found it difficult to establish themselves in the craft.

---

[10] Nash, *Urban Crucible*, pp. 82–83; *Suffolk County Probate Records*, no. 4086; William H. Whitmore, comp., *Port Arrivals and Immigrants to the City of Boston, 1715–1716 and 1762–1769* (Baltimore: Genealogical Publishing Co., 1973), p. 12; Winifred Lovering Holman, "Legaré—L'Egaré Notes: Francis of Boston and Braintree, Massachusetts, and His Son Daniel" (genealogy), New England Historic Genealogical Society.

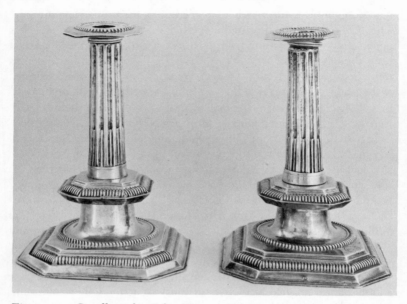

Figure 2.   Candlesticks, John Noyes. Boston, 1695–1700. Silver; H. 9¼″, W. (base) 6⅜″. (Museum of Fine Arts, Boston.)

Among them were men like John Burt and Jacob Hurd, who, with their sons, would dominate the goldsmithing trade in Boston for the next two decades. Edward Winslow increasingly devoted his energy and time to public duties, particularly after his appointment as sheriff of Suffolk County. It can be assumed that he left most of his routine work to his journeymen, as nothing of significance survives from this period and documentary references mention only minor pieces from his shop.[11]

The Edwards family also played a major role in the trade, with Thomas and Samuel joining their father, John, in the business. Paul Revere I, father of the patriot, won his freedom after the death of his master, John Coney, in 1722 and established himself in the craft. John Potwine, George Hanners, Samuel Burrill, and Joseph Goldthwait finished their apprenticeships during this decade and enjoyed moderate

[11] G. B. Warden, "Inequality and Instability in Eighteenth-Century Boston: A Reappraisal," *Journal of Interdisciplinary History* 6, no. 4 (Spring 1976): 589; Nash, *Urban Crucible,* pp. 110–18; Buhler, *American Silver,* 1:79; Bigelow-Phillips notes.

success. Knight Leverett had difficulty making a living in the craft, in spite of the skill demonstrated in his surviving works.

Of the fifty-five goldsmiths who began working in Boston between 1700 and 1730, approximately 73 percent achieved some degree of independence as artisans, and marks can be identified for 69 percent. Thirty-five men operated shops large enough to require the services of journeymen, and another 11 percent worked alone and were reasonably successful. Those who were semidependent or who operated marginal independent shops account for another 33 percent. Approximately 20 percent of the second-generation goldsmiths, as opposed to approximately 7 percent of the first-generation goldsmiths, were wholly dependent journeymen for most of their careers. John Edwards and his sons Samuel and Thomas owned adult male slaves who may have worked as goldsmiths, but slaves appear to have made up only a very small proportion of the craft, and there is no definite reference in the records to any slave goldsmiths. Only the very high valuations of the slaves owned by the Edwardses suggest that some slaves may have worked in Boston as goldsmiths.[12] Other members of the craft owned youths who may have been apprentices or general errand boys, but the need for strict security within the goldsmith's shop may have discouraged the practice of taking slave apprentices.

During the 1690s goldsmithing was a promising trade for a young man to enter, but by the 1730s Boston was no longer an attractive place to send one's son for training in the craft. Immigration of craftsmen from abroad also decreased significantly during the period. Whereas 60 percent of the young men who began their careers in Boston during the 1690s were foreign born, by the 1720s the makeup of the craft was increasingly native Bostonian (65 percent) and native colonial (79 percent). The ratio of goldsmiths to inhabitants fell from 1 in 240 in the 1690s to 1 in 290 in the 1720s. It then took a precipitous drop in the 1730s, and by 1742 only 1 of every 430 inhabitants was a goldsmith. This decline not only reflects the fact that fewer young men were entering the trade but also shows the extent to which out-migration of craftsmen weakened the goldsmithing trade. Epidemics and hard economic conditions forced many craftsmen—like John Potwine, William Pollard, Benjamin Savage, and Thomas Edwards—to try their luck elsewhere.

[12] *Suffolk County Probate Records*, nos. 8478, 12962.

Although probate information is available for only 48 percent of the goldsmiths in the study, it seems clear that only a few individuals gained a substantial fortune from goldsmithing. Figures published by Gary Nash allow us to compare the wealth distribution among goldsmiths to the population in general.[13] The figures that follow are based on estate inventories and therefore represent wealth at the time of death.

Of the twenty-seven men who were trained and working in Boston before 1700 (Appendix 1), estate information is available for fourteen (52 percent).[14] Of these, five (18.5 percent of total) had estates sufficient to place them in the wealthiest 10 percent of Boston's population. Only three—John Coney, John Edwards, and Edward Winslow—made their fortunes in Boston. The other two, René Grignon, who died in Norwich, Connecticut, and F. Solomon Legaré, who died in Charleston, South Carolina, failed to achieve financial success until they left Boston. Another six (22 percent) fall within the upper middle class (61st to 90th percentile), and another three (11 percent) fall within the lower middle class (31st to 60th percentile). None of the goldsmiths probated from this generation had estates placing them within the poorest 30 percent of the population. Some transient individuals may have had lower incomes, but the shortness of their stay in Boston makes it impossible to determine their economic status.

The next generation of goldsmiths, those who came of age after 1700 (Appendix 2), fared less well. Of the fifty-five men in this group, estate information is available for twenty-five (45 percent). Seven men

---

[13] Nash, *Urban Crucible*, p. 400. Monetary figures have been converted to pounds sterling based on the changes in the price of silver as recorded in *The Statistical History of the United States from Colonial Times to the Present* (Stamford, Conn.: Fairfield Publishers, 1966), p. 773; and in the tables included in John J. McCusker, *Money and Exchange in Europe and America, 1660–1775: A Handbook* (Chapel Hill: University of North Carolina Press, 1978).

[14] Inventories exist for Benjamin Coney (Connecticut Probate, Town of Stratford, Fairfield Probate District, file 1707) John Coney (Suffolk County Probate [hereafter cited as SCP], 22:813–16), Richard Conyers (SCP, new ser., 4:421), Timothy Dwight (SCP, 8:228), John Edwards (SCP, 38:515–18), René Grignon (Connecticut Probate, Town of Norwich, New London Probate District, file 2317), Samuel Haugh (inventory missing, value of estate given in administration accounts, SCP, 22:405–6), Henry Hurst (SCP, 21:276–77), David Jesse (SCP, 16:143–45), Francis Legaré (SCP, 17:374–75), F. Solomon Legaré (E. Milby Burton, *South Carolina Silversmiths* [Charleston: Charleston Museum, 1968], pp. 109–10, records the value of Legaré's estate as probated in Charleston in 1760), William Rouse (SCP, 16:86–87), Robert Sanderson, Jr. (SCP, 21:170–71), and Edward Winslow (SCP, 49:341–44).

(12.7 percent of the total group) had estates that placed them within the wealthiest 10 percent of Boston's population.[15] Five of these seven spent most of their careers in Boston. Another eight had estates in the upper-middle wealth category (61st to 90th percentiles), and nine had estates in the lower-middle category (31st to 60th percentiles) or had estates that were declared insolvent.[16] Of those whose estates were insolvent, only two, those of Daniel Legaré and Knight Leverett ranked in the lowest wealth category before payment of debts. The mean value of probated goldsmith's estates for men who came of age between 1700 and 1730 was £484.18 sterling, and the median figure was £350.00 sterling with 60 percent of the estates falling below the average figure. Of those goldsmiths who came of age during the 1720s, however, 70 percent fell below the average of £527.00 for their group, and the median figure of approximately £175.00 indicates a highly unequal distribution of wealth. Whereas those goldsmiths who came of age during the first two decades of the eighteenth century fell for the most part in the moderate or the upper-middle wealth ranges, nearly 50 percent of those who came of age during the third decade of the century fell within the lower-middle range, and the estates of 24 percent were insolvent. Only two men (9.5 percent), Thomas and Samuel Edwards, died with estates

[15] The seven men were John Burt (SCP, 39:160–61), William Cowell (SCP, 33:66–67), Samuel Edwards (SCP, 63:37; Smith-Carter Family Manuscripts, notebook kept by Isaac Smith as one of the executors of the estate of Samuel Edwards, Massachusetts Historical Society, Boston [hereafter cited as MHS]), Thomas Edwards (SCP, 51:52), Samuel Gray (Connecticut Probate, Town of New London, New London Probate District, file 2276), Benjamin Savage (Probate Court, Charleston, S.C., inventories 1748–51, p. 333, as transcribed by Emma B. Richardson, Bigelow-Phillips notes), and Edward Webb (SCP, 21:261–62).

[16] The eight men in the upper-middle wealth category were John Dixwell (SCP, 25:274–80), Joseph Goldthwait (Middlesex County Probate, 64:4), George Hanners (SCP, 35:89–90), William Jones (Essex County Probate, no. 15237), Joseph Kneeland (SCP, 35:137, 168), Job Prince (SCP, 16:437); inventory missing from his docket in Connecticut Probate, Town of Milford, New Haven Probate District, file 8504), William Simpkins (SCP, 79:286–89), and Andrew Tyler (SCP, 66:74, partial figures only). The estate of Daniel Russell was inventoried but not valued, but it probably falls within this category (Ezra Stiles itinerary, May 9, 1780, p. 415, Stiles Papers, Bernecke Library, Yale University). The nine men in the lower-middle category were James Boyer, insolvent (SCP, 35:400–402, 37:293), Peter Feurt, insolvent (SCP, 36:186), John Gray (Connecticut Probate, Town of New London, New London Probate District, file 2274), Rufus Greene (SCP, 89:372–77), Jacob Hurd (SCP, 54:58), Daniel Legaré, insolvent (SCCF, no. 16553), Knight Leverett, insolvent (SCP, 48:460, 49:385, 50:712), Nathaniel Morse (SCP, 41:199, 42:160), and Jonathan Reed (SCP, 36:240–41).

large enough to rank them in the top 10 percent. These figures clearly demonstrate that by 1730 goldsmithing did not provide the financial security that it had prior to 1700.

There is also reason to believe that the social mobility of the goldsmith declined in the later period and that the goldsmith was becoming more entrenched as a member of the artisan class than he had been in the seventeenth century. Evidence for this view lies in the fact that more men trained sons in the craft than previously. Of the twenty-seven men trained before 1700, for instance, three were sons of clergymen, three of merchants, one of a gentleman, two of mariners, and one of a surgeon. Eight, or 30 percent, came from the families of artisans and, surprisingly, only two (7.4 percent), Robert Sanderson, Jr., and F. Solomon Legaré, were sons of goldsmiths. Of the craftsmen trained between 1700 and 1720, 38 percent came from artisan families and 12.7 percent were sons of goldsmiths. Those men who entered the craft after 1700 were more likely to follow the paths of their fathers than were their predecessors. Furthermore, several of the men in the later group—most notably William Cowell, John Burt, and Jacob Hurd—continued the tradition by training their sons in goldsmithing. While the most successful men from the earlier period saw their sons become wealthy merchants, like Joshua and Isaac Winslow, or public servants, like William and Jeremiah Dummer, Jr., the most successful men in the later period trained their sons to carry on their business.

Even for the goldsmith, "the most genteel of any in the Mechanic Way,"[17] success was a matter of good business sense, strong local connections, and skill in the craft. For the young man trying to establish himself in a highly competitive market, the surest way to advance in his profession was to serve an apprenticeship under one of the best goldsmiths in town. Another possible road to success was to work as a journeyman in a prestigious shop where one would have a chance to make his abilities known to the most influential clients.

The master goldsmith employed journeymen and accepted apprentices according to the size of his business. Kathryn Buhler credited the shop of John Coney with seven apprentices. In light of new evidence, we may tentatively add Peter Oliver, who chose Coney to be his guardian in 1697, and Coney's youngest brother, Benjamin, whose identity as a goldsmith was recently discovered by Edward S. Cooke, Jr. Count-

[17] Campbell, *London Tradesman*, pp. 141–42.

ing his apprentices alone, Coney could have had as many as five men working in his shop at any one time. A master craftsman would have had trouble supervising and teaching so many young men by himself, but he was probably aided by the older apprentices and one or two journeymen. In addition, as Carl Bridenbaugh has pointed out, the craftsman was often aided in his work by his wife.[18] Perhaps Mrs. Coney worked with the youngest boys, teaching them to polish the goods displayed in the glass case and to weigh the silver on the large scales usually kept in the showroom area of the shop. The fact that the goldsmith's wife often played a role in the management of the business is borne out by the apprenticeship agreement in general use for all the crafts in Boston. Although the actual indenture does not survive, the apprenticeship agreement between Joseph Soames and René Grignon, contracted in 1697, is referred to at length in a writ of 1704. This agreement bound Soames

unto the sd Rene Grignon to lerne his arts and with him and Mary his wife after the maner of an apprentice to serve from the first day of November unto the full end and term of five years from thence Next ensuing and fully to be Compleat and ending Duering all which sd Term the sd . . . Rene Grignon and his wife faithfully to serve their secrets keep Hose and Lawfull Commands Every where Gladly doe and obey he should do no damage to his sd Master or Mrs: nor Suffer to be Don of others but that he to his power should let or forthwith make knowne the same to them he should not purloin Imbezell wast or spend the moneys or Goods of his sd Master or Misrs nor Lend them to any without Leave he should not Commit fornication nor Contract matrimony within sd term nor frequent taverans ordniaryes nor places of gameing nor absent himself from the service of his Master or Misrs: by day nor by night unlawfuly but in all things a good faithfull and deligent and obedient servant and an apprentice should bear and behave himself towards his sd master and mistress During the sd Term In Cosideration where of the sd Rene Grignon the sd master for him selfe and in behalfe of his sd wife did Covenant Promise grant and agree to teach and In struct or cause the sd apprentice to be taught and Instructed in the arts trades and Callings of Goldsmith and Jeweller.[19]

Some agreements also bound the master to provide his apprentices with a basic education. A few required the apprentice's father to put up a

---

[18] Buhler, *Colonial Silversmiths*, pp. 30–32; *Suffolk County Probate Records*, no. 2518; Fairfield, Conn., Probate District, file 1707; Bridenbaugh, *Colonial Craftsman*, pp. 127, 129.
[19] SCCF, no. 6035.

sum of money to guarantee the boy's reliability or, as in the case of Kiliaen Van Rennselaer, as surety "in case he should undertake some big piece of work and spoil it, so that he would have to stand the loss."[20]

A good apprentice, particularly in the later years of his term, was a valuable asset to a goldsmith, allowing him to take on additional business without a large outlay of money for labor costs. At the end of their terms, the more talented apprentices were ready to work as journeymen, being paid either by the job or by the day. In spite of the evidence that journeymen goldsmiths existed in considerable numbers in Boston between 1690 and 1730, very little is known about their actual duties in the shop or their working arrangements with their masters. A rare document preserved in the court files of Suffolk County refers to an agreement between a journeyman and his master.

whereas by certain Articles of Agreemt had made concluded declared & agreed upon the Sixteenth day of October Anno Domini 1699 between the sd plt. [John House, citizen and goldsmith of London, the plaintiff] of the one part & the sd Hindrich Huss [later known as Henry Hurst] of the other part. It is amongst other things agreed upon that whereas the sd Hindrich Huss was willing & desirous by Gods permission suddenly to undertake a voyage [from London] to Boston in New England in order to serve Richard Conyers of Boston aforesd after the manner of a plateworker or worker in silver Imboster, Graver or otherwise howsoevr. according to the utmost of his skill & diligence for & during the full Term of Two years from the time of the sd Hindrich Huss his Entrance into the imediate service of the sd. Rich. Conyers in Boston in New England aforesd. after the rate of thirty pounds p anum to be paid quarterly by the sd Richd. Conyers to the sd Hindrich Huss & convenient meat drink & lodging during wch. sd term or space of two years And one whole year to comence from the expiration of the sd two years he the sd Hindrich Huss was not to serve any person in Boston aforesd in any quality or condition whatsoevr. neither to follow any manner of Imploymt. upon his own proper account. In pursuance of wch. sd agreemt. the sd Hinderich Huss for himself . . . did Covenant promise & agree to . . . diligently carefully & faithfully give his due attendance to the sd Rich. Conyers during the space of two whole years from the time of Entrance into his sd Masters service in Boston in New England aforesd & should work in plate Ingrave Imbost or hammer Silver at all reasonable & convenient times & seasons that his sd Master Richd. Conyers should think fit to appoint & desire him & for no other person or persons whatsoever.

[20] Quoted in Buhler, *Colonial Silversmiths*, p. 26.

Figure 3. Tankard, Henry Hurst. Boston, ca. 1700. Silver; H. 7″ (including thumbpiece); Diam. (base) 5³⁄₁₆″, (lip) 4⅜″. (Museum of Fine Arts, Boston.)

Hurst arrived in Boston on March 1, 1699 or 1700, and on June 6, 1701, "did depart & leave the sd Richd. Conyers."[21] From the surviving objects made by Hurst, particularly the tankard with chased handle and cover now in the Museum of Fine Arts, Boston (fig. 3), we know that he was a very competent craftsman. Once in the colonies, Hurst no

[21] SCCF, no. 5565a.

doubt realized that even a laborer could expect to earn £30 per year, and that as a skilled craftsman he could make double what Conyers was paying him. Even with the penalty of £100 that he was obliged to pay for forfeiting his contract, he could make a better living working for other Boston goldsmiths—or on his own—than he could if he remained in Conyers's employ. When Hurst was summoned by the court in 1702, Edward Winslow and James Barnes, Jr., "goldsmiths," came forward as sureties for Hurst and posted bond of £200. That they were willing to post bond strongly suggests that Hurst was working with them. If so, it is interesting to speculate on Hurst's contribution to the design and production of Winslow's magnificent sugar boxes, two of which are dated 1702. Perhaps Hurst did the chased work on the cover of the sugar box that Winslow retained for his own use (fig. 4). Certainly its fine workmanship and sophisticated iconography suggest that it was made by a craftsman who had worked in London.[22]

The fact that Conyers included a clause in Hurst's work contract prohibiting him from working for other Boston goldsmiths indicates that Conyers was aware of Hurst's skill and hoped that having Hurst at work in his shop would give him an advantage over his competitors. In most cases, the shortage of labor in Boston in the late seventeenth century necessitated the sharing of journeymen. Since an individual master would not have had several large commissions in progress at all times, the need for journeymen in many shops would have been occasional. Work was often sent out to pieceworkers who produced objects for several different shops. Conyers's stipulation that Hurst work only for him was therefore somewhat unusual and reflects common practice in England where long-term employment contracts were more usual.[23]

Lacking such evidence for other craftsmen, it is difficult to determine the contribution of journeymen to the appearance of surviving objects. Perhaps the talented Nathaniel Morse, who witnessed a deed for John Coney three years after his apprenticeship would have terminated, was responsible for some of the fine engraving of his master's

[22] Nash, *Urban Crucible*, p. 12; SCCF, no. 5565a; Edward J. Nygren, "Edward Winslow's Sugar Boxes: Colonial Echoes of Courtly Love," *Yale University Art Gallery Bulletin* 33, no. 2 (Autumn 1971): 38–52.

[23] Lawrence Towner, "A Good Master Well Served: A Social History of Servitude in Massachusetts" (Ph.D. diss., Northwestern University, 1955), p. 51; Richard B. Morris, *Government and Labor in Early America* (New York: Columbia University Press, 1946), pp. 208–13, 219–21.

Figure 4.   Sugar box, Edward Winslow. Boston, 1700–1710. Silver;
H. 5⅜″, W. 6⅝″, L. 7¹³⁄₁₆″. (Yale University Art Gallery, Mabel Brady
Garvan Collection.)

silver. It may have been this connection that led to his being chosen
successor to Coney as the engraver of Massachusetts currency.[24] Coney's
magnificent monteith may have required the work of specialists in chas-
ing and casting; the repoussé around the rim of the bowl and the fine
casting of the lion handles and the cherubs around its scalloped edge
show superb technical skill (fig. 5). Jeremiah Dummer may have
employed one Robert Punt, apparently a watchmaker, to mend watches
for his customers as early as 1670. A watch "was delivered to Robert
Punt at Mr Dumars shop brought there to be mended," and Dummer
testified in court as to the condition of the watch on December 3, 1670.
In 1697 partners John Allen and John Edwards sued goldsmith Jona-

[24] Buhler, *Colonial Silversmiths*, p. 31; Martha Gandy Fales, "Heraldic and
Emblematic Engravers of Colonial Boston," in *Boston Prints and Printmakers, 1670–
1775,* ed. Walter Muir Whitehill (Boston: Colonial Society of Massachusetts, 1973), p.
li.

Figure 5.   Monteith bowl, John Coney. Boston, 1700–1710. Silver; H. 8⅝″, Diam. (base) 6¹¹⁄₁₆″, (lip) 10¾″. (Yale University Art Gallery, Mabel Brady Garvan Collection.)

than Belcher for the cost of a coat, shoes, a hat, and "4 neckcloaths & 4 hankerchers" as well as "money lent him at Severall times." What business relationship existed among Belcher and Allen and Edwards remains pure speculation; possibly Belcher had served the partners as a journeyman and considered these perquisites due a journeyman. Belcher may also have served John Noyes who signed as his surety at the time of the suit. Edward Winslow employed a journeyman called Tom Cully (Thomas Maccollo) as early as 1743, and in his will Winslow stipulated that his wife was to pay Maccollo "twenty shillings a week weekly, that is to say fifteen shillings by herself & five shillings by Mr Hurd or any others that may employ him."[25] Martha Gandy Fales found that Philadelphia silversmith Joseph Richardson also employed jobbers, often

[25] SCCF, nos. 1043, 98567; Benjamin Walker diary, vol. 2, January 16, 1742 or 1743, MHS; *Suffolk County Probate Records*, no. 10609.

giving them silver on account and paying them for their labor when he received the finished object. There is little doubt that such practices were common in Boston by the 1730s. Brock Jobe found evidence of similar activity in the furniture-making trades.[26]

Division of labor was common in London where goldsmiths registered as small workers or large workers; some craftsmen were even more specialized, like those who referred to themselves as candlestick makers. The striking similarity in porringer handles, finials, thumbpieces, and handle terminals on objects made in Boston during this period suggests that some goldsmiths specialized in cast parts. Those specializing in casting may have found a lucrative trade in making and finishing candlesticks which, from the surviving examples, seem to have been produced by a relatively small number of goldsmiths using nearly identical molds (figs. 6, 7). Porringer handles occasionally bear the maker's mark in the casting which was later struck over by the mark of another maker (fig. 8). Other porringer handles are known with English marks in the casting. This may indicate that someone was casting handles from English porringers and selling them to local Boston craftsmen or that handles were imported from England.[27] Later documents reveal several instances of goldsmiths sending their pieces out to be engraved in other shops, and, although no such direct evidence exists for the period in question, detailed inventories of goldsmiths' tools show that many shops lacked even the simplest engraving tools. The presence of quicksilver, or mercury, and touchstones in some inventory listings and not in others suggests specialization. The processes of refining and gilding required the use of mercury, the vapors from which were known to be dangerous even in the seventeenth century. It is reasonable to assume, therefore, that not all goldsmiths were anxious to take on these tasks themselves. The larger shops may have found it necessary to perform these functions in order to assure that they had enough refined metal on hand to meet their demands, and John Coney's shop was so equipped. Smaller shops could then rely on his expertise (or that of his journeymen) as needed.

---

[26] Martha Gandy Fales, *Joseph Richardson and Family, Philadelphia Silversmiths* (Middletown, Conn.: Wesleyan University Press, 1974), pp. 66–67; Jobe, "Boston Furniture Industry," pp. 12–26.

[27] Arthur G. Grimwade, *London Goldsmiths, 1697–1837: Their Marks and Lives from the Original Registers at Goldsmiths' Hall and Other Sources* (London: Faber and Faber, 1976); Wendy A. Cooper, "New Findings on Colonial New England Goldsmiths and English Sources," *American Art Journal* 10, no. 2 (November 1978): 107–9.

Figure 6. Candlesticks, John Coney. Boston, 1716. Silver; H. 7½",
W. (base) 4¹⁄₁₆". (Historic Deerfield.)

Figure 7. Candlestick,
Nathaniel Morse. Boston,
ca. 1720. Silver; H. 7¼".
(Historic Deerfield.)

Figure 8. Detail of silver porringer handle, bearing marks of both Samuel Edwards and Joseph Edwards (1737–83). Boston, ca. 1750. (Gebelein Silversmiths: Photo, G. M. Cushing.)

Others, like Richard Conyers whose inventory lists an incredible variety of working tools, may have been importers and retailers of fine-quality tools as well as goldsmiths. Given Conyers's dismal financial situation (he was imprisoned for debt in 1701), it is unlikely that he would have had use for so many tools himself.[28] He may have found that with his

[28] *Suffolk County Probate Records*, no. 4641. The inventory of Conyers's shop tools was published in John Marshall Phillips, *American Silver* (New York: Chanticleer Press,

connections in England he was able to supplement his income by importing the tools that were constantly in demand by Boston goldsmiths.

In a barter economy where goldsmiths, like other craftsmen, were sometimes paid in kind, it was occasionally necessary for craftsmen to sell items unrelated to their craft. In 1696 David Jesse sold to one Mrs. Hill:

Twelf yards & ½ of Caliminco att	
6s 4d = pyd	3.19.2
five pare of hose att 9 = ppr	2.05.0
one pare of Silver Shoe buckles	0.08.6
	6.12.8 [29]

Five years later Jesse performed an unusual task for a business acquaintance named Joseph Mallinson, which resulted in a long and bitter court battle. According to a bill filed with the court, Mallinson delivered 948 pieces of eight "to sd Jesse . . . wch Mr Mallinson saith he was to hand Cutt to twelve penny weight & is willing to allow two pence per pieice for the Cutting, but Mr Jesse saith he will give his oath he was to have five shillings for Each peice of Eight when Cutt as aforesd."[30] The act of clipping coins, usually a criminal offense, was not a matter of concern to the court, for by this time it had become common practice to weigh all coins used in payment of debts. Why Mallinson wanted the coins clipped is a mystery; perhaps there was a shortage of coins of this weight. The goldsmith, then, was called on to do all sorts of work involving gold and silver, some of which has little meaning in today's terms.

Little has been said about the import/export business in the goldsmithing trade. Fales found ample evidence of this activity in the letter books of Joseph Richardson, but there is little documentation of the practice in the period treated by this paper. A few pieces, such as a tobacco box marked by John Coney (fig. 9), also bear the mark of a London goldsmith. Other English pieces that belonged to Bostonians in this period are known, and many of these were published by E.

1949), pp. 14–16. Richard Conyers, Petition to the Inferior Court of Common Pleas, Suffolk County, Mass., December 16, 1701, Photostat, Miscellaneous Bound Volumes of Manuscripts, MHS.

[29] SCCF, no. 3475.
[30] SCCF, no. 5559.

Figure 9. Tobacco box, bearing marks of both John Coney (Boston) and L. S. (London). Ca. 1701. Silver; H. ¹⁵⁄₁₆″, W. 3⅛″, L. 3¹³⁄₁₆″. (Yale University Art Gallery, Mabel Brady Garvan Collection.)

Alfred Jones in *The Old Silver of American Churches*. Other notable examples have been discovered by Fales and Buhler in small local museums and in private collections. We do not know if these pieces were ordered directly from England (or Europe) by their owners, as seems to have been the custom in the South, or if they were purchased through local goldsmiths.[31] Inventories sometimes mention foreign silver, such as the "spanish dishes" owned by Wait Winthrop and the "french cup" mentioned in the will of Daniel Gookin, Sr., in 1685. It has been said that, aside from special orders, most goods imported by Boston goldsmiths were probably small items such as buckles and rings. In 1699 Samuel Shrimpton, a local merchant, sent plate from Boston "to be disposed of either at Amsterdam or London." Samuel Sewall sent "a Skillet of fine silver" to Edward Hull of London in 1688 in payment for goods he had received. According to an account dated April 1, 1700, between Richard Conyers of Boston and Charles Groome of Saint Martin in the Fields, Middlesex, England, Groome owed Conyers fourteen

---

[31] Fales, *Richardson*, pp. 2310–60; Kathryn C. Buhler and Graham Hood, *American Silver, Garvan and Other Collections in the Yale University Art Gallery*, vol. 1 (New Haven: Yale University Press, 1970), pp. 41–42; "Letters of William Fitzhugh," *Virginia Magazine of History and Biography* 6, no. 1 (July 1898): 71.

shillings for "18 Silver buttons wt 1 oz: 11 pt fashion & silver agreed."[32] Conyers apparently exported the buttons in return for which he ordered from Groome two swords (which he may have planned to equip with silver grips), various flasks, pots, a hammer, pumice, files, linen, and scales. How many other Boston silversmiths were in the habit of exporting wrought silver to England is still a matter of speculation. The Conyers bill at least suggests the possibility that paying for imports with the products of one's own shop was a distinct possibility at the time and was thoroughly consistent with prevailing trade practices.

The question of whether the goldsmith also acted as a banker has been debated for several decades. As the title of a London treatise of 1676 would indicate—*The Mystery of the New Fashioned Goldsmiths or Bankers*—there were men working in London who called themselves goldsmiths but who devoted themselves completely to the business of banking. In Boston there is evidence that some goldsmiths accepted money for safekeeping. In 1694, for instance, Daniel Westfield of Boston bequeathed twenty pounds to a minor named Thomas Pemberton. The will stipulates, "[the money is] to be put into the hands of my very good Friend Jeremiah Dummer of Boston aforesd. Esqr. to be put out at Interest for the use of the sd. Thomas Pemberton until he comes of age and then to be paid him with the improvement thereof." Francis Legaré, who was called a "Merchant Goldsmith" by one of his fellow Huguenot émigrés, is known to have held mortgages on the property of at least two citizens of the town of Braintree in 1707.[33] Such activities, however, were commonplace among merchants in Boston and the surrounding area. Probably only those goldsmiths deeply engaged in general mercantile activities accepted deposits of cash for safekeeping. As

[32]Buhler and Hood, *American Silver*, 1:19; *Suffolk County Probate Records*, no. 1553; Martha Gandy Fales, *Early American Silver* (rev. ed.; New York: E. P. Dutton, 1973), pp. 195–212; Records of the Inferior Court of Common Pleas for Suffolk County, Docket Book 1701–6, p. 80; "Letter Book of Samuel Sewall," in *Collections of the Massachusetts Historical Society*, vol. 1, 6th ser. (Boston: By the society, 1886), pp. 85–86; SCCF, no. 4825.

[33]*The Mystery of the New Fashioned Goldsmiths or Bankers. Their Rise, Growth, State and Decay. Discovered in a Merchants Letter to a County Gent. Who Desired to Bind His Son Apprentice to a Goldsmith* (London, 1676; reprinted in *Quarterly Journal of Economics* [January 1888]: 253–62). I wish to thank Edward S. Cooke, Jr., for bringing this piece to my attention. *Suffolk County Probate Records*, no. 2180½; E. T. Fisher, trans., *Report of a French Protestant Refugee in Boston, 1687* (Brooklyn, 1868), p. 35; Holman, "Legaré," p. 7.

yet there is no evidence that these activities were especially reserved for goldsmiths.

In addition to their goldsmithing activities, many craftsmen branched out into other kinds of business. David Jesse is just one of many engaged in general shopkeeping; others, such as William Cowell, Sr., William Rouse, and Francis Legaré, are known to have been innkeepers or taverners. In 1715 Samuel Sewall hired a horse from William Cowell, Sr., which suggests that Cowell may have had a stable of sorts in addition to his tavern. Samuel Clark is mentioned as a mariner as well as a goldsmith. John Coney, Jeremiah Dummer, and Edward Winslow invested in land, and each of them held interests in Boston wharves. When he left Boston and set up shop in Hartford, Connecticut, John Potwine gradually changed his business and became more a dry-goods merchant as he got older. René Grignon held an interest in a wash-leather mill with Gabriel Bernon at Oxford, Massachusetts, and later, when he went to Norwich, Connecticut, he was called a mariner as well as a goldsmith.[34] Other goldsmiths, particularly those who did not achieve financial success in the trade, turned to professions that seemed more lucrative.

Such extraordinary diversity prevented the goldsmiths of Boston from developing a strong group identity. Although there is evidence that members of the craft had numerous business dealings with one another, there is no evidence that they ever joined together for group action. It is perhaps the freedom of endeavor allowed in Boston and other colonial seaport towns that helps to explain why American craftsmen of the early eighteenth century never established strong guild organizations such as those known in Europe.

It appears that the craft of goldsmithing, while it could be a very lucrative trade, was not necessarily a sure route to financial success. The men at the top of the profession, particularly those who came of age before 1700, sometimes became respected public servants and wealthy

---

[34] James and Jameson, *Journal of Danckaerts*, p. 260; SCCF, no. 5591; Buhler, *American Silver*, 1:123; Samuel Sewall ledger, April 11, 1715; Thomas, *Diary of Sewall*, 1:77; SCCF, no. 14367; *Suffolk County Probate Records*, no. 10609; Clarke and Foote, *Jeremiah Dummer*, pp. 22–44; George F. Daniels, *History of the Town of Oxford, Massachusetts* (Oxford, 1892), pp. 23–24; A. R. Chase, "René Grignon, Silversmith," *Antiques* 34, no. 1 (July 1938): 26–27.

merchants, but the great majority of goldsmiths were men of modest families who earned modest incomes. Although people from outside of Boston continued to patronize Boston goldsmiths regularly up through the end of the eighteenth century, those goldsmiths who left Boston for the outlying towns achieved a status far above what would have been possible for them in New England's metropolis. Further statistical analysis of the craftsmen and their place in the society promises to yield interesting new information. So far the evidence is that Boston's goldsmiths were constantly in contact with one another and that, probably, a substantial proportion of the men whose names we know served as journeymen or jobbers during some portion of their careers. In addition, accounts and court records suggest some interesting connections among craftsmen. Unfortunately, in the absence of documentary evidence, the work of the men who never became master craftsmen—and thus never used their own maker's marks—may remain a mystery. Perhaps through the analysis of construction techniques known to have been used in the shops of certain goldsmiths, it will be possible to substantiate the presence of identifiable apprentices and journeymen. It may also be possible to suggest additional relationships and areas of specialization from the physical evidence. The role of the immigrant craftsman and his status in relation to the native craftsman also need study. Clearly many questions remain in our efforts to fully understand the early American goldsmith.

APPENDIX 1

Goldsmiths Included in This Study Whose Careers in Boston Began before 1700

NOTE.—A plus sign indicates that I believe the goldsmith lived or worked past the latter date, which is based on the last recorded reference to him as a working goldsmith in Boston.

Goldsmith	Life dates	Working in Boston
John Allen	1671/72–1760	1693–1736 +
Francis Bassett	1678–1715	1699–1715 *
Jonathan Belcher	1661–1703 +	1682–1703 +
Samuel Clark	1659–1705	1681–1705
Benjamin Coney	1673–1721	ca. 1694
John Coney	1655/56–1722	1677–1722
Richard Conyers	1668–1709	ca. 1697–1709
William Cross	1658–1716 +	1692–95 +
Jeremiah Dummer	1645–1718	1667–1710
Timothy Dwight	1654–92	1675–92
John Edwards	1671–1746	1692–1746
Samuel Foster	1676–1702	1697–1702
René Grignon	1652/53–1715	1696–1700
Samuel Haugh	1676–1717	1698–1717
Henry Hurst	1666–1718	1699–1718
David Jesse	1668–1705/6	ca. 1692–1705/6
F. Solomon Legaré	1674–1760	1687–95
Francis Legaré	1636–1711	1687–95
John Noyes	1674–1749	1695–1749
Moses Prevereau	ca. 1675–1701 +	ca. 1699–1701
Daniel Quincy	1651–90	1672–90
William Rouse	1641–1704/5	ca. 1675–1704/5
Eliezur Russell	1663–91/92	1684–91/92
Robert Sanderson, Jr.	1652–1714	1673–1714
Thomas Savage	1664–1749	1685–1705, 1714–37
Edward Winslow	1669–1753	1690–1735 +
Thomas Wyllys	1666–pre-1720	ca. 1690–94

* And in Charlestown.

APPENDIX 2

Goldsmiths Included in This Study Whose Careers in Boston Began after 1700 and before 1730

NOTE.—A plus sign indicates that I believe the goldsmith lived or worked past the latter date, which is based on the last recorded reference to him as a working goldsmith in Boston.

Goldsmith	Life dates	Working in Boston
Isaac Anthony	1690–1773	1711–ca. 1727
John Banks	1696–1737+	1717–37+
Abraham Barnes	ca. 1692–1716+	1716
James Barnes	1680–1703+	1702–3
Peter Boutet	ca. 1685–1715+	1714–15
James Boyer	ca. 1700–1741	1723–41
Thomas Bradford	1697–1740	1718–40
Samuel Burrill	1704–40	1725–40
John Burt	1692/93–1746	1714–46
William Caddow	ca. 1692–pre-1746	1726–38+
Thomas Coverly	1708–78	1729–78
John Cowell	1707–pre-1736	1727–31+
William Cowell	1682/83–1736	1704–36
Mathew Delaney	ca. 1698–1723+	ca. 1722–23
Peter Denman	—	ca. 1710–12
John Dixwell	1680/81–1725	1702–25
Shubael Dummer	1687–1709+	1708–9
Samuel Edwards	1705–62	1726–62
Thomas Edwards	1701/2–55	1723–30, 1745–55
Peter Feurt	1703–37	1727–37
Daniel Gibbs	ca. 1691–1716+	ca. 1716
Joseph Goldthwait	1706–80	1727–73
Daniel Gookin	1683–1705	1704–5
John Gray	1692–1720	1713–19
Samuel Gray	1684–1713	1705–7
Bartholomew Green	1697–pre-1746	1718–34+
Rufus Greene	1707–77	1728–75
George Hanners	1696–1740	1717–40
Benjamin Hiller	1688–1739+	1709–39+
Jacob Hurd	1702/3–58	1724–55
William Jones	1695–1730	1716–21
Joseph Kneeland	1700–1740	1721–40
Daniel Legaré	1689–1725	1714–25

Goldsmith	Life dates	Working in Boston
John LeRoux	1695–1725 +	1723–24
Knight Leverett	1702/3–53	1724–53
Thomas Maccollo	ca. 1708–53 +	ca. 1729–53 +
Thomas Milner	ca. 1682–1745 +	ca. 1708–45 +
Nathaniel Morse	ca. 1688–1748	1709–48
Thomas Mullins	ca. 1680–ca. 1752	1708–ca. 1752
Peter Oliver	1682–1712	1703–12
John Pitts	—	ca. 1728–30
William Pollard	1690–1740	1711–30
John Potwine	1698–1792	1719–ca. 1737
Job Prince	1680–1703/4	ca. 1701
Jonathan Reed	ca. 1695–1742	ca. 1724–42
Paul Revere I	1702–54	ca. 1725–54
Michael Rouse	1687–1711 +	1708–11
Daniel Russell	1698–1780	1719–22
Moody Russell	1694–1761	ca. 1715
Benjamin Savage	1699–1750	1720–32
William Simpkins	1704–80	1725–80
Joseph Soames	1681–1705	1702–5
Thomas Townsend	1704–52 +	1725–52 +
Andrew Tyler	1692–1741	1713–41
Edward Webb	1666–1718	ca. 1706–18

The Glassmakers of Early
America
Arlene Palmer Schwind

Throughout history there has been an aura of mystery and magic surrounding the craft of the glassmaker. As one Englishman observed in
1620, it was "a rare kind of Knowledge and Chymistry to transmute
Dust and Sand . . . to such a diaphanous pellucid dainty Body as you
see a Crystal-Glass is." Although published technical treatises dispelled
some of the magic,[1] successful glassmaking in the seventeenth and eighteenth centuries still depended chiefly on the craftsman's experience in
evaluating raw materials and his practiced skill in mixing and manipu-
lating them. The style of a glass object, its shape and decorative detail,
will reflect the glassmaker's origins and training. At the same time, the
peculiar properties of glass and the way it must be worked insure the
prevalence of certain techniques regardless of time and place.

Glassmakers were among the first craftsmen in America, arriving
in Jamestown, Virginia, in 1608. From then on, there was an almost
continuous interest in glassmaking in this country, encouraged by the
abundance of raw materials, especially wood fuel, and the universal
need for window glass, bottles, and drinking vessels. This interest in
glass led to the establishment of at least twelve factories in the colonial

---

[1]James Howell to his brother, as quoted in Eleanor S. Godfrey, *The Development
of English Glassmaking 1560–1640* (Chapel Hill: University of North Carolina Press,
1975), p. 156. The first printed work devoted exclusively to glassmaking was *L'Arte Vetraria*,
published in Florence in 1612 by Antonio Neri. Christopher Merret published an English
edition with additions and comments in 1662.

period and another fourteen in the years immediately following the Revolution, although by no means did they all prosper.

The exact number of glass craftsmen practicing their art in the factories built before 1800 cannot be determined. The 1820 Census of Manufactures records 1,031 workers in thirty glasshouses, and by 1843 eighty-two factories employed 4,236 people.[2] These numbers represent the entire labor force of glassmaking, only a minority of whom were skilled glassblowers, cutters, or engravers. For example, in 1820 at the Cincinnati Glass Works of Pugh and Teater only ten of the staff of thirty-one were glassblowers. The rest performed such necessary duties as washing and otherwise preparing ingredients for the batch, building and maintaining the furnaces, chopping wood and keeping the fires going, and packing and delivering the finished glassware.

Because of the large physical plant and the number of employees required, glassmaking has not fit comfortably into the category of handicraft. The actual process of glassblowing, however, is very much a craft that requires a trained eye, skillful hands, and powerful lungs and mouth. The tools are simple, the same as those used when glassblowing was invented in the first century b.c., yet the shaping of the simplest object entails the cooperation of at least two people. In large establishments the tasks of the workers were highly specialized, but machinery did not begin to reduce the need for skilled labor until 1825 with the introduction of mechanical pressing. None of the other factory-type crafts in America required laborers with skills as developed as those of glassmakers, and probably no other craftsmen produced their goods against such persistent competition from foreign manufacturers. The glassblowers themselves were overwhelmingly foreign-born and foreign-trained. All of the twelve colonial factories employed craftsmen who came to America from Europe for the express purpose of making glass. Native-born craftsmen began to penetrate the glass industry at the end of the eighteenth century, but the labor force remained predominantly immigrant until the mid nineteenth century.

In these and other ways, glass craftsmen occupy a unique and interesting position in the history of American industry. Nevertheless, as a

---

[2] United States Bureau of the Census, "Record of the 1820 Census of Manufactures," National Archives, Washington, D.C. (microfilm, Joseph Downs Manuscript and Microfilm Collection, Winterthur Museum Library [hereafter cited as DMMC]); T. B. Wakeman, "Glass," in *The American Laborer* (New York: Greeley & McElrath, 1843), p. 78.

Figure 1. Tobacco box made for Richard Wistar by Thomas Shaw. London, 1756. Steel. (Collection of the late Vincent D. Andrus: Photo, Winterthur.) Although Wistar owned a glassworks in New Jersey, he was by training a brass-button maker. The engraving on the box illustrates the tools of both trades.

group and as individuals the glassmakers of early America have been ignored by historians and, ironically, by historians of the glass industry in particular. Attention has centered instead on those who owned the glass factories, men who were glassmakers by virtue of investment, not skill. Caspar and Richard Wistar, owners of America's first successful glassworks, were brass-button makers by trade (see fig. 1), while the flamboyant Henry William Stiegel was an ironmaster. Benjamin Bakewell was a merchant, in both England and America, before he opened the glasshouse in Pittsburgh. Of the owners of the major glass factories in early America, only John Frederick Amelung, of the New Bremen works in Maryland, had practical experience as a glassmaker.[3]

This paper summarizes research in progress on the glassblowers, cutters, and engravers in America before 1860, over 900 of whom have been identified by name. Information is being gathered about their

[3] See Arlene Palmer, "Glass Production in Eighteenth-Century America: The Wistarburgh Enterprise," in *Winterthur Portfolio 11*, ed. Ian M. G. Quimby (Charlottesville: University Press of Virginia, 1976), pp. 75–101; Frederick William Hunter, *Stiegel Glass* (Boston: Houghton Mifflin Co., 1914); and Dwight P. Lanmon and Arlene M. Palmer. "John Frederick Amelung and the New Bremen Glassmanufactory," *Journal of Glass Studies* 18 (1976): 9–136.

European origins, migration patterns, families, status, and so on.[4] Research sources include factory records and other manuscripts, newspapers, city directories, and official documents. Few letters or diaries written by glassmakers survive. Many were illiterate or were fluent only in German or another foreign language, while their foreign-sounding names stymied census takers and directory compilers. Glassblower William Hinds, for example, is listed in the Boston directories at the same address over a twenty-year period with his name spelled five different ways; Adam Kersthaler is recorded variously as Keftoaler, Kinthaler, and Keasbelter.

The first two factories in America, erected in Jamestown, were run by Polish and Venetian glassblowers. The Virginia Company sponsored these works to bolster England's floundering industry by providing some of the glassware needed by British consumers. Of the remaining glasshouses in the colonial period, two were staffed with English-trained artisans and the rest with glassblowers from central Europe. These factories competed with English manufacturers in their attempts to supply the colonists with bottles, windowpanes, and table glass. Caspar Wistar unabashedly pointed out to the New Jersey provincial House of Representatives, "the Making of Glass is . . . a Considerable Advantage to the Country, not only as it saves the Money that must otherwise be sent abroad for that Commodity, but as it brings Cash in, for Quantities exported to other Colonies." At the very heart of the colonial system, however, was the idea that colonies did send money abroad for the manufactured goods of the mother country. Therefore, as Caspar's son Richard observed in 1760, "It was not for the Honour of England to Suffer Manufactories in the Colonies."[5]

Although contrary to official policy, glasshouses were suffered. During the Seven Years' War, Richard Wistar petitioned the earl of Loudon, saying, "if his Majesties Officers continued to Inlist our Servants, we shall be disabled from carrying on the Works, to our great

[4] The author's research of the European origins of American glass craftsmen was funded partially by a grant from the American Philosophical Society.
[5] See Godfrey, *English Glassmaking*, for discussion of the English context of the Jamestown glasshouses; "Petition to exempt the Glass works from Taxes," Caspar Wistar, Martin Haltar, and Johann William Wentzel to the House of Representatives, Province of New Jersey, January 29, 1752, New Jersey State Library, Trenton; Richard Wistar to Daniel Taylor, October 21, 1760, Richard Wistar Letterbook (microfilm), DMMC.

Prejudice and Ruin." The request was, apparently, granted, and the works remained open. Colonial entrepreneurs openly sought craftsmen in England, and at least one placed advertisements in British newspapers for glassmakers wanted in Boston.[6] Before 1770, however, so few glasshouses sustained any measure of success, particularly in tableware, that the English glass industry was by no means threatened.

In 1767 the Townshend Acts levied increased duties on imported glass which had the effect of greatly encouraging American manufacturers. Their successes were minimized in the reports of colonial officials, but within two years the secret of lead-glass technology—the core of England's vitreous supremacy—had arrived in America. The bearer of the secret, John Allman, realized full well the importance of this knowledge when he petitioned the Pennsylvania legislature for recognition, claiming, "without his Assistance and particular Management of American materials at the Glass Work of Henry William Stiegel . . . The Manufacture of white Flint Glass could not have been brought to its Present Degree of Perfection." But Stiegel, not Allman, received the £150 premium, and Allman took his secrets to a rival firm in the Kensington section of Philadelphia. That venture was beset with so many problems that the owners were convinced Allman was a saboteur, "an artful designing man, one who probably was sent to America to blast such undertakings." Nonetheless, lead glass continued to be made at Kensington. In 1773 William Logan sent a box of Kensington-made wine glasses to Bristol to prove that glass equal in quality to England's export ware—and actually cheaper—was being made in America.[7]

After the Revolution, Britain's fear of American competition seems to have increased. In 1784 as Amelung prepared to leave Hanover for America, with a large crew of glassblowers, English merchants conspired to detain him. Amelung reported:

some English Merchants, and sea Captains, who were at that time in Bremen, wrote to England about it, and this jealous Nation, who look on the glass trade as an important one, desired the Government of Hanover, to do all that was in

---

[6] Petition of Richard Wistar to John, earl of Loudon [1756–57], Henry E. Huntington Library, San Marino, Calif.; F[elix] F[arley's] Bristol Journal (January 11, 1766).

[7] T. Kenneth Wood, "A Gratuity for Baron Stiegel," Antiques 7, no. 1 (January 1925): 30; Joseph Leacock to John Nicholson, December 23, 1794, John Nicholson General Correspondence, 1772–1819, John Nicholson Collection, Manuscript Group 96, Division of History and Archives, Pennsylvania Historical and Museum Commission, Harrisburg (hereafter cited as NGC); William Logan to Cornelius Fry, May 17, [1773], Smith Papers, Library Company of Philadelphia.

their power to frustrate a plan which they feared, would be to their loss, and greatly to the benefit of this country. Brunswick, Hesse, and other neighbouring Princes of the Roman Empire, were called upon to join for that purpose—now all possible obstacles were partly by intrigue, partly by force and despotic behaviour thrown in my way—the workmen I had engaged were detained, and nothing left untried to oppose me.[8]

When the city of Hanover declared it illegal to advertise for emigrants, Amelung immediately left with what workmen he had assembled. He claimed his ship eluded capture by the English only by virtue of an unusually quick passage. Great Britain continued to monitor the growth of the American glass industry in the early nineteenth century. When the agent of the Rensselaer Glass Factory at Sandlake, New York, was sent to England to hire workers in 1806, he had to resort to clandestine tactics: "dressed as a beggar, he travelled as a bag-pipe player and visited the principal glass manufacturing districts and engaged the number of employees desired." Getting workmen out of England could also be a problem, as evidenced by the arrest of five glass craftsmen as they boarded an America-bound ship at Liverpool in 1815.[9]

The constraints of governments and employers aside, it was often difficult to find glassblowers who were willing to leave Europe for America. In their search for blowers for their Philadelphia glasshouse, Robert Towers and Joseph Leacock sought the aid of Benjamin Franklin who was then in London. According to Franklin, it was "always a Difficulty here to meet with good Workmen and sober that [were] willing to go abroad." Glassblowers were probably among the craftsmen least anxious to set off into the unknown because their livelihood depended not just on their own skill but also on the investment of others in land, buildings, and raw materials and on an auxiliary labor force. As one glasshouse clerk reminded his employer, the "teazers, the men that smelts the Glass, takers-in &c. . . . [were] a[s] much if not more necessary to keep [the works] together, [men] without whose help the Glass Blowers can do nothing."[10]

---

[8]John F. Amelung, "Remarks on Manufactures, Principally on the New Established Glass-House, near Frederick-Town . . . ," 1787, p. 11 (facsimile in Lanmon and Palmer, "John Frederick Amelung," p. 135).

[9]Arthur J. Wiese, *History of the 17 Towns of Rensselaer County* (Troy, N.Y., 1880), pp. 136–37; *Raleigh Star* (December 22, 1815).

[10]Benjamin Franklin to Robert Tower and Joseph Leacock, August 22, 1772, American Philosophical Society, Philadelphia; Thomas Joubert to Nicholson, May 29, 1797, NGC.

A major concern of potential emigrants was the availability of suitable raw materials in America, because without ingredients of very specific type and quality glass could not be made. Good glassmaking sand does not occur on every beach. More difficult to locate was the fireclay needed to make the pots, or crucibles, in which the sand and other ingredients were melted. John Winthrop, Jr., of the Massachusetts Bay Colony, received word from London in 1636 that the glassmen recruited for a works at Salem would "not undertake to goe over till there be claye found out fitt for them: least They should be a burthen to those that transport them, or else live miserably; for they have not wherewithall to defray theire owne charges over." As it happened, their fears were well founded; the lack of suitable clay plagued the enterprise and led to its abandonment.[11]

Another concern of emigrant glass craftsmen must have been the potentiality of the American market. The need for windowpanes, bottles, and drinking glasses was great, but the willingness of the American consumer to eschew fashionable imported glass in favor of domestic products was uncertain.

In two cases foreign craftsmen themselves were willing to take the risk and made unsolicited offers to establish glasshouses in America. In 1709 Philadelphia merchants considered a proposal from Daniel Tittery of Bristol, whose brother, Joshua, had come to Philadelphia in 1683 to manage a glassworks for the Free Society of Traders. Probably because the earlier venture had not been successful, the Philadelphians forwarded Tittery's plan to acquaintances in Boston, but nothing came of it there. At the end of the century some Norman plate-glass makers petitioned Franklin for help with their scheme to build a manufactory in America. Again, no support was forthcoming.[12]

There is some evidence, however, that the Wistarburgh glassworks,

[11] From medieval times *glassman* was the term used to describe one who actually made glass. Later, after the seventeenth century, it meant only merchants involved in the glass trade. Samuel Reade to John Winthrop, Jr., March 5, 1635/36, as quoted in Allyn Bailey Forbes, ed., *Winthrop Papers*, 5 vols. (Boston: Massachusetts Historical Society, 1943), 3:234; Robert Child to Winthrop, March 15, 1646/47, as quoted in Forbes, *Winthrop Papers*, 5:141; Petition of John Conklin and Ananias Conkloyne, October 1, 1645, Massachusetts Archives, vol. 59, p. 21 (Photostat, Massachusetts Historical Society, Boston).

[12] Thomas Fitch to Edward Shippen, August 15, 1709, Thomas Fitch Letterbook 1702–11, American Antiquarian Society (microfilm, DMMC) (courtesy Neil Kamil); Franklin Manuscripts, vol. 4, p. 58, Historical Society of Pennsylvania (hereafter cited as HSP).

which operated in Salem County, New Jersey, between 1738 and 1777, may also have been the result of foreign initiative and not Caspar Wistar's own vision. Wistar's agreement with the four glassblowers who built and carried on the factory proves they had a partnership in which the craftsmen would share in the profits. Known as the United Glass Company, it was a unique arrangement among eighteenth-century American glasshouses.

Some laborers employed by the Wistars and other glass manufacturers in the colonial period came to America as indentured servants. In return for their passage across the Atlantic they agreed to work for a specific length of time. The evidence for indentured servitude in the glass industry comes largely from newspaper advertisements for runaways. Unskilled laborers, or those with no glass skills like stonemason Philip Jacobe, were often indentured servants (fig. 2). In the 1770s, however, three glassblowers, one glass cutter, and one glass polisher traveled from England to be bound by indenture for service in colonies where no glasshouses existed.[13]

Occasionally, political circumstances abroad compelled glass craftsmen to emigrate without previous arrangements for employment. Such was the case of Saxon-born Peter William Eichbaum, a glass cutter at the court of Louis XVI, who, with six glassblowers, fled the French Revolution and landed in Philadelphia on May 31, 1794. They were fortunate in securing immediate employment with entrepreneur John Nicholson, who was eager to implement his plans, drawn up the previous summer, for a glasshouse in the Philadelphia area.[14]

Few details are known of the hiring procedures used by glasshouse proprietors to obtain workmen from overseas. Some relied on the assistance of friends and factors who lived abroad, while others sent agents or traveled themselves. When Philip Friese journeyed to Germany in the early 1800s, he hired blowers not only for his own factory in Baltimore but also for the Chelmsford, Massachusetts, glasshouse. After the War of 1812 Benjamin Bakewell sent representatives to England to engage glassworkers for his Pittsburgh glasshouse. When one of them, Thomas Pears, had no luck in England, he proceeded to Paris. There he found

---

[13] Those glassworkers were Francis Simpson, William Oakes, Joseph Brittle, John Mackay, and Jacob Johnson (Gerald Fothergill, trans., *Emigrants from England, 1773–1776* [Baltimore: Genealogical Publishing Co., 1976], pp. 29, 39, 78, 83).

[14] For an account of the Nicholson glassworks, see Arlene M. Palmer, "A Philadelphia Glasshouse, 1794–1797," *Journal of Glass Studies* 21 (1979): 102–14.

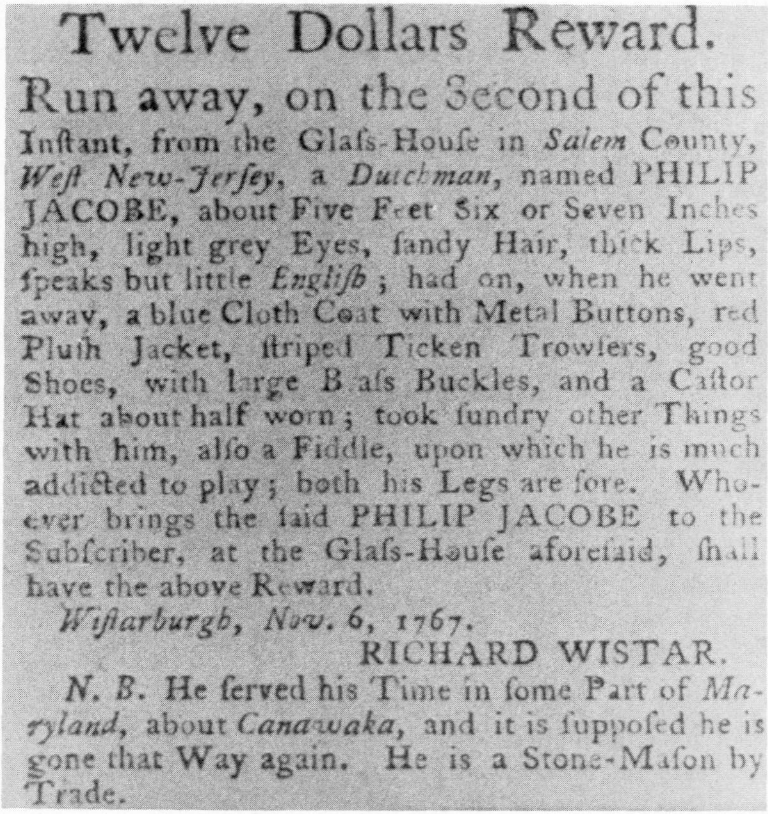

Twelve Dollars Reward.

Run away, on the Second of this
Inftant, from the Glafs-Houfe in *Salem* County,
Weft New-Jerfey, a *Dutchman*, named PHILIP
JACOBE, about Five Feet Six or Seven Inches
high, light grey Eyes, fandy Hair, thick Lips,
fpeaks but little *Englifh*; had on, when he went
away, a blue Cloth Coat with Metal Buttons, red
Pluth Jacket, ftriped Ticken Trowfers, good
Shoes, with large Bafs Buckles, and a Caftor
Hat about half worn; took fundry other Things
with him, alfo a Fiddle, upon which he is much
addicted to play; both his Legs are fore. Who-
ever brings the faid PHILIP JACOBE to the
Subfcriber, at the Glafs-Houfe aforefaid, fhall
have the above Reward.
Wiftarburgh, Nov. 6, 1767.
                              RICHARD WISTAR.
N. B. He ferved his Time in fome Part of *Ma-*
ryland, about *Canawaka*, and it is fuppofed he is
gone that Way again. He is a Stone-Mafon by
Trade.

Figure 2.   Advertisement for runaway stonemason Philip Jacobe placed
by Richard Wistar in the *Pennsylvania Chronicle* (November 9, 1767).
(Collection of Elizabeth Morris Wistar: Photo, Winterthur.)

that glassblowers were difficult to hire because they were in great demand
to make wine bottles, so many having been destroyed during the Napoleonic Wars. Although he offered three-, six-, and nine-year contracts,
with passage paid overseas and wages starting immediately upon signing
a contract, Pears was able to hire only one glass cutter. Two years later
he traveled to France on his own behalf and was more successful,
returning with a foreman, four glassblowers, four journeymen, and two
apprentices. Sometimes families migrated to America as family units,

but many more craftsmen came on their own. Single men were preferred by some glasshouse owners because, in the words of one of them,
married glassblowers bred "like minks."[15]

In general, the cream of the craft did not choose to emigrate. Some
of those who did so choose may have been prompted because they had
neither the skills nor the temperament to retain their employment at
home. Joshua Tittery was "accompted no workman" by his peers who
claimed he had been dismissed from an English factory and had never
made any broad (window) glass. In 1772 Stiegel complained his workmen were "bunglers," while in the opinion of a Connecticut manufacturer, in 1790, there were in this country "very few if any of them
[glassblowers] who [were] expert in the trade."[16]

Some competent glassblowers were doubtless willing to emigrate
from the Continent because, for them, the trade had traditionally been
a migratory one. In medieval times, entire glasshouses moved at regular
intervals as forests were denuded for furnace fuel and new wooded areas
were sought. Indeed, glassmakers were often hired by local rulers for
the specific purpose of clearing a forest. By the seventeenth century
wandering was confined to the workers. Journeymen glassblowers were
expected to "journey," and master blowers, or gaffers, and factory
superintendents were just as likely to change jobs frequently. Historian
Ada Polak offered an explanation of the glassmaker "on the move":
"Tempted by monetary rewards, by the wish for adventure and the desire
to break out of the closed family circle, many glassmakers were persuaded to leave their homes and use their skills in countries where these
were not taken for granted but considered as something out of the ordinary, and where they had chances of reaching higher grades than at
home."[17]

The experience of John Martin Griesmayer and his family may be
typical. In 1702 Griesmayer is known to have left the glasshouse at
Herrenberg to blow glass at Klosterwald. After seven years he joined the

[15] Kenneth M. Wilson, *New England Glass and Glassmaking* (New York: Thomas
Y. Crowell Co., 1972), p. 86; Lowell Innes, *Pittsburgh Glass, 1797–1891: A History
and Guide for Collectors* (Boston: Houghton Mifflin Co., 1976), pp. 15–16, 13.

[16] Richard B. Morris, *Government and Labor in Early America* (1946; New York:
Octagon Books, 1965), p. 217; H. W. Stiegel to John Dickinson, December 2, 1772,
Logan Papers, vol. 38, p. 91, HSP; Mark Leavenworth, May 18, 1790, as quoted in
Wilson, *Glass and Glassmaking*, p. 75.

[17] Ada Polak, *Glass: Its Makers and Its Public* (London: Weidenfeld & Nicholson,
1975), p. 25.

works at Zwiefalten but by 1712 had moved to Mattsthal. The Rodalben glasshouse was his next employer, between 1715 and 1723. Then he became superintendent of the Hassell glassworks and remained there until 1730. Griesmayer then returned to Mattsthal where he finished his glassmaking career. His sons did not accompany him on his final move but set out on their own. John George Griesmayer went to the glasshouse at Forbach where he made glass from 1731 until 1737, and then he spent four years at Dunkerque. Before his death in 1768 or 1769 he worked for five more glasshouses: Amblève, Bruxelles, Amblève again, Chênée-lez-Liège, Monthermé, and Eikenvliet. Another son, Simeon, left his brother at Forbach in 1737, traveled to Rotterdam, and sailed from there to Philadelphia.[18] Along with Martin Halter, Caspar Halter, and John William Wentzel, Griesmayer built the glasshouse in New Jersey for Caspar Wistar. Griesmayer remained at Wistarburgh until his death in 1748. He had no opportunity to wander because Wistar's was the only glassworks known to have been in operation in America during those years.

By 1817, when Franz Georg Hirsch came to this country, there were many glasshouses, yet it appeared that he worked only at the Chelmsford, Massachusetts, glasshouse for his entire career, in marked contrast to his experience abroad. Born in Bohemia, Hirsch blew glass at Habichsbach, Alsberg, Theissen, Schmalenburg, and Ober Alsbach. His peregrination throughout central Europe caused no ill will with management, as notes written by two of his employers demonstrate. "Because Mr. Hirsch has been so loyal and honest a worker," wrote Ludwig Greiner at Ober Alsbach, "I am happy to give him this certificate and impress on it our seal."[19] The labor pool was large, and other migrant workers would undoubtedly fill the places of Hirsch and others who left.

This was not the case in eighteenth-century America where there was a handful of skilled glass craftsmen. Because of this, glasshouse proprietors viewed their competition with suspicion. Their fears were well founded because several manufacturers sought their blowers not in Europe but among the ranks of their rivals in America. At least one

[18] Léon-Maurice Crismer, "Origines et Mouvements des Verriers Venus en Belgique au XVIIIe Siècle," in *Annales du 7e Congrès International d'Etude Historique du Verre, Berlin-Leipzig, 15–21 août 1977* (Liége: Edition du Secrétariat Général, Association pour l'Histoire du Verre, 1978), p. 351.

[19] Hirsch Papers, translation, Chelmsford Historical Society, Chelmsford, Mass.

Wistarburgh blower yielded to offers from Stiegel when the ironmaster started a glassworks in Lancaster County, Pennsylvania. In 1795, when John Brown planned to build a glassworks in Providence, his agent, John Hurley, journeyed to factories in East Hartford, Philadelphia, and New Jersey to procure a staff.[20] Such recruiting methods sometimes prompted reciprocal action. James O'Hara of Pittsburgh complained to a friend about Frederick Magnus Amelung, then manager of the Port Elizabeth, New Jersey, glassworks, claiming, "he is employed in endeavors to get my best glassblowers to desert my works." O'Hara then urged his friend to do what he could to get two or three of Amelung's best. Proprietors of Lake Dunmore Glass Company took great pains to see that their recruiting agent reached the Keene, Clyde, and Geneva factories before the agent of a rival firm.[21] Some factories agreed to avoid competing for labor. When Isaac Craig, O'Hara's partner, noted the disappearance of blower James Clark, he reminded the owner of the nearby New Geneva glasshouse, "You will not employ him particularly as we have in all our transactions since the establishment of our works scrupulously avoided a Competition or rivalship." Craig bolstered his request with threats of a lawsuit.[22]

Craig, like many other glasshouse owners, had signed a contract with his blower. That Clark chose to ignore it was not uncommon in the glass trade. An indentured servant at a glassworks in Hilltown, Pennsylvania, deserted his master no less than six times, while at least four apprentices are known to have run away from their masters.

As the numbers of glass factories increased in the late eighteenth and early nineteenth centuries, there were more opportunities for employment, and many glass craftsmen resumed the traditional migratory ways of the Continent. Within the Middle Atlantic region alone, there is considerable evidence of migration. Wistar blowers went to Stiegel's factory in Lancaster County; Stiegel workers went to Kensington, Philadelphia, and to Frederick, Maryland, where they started a factory that Amelung later bought. Some Amelung craftsmen worked

[20] Messrs. Brown and Francis in Account with John Hurley, 1795, Brown-Francis Papers, private collection, as quoted in Wendy A. Cooper, "The Furniture and Furnishings of John Brown, Merchant of Providence, 1736–1803" (M.A. thesis, University of Delaware, 1971), app. 3.

[21] Quoted in Innes, *Pittsburgh Glass*, pp. 19–20; Peter H. Templeton, "Glassmaking in Addison County, Vermont," p. 36 (Course paper, Middlebury College, 1978), copy, author's collection.

[22] Quoted in Innes, *Pittsburgh Glass*, p. 13.

for Nicholson in Philadelphia, and some moved to Baltimore, while others operated the Gallatin works at New Geneva near Pittsburgh. Kensington people advised Nicholson, then Nicholson blowers went to Kensington. They also headed for Boston and Pittsburgh. Glassblowers in New York and New Jersey have been traced to Pittsburgh, and artisans from New Geneva migrated to Baltimore.

The mobility of glass craftsmen has certain important implications for the identification of glassware from a particular region or factory. Just as an immigrant blower continued to fashion the shapes and decorations he had learned in Europe, so too did he carry his own particular style—and sometimes his tools. Iron and brass molds, even more than hand tools, directly determined the shape, size, or pattern of an object, and they, too, traveled back and forth with the craftsmen. The evidence of migratory craftsmen suggests that the traditional regional approach to the identification of American glass is in need of revision.

Mobility was not always a matter of choice. When glassblowers signed on, they had no assurances that the glasshouse would survive the vicissitudes of the marketplace. Of the twelve glasshouses of colonial America, only Wistarburgh endured more than twelve years. When glass craftsmen found themselves out of work, they sought employment at other glasshouses or encouraged new investors to try their luck. Fearing that the troubled Boston Glass Manufactory would not last another season, "the complete set of Glass Blowers" advertised their "wish to be employed in the same line, by any Gentleman or Company" with an agreement for one or two years.[23] Sometimes, as in the case of Basil and Louis Fertner, glassblowers pooled their resources and opened works of their own. When the glassworks of John Frederick Amelung closed in 1795, a group of workers leased one of the furnaces to keep the craft alive at New Bremen.

Many circumstances other than closing of the factory could lead a glassblower to leave his situation to seek employment elsewhere, but lack of payment was the most frequently recorded complaint. Joshua Tittery, for example, sued the president of the Free Society of Traders in 1685 for back wages and won.[24]

Often workers were not paid because the great capital investment required to set up a glasshouse left insufficient funds for operating

[23] *Columbian Centinel* (Boston) (June 1, 1796).
[24] Morris, *Government and Labor*, p. 217.

expenses. No one had more problems of this nature than Nicholson, who included a glassworks among his many ill-fated ventures of the 1790s.[25] The glasshouse superintendent, William Eichbaum, reported to Nicholson in June 1795, "[I have] Experienced of the Fertners so much Insolence which I can't account for any other Reason then that the Money is not here." In September he reported, "our people an[d] my Self are so Distreset for Money that [w]e must Endeavoar to Seek other [e]mployment in order to procure Subsistance." In October the Fertner family declared that they would not work beyond the end of the month. They took their case to the German Society, established to assist German immigrants, and through that organization put pressure on Nicholson to pay. The relief was temporary, however, because Nicholson had greatly overextended himself and the end was in sight. In 1797 Nicholson vainly tried to reduce his mountain of debt by paying his creditors in glassware and urged his staff to produce. The glassblowers, however, staged a sit-in strike in Nicholson's office. The company clerk "went to see each of them to order them to their work, their answer was that they will not work a stroke unless they get all the money which is due to them."[26]

Little information survives concerning the wages of glassmakers. In Europe, in all periods, glassblowers were among the most highly paid craftsmen. In America, as Mark Leavenworth noted on May 18, 1790, they were "in such demand that they obtain[ed] very high pay."[27] At the top of each factory organization was the glasshouse master, or superintendent, whose duties in American glasshouses would have varied little from those spelled out by the elector of Brandenburg in 1674:

He is to keep a watchful eye on the furnace and see that all that is necessary to bring and keep the furnace and glasshouse in good order is there: wood for fuel, clay, stone for the furnace, ash and other materials, and take care that nothing is missing as great trouble can ensue; he shall see to it that hard-working journeymen are retained, and he shall keep them in order, also see that nobody

[25] See Robert D. Arbuckle, *Pennsylvania Speculator and Patriot: The Entrepreneurial John Nicholson, 1757–1800* (University Park: Pennsylvania State University Press, 1975).

[26] William Eichbaum to Nicholson, June 5, September 18, October 30, 1795, and Joubert to Nicholson, June 1, 1797, NGC; Nicholson to Henry Keppele, December 14 and 28, 1795, John Nicholson Letterbooks, vol. 3, pp. 286, 303, HSP.

[27] See, for example, Joan Wallach Scott, *The Glassworkers of Carmaux* (Cambridge, Mass.: Harvard University Press, 1974), pp. 38–42; quoted in Wilson, *Glass and Glassmaking*, p. 75.

sells and takes home his work of the week, but make sure that everyone each week gives what he had done to the glass-house clerk.[28]

The master of a European glasshouse generally came from the ranks of the glassblowers, but in America superintendents had diverse backgrounds. Although Edward Lambert had been hired only to keep the books, he felt he had become, in effect, the "master overseer" and clerk of the Germantown, Massachusetts, glassworks in the 1750s. Ebenezer Hall came to the Franklin Glassworks in Warwick, Massachusetts, with experience as a teacher and physician. Hall left Warwick in 1815 to become superintendent of the Keene, New Hampshire, glasshouse for an annual salary of $500. The glasshouse in Woodstock, New York, then hired him for $600 per year. Henry Schoolcraft at the age of twenty-one was hired as superintendent by the Vermont Glass Works for $1,000.[29]

The only complete record of the activities of an American glassworks superintendent dates from 1795–97 and was made by Eichbaum at Nicholson's factory at Falls of the Schuylkill near Philadelphia. His duties were the same as those outlined for the Potsdam master, but they also included control of worker housing. Eichbaum's problems were probably atypical because of Nicholson's constant interference and mismanagement. At one point, when Eichbaum felt his authority threatened, he complained:

I cannot omit to mention the Disagreable news at my arival on Saturday night last which Mr. Groves had Published that Mr. Nicholson was going to Confine in joal the Glass Makers for Burning the Coals & making no Glass, now Sir if you have anything to alidge to my misconduct I should be very Glad if you would be pleased to acquaint me of it yourself & not let it come through the means of such a worthless old villian as he is.[30]

For his efforts Eichbaum received $1,000 per year—about £31 per month—three times the salary of a glassblower.

At Falls of the Schuylkill, as at many other glasshouses, the wages of a glassblower depended directly on the amount of glass he produced.

[28]Quoted in Polak, *Glass*, p. 18.

[29]Edward Lambert to Thomas Flucker and Isaac Winslow, February 13, 1754, as quoted in Wilson, *Glass and Glassmaking*, p. 45; Julia D. Sophronia Snow, "The Franklin Glass Factory—Warwick's Venture," *Antiques* 12, no. 2 (August 1927): 133–39; Templeton, "Glassmaking," p. 8.

[30]Eichbaum to Nicholson, October 17, 1795, NGC. The coal-fired furnaces at the Nicholson works were the first in America.

Records for 1797 show that Nicholson's seven gaffers were given one-fifth the value of the glass each made. For the month of March their wages ranged from £8.13.4 to £12.4.1½, with an average wage of £10.15.1, calculated on a total of 12,338 claret, snuff, and square bottles blown. The average wages for February, April, and May were £13.14.11, £13.10.1, and £10.17.2 respectively.

Caspar Wistar and his glassblowing partners shared in various proportions the value of glass bottles and windowpanes blown. For the eight-month season, or "blast," between October 1745 and May 1746, Wentzel was responsible for making glass worth £400.18.3; he received a third of that sum, £133.12.9, or approximately £16.14.1 per month. Martin Halter and Simeon Griesmayer apparently worked together, and for the 1745–46 blast they produced glass to the value of £953.8.7. They each received one-sixth of the total, or £158.18.1. Eleven years later when only Wentzel and Halter remained of the original partnership, each of them earned £359.12.7.

For some glass craftsmen income depended not only on their productivity but also on the type of object manufactured. According to the terms of his contract drawn in 1752, John Martin Greiner of Saxe-Weimer was required to inform his New York employers "in Ev'ry respect in the Art & Mistery of Erecting and Building a Glass House & allso in Blowing & Making of Glass." In return Greiner would be paid twenty-four stivers for every 100 one-quart bottles made and three gilders per 100 half-gallon flasks. An 1825 contract between the owners and employees of the Chelmsford, Massachusetts, glasshouse set forth a salary based on the size of the windowpanes made: for 8-by-10-inch and smaller sizes the glassblower got £0.6.9 per 100 feet and £0.8.3 for larger sizes.[31]

Although early American glassmakers primarily blew bottles and windowpanes, it is the table articles fashioned of the same melts that have survived in collections. These are described in the literature as "offhand" or "end-of-day" wares (fig. 3), the assumption being that blowers worked on a quota per diem basis. Supposedly, after he had completed the stipulated number of bottles or cylinders, the blower was free to empty the pot by shaping items of his own desire and for his own use, but this is not well documented. While certain whimsies were undoubt-

[31] Draft of agreement, New-York Historical Society; "Articles of Agreement between the Proprietors & the Blowers at the Chelmsford Glass Works," August 16, 1825, Corning Museum of Glass.

Figure 3.   Covered bowl, green glass. Probably New Jersey, early nineteenth century. H. 8⅞". (Winterthur 59.3018.) Often considered "offhand" glass, such wares blown of unrefined glass were probably made
for commercial sale and not solely for the glassblower's amusement.

edly made for pleasure, factory records suggest that table forms of common glass were intended for commercial sale. From one glassblower's diary it is clear that his daily goal was to "finish" his pot, whether it be with bottles or bowls.[32]

Entries in the record books of Stiegel show that he paid his workers a flat rate rather than base their wages on productivity, a system that was also practiced at several English factories. A fragmentary wage record for 1768 from the Taylor glasshouse in Bristol shows that master blowers received £1.7.9 for seven days' work, or £5.11 per month. At the Northumberland glassworks of Lord Delaval, master craftsmen earned £1.0.0 per week in 1773, while journeymen were paid between 20s. and 14s. At about the same time, Stiegel was paying his master blowers £5.10.0 per month. To the parents of apprentices he paid £0.1.5 per month. In 1773 Stiegel signed a contract with an English-trained glass engraver, Lazarus Isaac, and agreed to pay him £5.10.0 each month for twelve months. In addition, Isaac would receive a house, land for a garden, and, like all the other employees at Manheim, firewood hauled to his door for 5s. a cord. Monthly wages may also have been paid at the New Bremen Glassmanufactory of John Frederick Amelung. When it closed in 1795, several glassblowers, sought employment with Nicholson, informing him, "it will be out of our power to work for less than Thirty dollars per Month if the Furnace is inclos'd and if not then half the wages are usually given, and a free house includet."[33]

When evaluating the wages of glass craftsmen in early America, two points should be kept in mind. First, piecework wages may have been paid to a team, not to an individual. Second, there were other forms of remuneration in the glass industry besides cash. The glasshouse labor force was usually organized into teams, or "chairs," with one team assigned to each pot of molten glass in the furnace. Christopher Triepel and Charles Ehrhard informed Nicholson that they were "able to furnish good capable Glass blowers for one oven." Louis Fertner was described at one point as Triepel's "pot companion."[34] The

[32] George Whitefield Foster, diary, as quoted in John Morrill Foster, *Old Bottle Foster and His Glass-Making Descendants* (Fort Wayne, Ind.: Keefer Printing Co., 1972).

[33] Taylor Records, Bristol Record Office, Bristol, Gloucestershire; Royal Northumberland Glassworks, Delaval Papers, Northumberland Record Office, Newcastle upon Tyne; facsimile reproduction of Lazarus Isaac contract in Hunter, *Stiegel Glass*, after p. 72; Christopher Triepel and Charles Ehrhard to Nicholson, June 14, 1795, NGC.

[34] Triepel and Ehrhard to Nicholson, June 14, 1795, and Eichbaum to Nicholson, January 29[?], 1796, NGC.

master blower, or gaffer, occupied the glassmaker's chair. He was responsible for the final shape and finish of the object. He was assisted by journeymen, apprentices, and boys. The wages recorded at Wistarburgh and at Nicholson's works were, apparently, paid to heads of teams who were then responsible for distributing shares to their assistants. The exact number of assistant positions depended on the type of vessel made and the scope of the establishment. There could be, for example, a gatherer who took up the initial gather of glass from the melting pot onto the blowpipe, a marverer who shaped the parison on a marver, while a boy may have had the task of opening molds, applying the pontil, or carrying off finished ware to the annealing oven.

As Stiegel's contract with Isaac and the Triepel letter demonstrate, glassworkers were often provided with living quarters. There was a practical reason for this because glassworks were often located in remote areas. Before 1795 all the furnaces of American glasshouses were wood fired, and in order to minimize the expense, factories were located within or near wooded areas. Caspar Wistar acquired over 2,000 wooded acres eight miles from Salem, New Jersey, and his ovens consumed 2,400 cords of wood annually. The ambitions of John Frederick Amelung were such that New Bremen became a manufacturing town containing, by 1787, dwellings for 135 people. Schools were built for the children, and a Masonic lodge was founded for the workers.

Three eighteenth-century glasshouses existed as part of larger industrial communities. The Germantown (now Braintree), Massachusetts, settlement of the 1750s included, besides a glasshouse, a chocolate factory, a pottery, weaving establishments, and a spermaceti processing plant. A town was laid out to accommodate the workers, all of whom were German immigrants. Stiegel founded and administered the town of Manheim for his glass- and ironworkers. At Falls of the Schuylkill Nicholson followed the pattern of the Paterson, New Jersey, textile experiment because he believed that diversification was the key to success. Nicholson built an ironworks, a button factory, and a glasshouse in addition to the textile factory. The complex was never completed, however, and surviving records suggest that worker housing was inadequate. Glassblower Mathias Fertner lamented, "[I am] under an Obligation to make a Complaint [as] . . . the Condition that I now labour under Is too tedicous and hard for any human Mortal to bear As there is no regulation to be had here [and] I have to Lay on the flore & have not where[withal] to accomplish my Dyet."[35] Five months later he died of a fever.

Many of the nineteenth-century glasshouses were built as independent undertakings in rural areas. Written descriptions and pictorial views prove that workers continued to be furnished with lodgings. Even in urban areas housing for the workers was often available. "Glasshouse Row" on Hughes Street, Baltimore, housed the first workers at the Baltimore Glassworks in 1800, while the Boston tax lists for 1798 show that three glassblowers for the Boston Crown Glass Works occupied company-owned houses in South Boston. Other workers for the company were tenants in noncompany houses, while blower Adam Hartwick owned and occupied his own two-story wooden dwelling on a 3,600-square-foot lot near the factory.

Whether in countryside or in town, American glassblowers were a group apart. Their physical isolation made political involvement difficult, and social intercourse beyond the glassworks was limited. To the outside world, the practitioners of this mysterious art were even more mysterious because so many spoke only a foreign tongue. As late as 1850 a visitor to Pittsburgh reported hearing only German in one glasshouse. Their isolation was strengthened by the peculiarities of the manufacturing process. They kept unusual hours, often working in six-hour shifts around the clock. The furnaces were tended constantly, and when the batch was ready it had to be worked, regardless of the hour. During the glassblowers' strike at Nicholson's factory, the clerk reported of Nicholas Fertner, the founder, or mixer of the ingredients, "[he cannot] continue longer the Glass blowers having not been working he is forced to stay in the Glasshouse in order to Watch the Glass and this evening he will have been 30 hours on duty without taking any rest."[36]

Glassmaking was a business full of risks, and if disaster struck all hands were needed to help out. Melting pots frequently broke in the oven; during the month of March 1797, nine pots broke at Falls of the Schuylkill. When this happened the broken fragments had to be removed and a new pot filled with batch and reset. Joseph Leacock, part owner of the Kensington glassworks in Philadelphia in 1771, vividly recalled his joy at seeing the first table glass made. He reported, however,

---

[35] Mathias Fertner to Nicholson, February 19, 1795, NGC.
[36] Joubert to Nicholson, June 2, 1797, NGC.

[My joy was] quickly damped by the terrific Cry "A pot is broke"—O the confusion that ensued. The Palace of a King in flames could not have created more hurry & hubbub—away all hurry to the furnace, down comes the side on which the pot had broke, out it was ha[u]led—another introduced in its place—the side of the furnace built up again, & all well once more. ["]O these little misfortunes must happen now and then["] cry'd out the pot maker—["]I suppose so["] was my reply ["]but I hope not too often or the glass men must be metamorphosed into Salamanders to Endure such hot work.["][37]

The work of a glassblower was indeed long, hot, and difficult. Glassblowing required strong lungs and arms. In making crown window glass a blower might have as much as thirty-two pounds of glass at the end of his blowpipe, and forty-pound cylinders up to seventy inches in length had to be swung on the blowpipe in the manufacture of cylinder glass (see fig. 4). Glassblowers were susceptible to lung diseases, and infections of any sort spread rapidly because the blowpipe passed from mouth to mouth in the manufacturing process.

With the physical efforts required of their lungs and mouth and the intense heat to which they were exposed, glassblowers were constantly thirsty. Beverages of alcoholic content were the usual thirst quenchers, and without them little glass was made. The clerk at Falls of the Schuylkill glassworks beseeched his employer saying, "if you have some *good Wine* pray send us some, even if it is *coloured tarr.*" A few weeks later he was again in want and argued that "a few Gall[ons] of any thing might operate wonders among the Glassmakers."[38]

Nicholson's reluctance to send liquor is understandable considering the drunken brawl that had occurred at his factory a few months before. According to the factory superintendent, three blowers, Louis Fertner, Christopher Triepel, and Frederick Wendt, had been drinking all afternoon.

& when the two George & Bassil [Fertner] Came up to persuade Louis to bed upon which he was obsternate and a Quarel insued and Blows, upon which Triepel went to the assistance of Louis and his Pot Companion and used the other two George & Bassil as you find them. and followed Them to Their house and got no admitance there. I had pot setting to do which could not be done till this morning about ten O'Clok, which ou[gh]t to have be done last night about the same hour. but having most hands Intoxicated and others Bruised was obliged to Defer it till this morning and how it will go this Day I know not

[37]Leacock to Nicholson, December 23, 1794, NGC.
[38]Joubert to Nicholson, April 27, May 20, 1796, NGC.

Figure 4.   Scrip notes for 50¢ and 75¢, Redford Glass Co. Redford, N.Y., 1831–51. Paper. (Winterthur 73.248.) Redeemable at the company store, these notes illustrate the manufacture of window glass by the crown method.

as drinking has been gone on all this day, and George Godwald living so very handy and so very agreeable to Drinkers, makes it impossible to have the place, but I shall wait on you as Soon as Bacchus Reign is over."[39]

Inebriation was a widespread problem. At Stiegel's works Henry Sharman had to pay five shillings "for getting Drunk and Leaving an [pot] Arch Empty about three hours." James O'Hara fired two workers from his Pittsburgh plant in 1806. In his opinion, blower Charles Haines "forfeited all claim to indulgence by his constant practice of getting drunk and neglecting his business to the great loss and disgrace of the works." The other became "unworthy of any confidence" in conse-

[39] Eichbaum to Nicholson, January 29[?], 1796, NGC.

quence of his "many repeated abuses of his duty in being drunk in the composition room."[40]

The absence of "spiritous beverages" in the factory at Sandwich, Massachusetts, was a source of pride and a matter of comment. An 1832 newspaper account reported: "No ardent spirit has been admitted within the factory for the last four years. . . . Of the 200 employed at the Factory, not more than 100 drink ardent spirits on any occasion; and of the 100 who occasionally drink, five of that number only, have ever been intoxicated."[41]

When Philadelphia entrepreneur and self-styled physician Thomas W. Dyott reorganized his glassworks as a model temperate manufacturing village, he found it necessary to dismiss those "workmen from Europe, tainted by the habits of a degenerate caste, which rendered intemperance an inveterate habit." He concentrated instead on instilling temperate habits into apprentices.[42] Dyott's crusade against alcohol did not extend beyond the factory gates, however, because wine bottles and fancy pocket liquor flasks were among his staple products.

Rules and regulations—and Dyott was not the first to prescribe them—did not insure that employer-employee relations in the glasshouse were always smooth. The Eichbaum–Nicholson correspondence illustrates some of the difficulties between superintendent and workers, albeit in a glassworks that was more or less doomed from the start. Similar problems must have plagued the Germantown glasshouse in the 1750s; clerk Edward Lambert stated, "[I am] certain there's not one young man in fifty would have stayed here and been so oppressed, threatened and abused by the glassman as I have."[43]

The failure of glassblowers to "perform their duty in a sober peaceable & workmanlike manner" could lead to disaster. Although the crew at the Rensselaer glassworks was described as "a set of the best workmen," they proved to be lazy and "addicted to carousing and extravagance." During a card game in 1815 they accidentally set fire to the works. The carelessness of the furnace stokers at the Vermont Glass

---

[40] H. W. Stiegel Records, Glass Factory Day Book, September 17, 1771, HSP; quoted in Innes, *Pittsburgh Glass*, p. 13.

[41] *Daily Evening Transcript* (Boston) (September 8, 1832) as quoted in Wilson, *Glass and Glassmaking*, p. 264.

[42] T. W. Dyott, *An Exposition of the System of Moral and Mental Labor Established at the Glass Factory of Dyottsville* (Philadelphia, 1833).

[43] Quoted in Wilson, *Glass and Glassmaking*, p. 44.

Figure 5. Vermont Glass Factory $1.75 bank note drawn on Farmers Bank, Troy, N.Y. Salisbury, Vt., 1815. Paper. (Joseph Downs Manuscript and Microfilm Collection 74 x 14.1, Winterthur Museum Library.) Shows factory as it appeared prior to a fire carelessly set by workers.

Factory near Lake Dunmore caused the destruction of that works by fire in 1815 (see Fig. 5).[44]

When they were not coping with such major disasters, superintendents tried to keep peace among workers on the factory floor. The creation of every glass object required the cooperation of at least two individuals, and a spirit of teamwork was essential. Caroline Harrison, visiting the Brooklyn Flint Glass Works in 1824, "looked with astonishment" at the process she observed: "every man seems to have his part to perform—they work into each others hands as it were—Therefore none of them can spend any idle time." The pressure on the workers was increased by the fact that glass can only be manipulated at a certain temperature maintained by constant reheating. Harrison marveled at "the red hot ball of Glass flying in all directions."[45] The material and the manufacturing process gave to glassmaking a sense of urgency unparalleled in other crafts.

There was another side of the glass business where the individual craftsman could act alone, and that concerned lampwork production

---

[44] "Articles of agreement"; *Columbia Patriot* (March 29, 1815) as quoted in Templeton, "Glassmaking," pp. 24–25.

[45] Caroline Harrison to Thomas Harrison, July 1, 1824, Leib-Harrison Papers, Miscellaneous Collections, HSP.

Figure 6.   Broadside, J. Tilley. Possibly Philadelphia, ca. 1820. Paper.
(Joseph Downs Manuscript and Microfilm Collection 76 x 404.1, Winterthur Museum Library.)

and certain decoration that took place outside the factory setting. Men
and women with skills in these areas emigrated on their own intiative
to seek their fortunes in America. Perhaps more in the category of enter-
tainers than craftsmen, were "fancy glassblowers," or lampworkers, who
fashioned whimsical articles from prefabricated glass rods softened at a
concentrated heat source. Men like James Tilley and Lawrence Finn
traveled throughout the states in the nineteenth century demonstrating
the remarkable qualities of glass to admiring audiences (fig. 6).

Decorators of glass, wheel cutters, engravers, and painters on glass
did not need to be associated with a glassworks and could set up independent shops. They obtained their blanks from private clients or factory agents or purchased them at auction. The identification of their
work is problematical; they undoubtedly embellished glass of both
American and European manufacture. Patterns of their work could be
seen in their shops, but they also executed designs on order. In spite of
their flexibility and a desire to please, it is certain that their training and
experience would be reflected in the style of their work.

The first glass engraver known to have practiced the art in America
was Lazarus Isaac who came to Philadelphia from London in 1773.
From his advertisement in the *Pennsylvania Packet* (May 17, 1773), it

Figure 7. Blown goblet, attributed to Henry William Stiegel, American Glass Manufactory, and probably engraved by Lazarus Isaac. Manheim, Pa., ca. 1773. H. 7″. (Private collection: Photo, Sheldon Butts.)

is clear that Isaac was prepared to decorate glass in the English manner: "he undertakes to cut and engrave on glass of every kind, in any figure whatsoever, either coats of arms, flowers, names, or figures. . . . He cuts upon decanters a name of the wine, &c. for 1s tumblers for 6d each, wine glasses for 2s per dozen, and the stems cut in diamonds at 2/6 per dozen." Isaac worked under contract with Stiegel starting in June 1773, but he may have returned to London at the outbreak of the Revolution.[46]

A lead-glass goblet recently discovered in the possession of Stiegel descendants appears to be an example of Isaac's work (fig. 7). It is engraved W & E / OLD for Stiegel's daughter Elizabeth who married William Old in 1773. On the reverse is a rose reminiscent of English work of

[46] No mention of Isaac has been found in American post-Revolutionary records. A Lazarus Isaacs was a warden ca. 1830 in the Western Synagogue of London (Arthur Barnett, *The Western Synagogue through Two Centuries* (1761–1961) [London: Valentine Mitchell, 1961], p. 159).

the period. The goblet has an opaque enamel twist stem, conforming to the fashion of the 1770s and fitting the contemporary description of "enameled" glass found in Stiegel's advertisements. The glass supports the theory that Stiegel's engraved glass would have been in the English style because Isaac learned his craft in England. Over the years, enormous quantities of nonlead glass engraved in a Continental folk style have been attributed to Stiegel. The designs on these glasses resemble those in a Bohemian glassmaker's catalogue of about 1800. They could not have been the work of Isaac, and, as yet, no engravers of Germanic origin have been identified for the colonial period.

Between 1788 and 1792 an anonymous craftsman of Germanic origin engraved glass for John Frederick Amelung (fig. 8). Close examination of the two dozen surviving decorated glasses suggests that he worked alone in a consistent manner. No evidence of his pre– or post–New Bremen activity has come to light. Besides Isaac there were at least three other engravers and cutters with English training practicing their art in late eighteenth-century America. Among them was John Moss who worked for Turner and Abbott in their Fleet Street, London, shop. After at least eight years as an independent glass engraver in Philadelphia, he became a general merchant. One of the few women in the early American glass industry was Madame Descamps from Paris who opened a glass-engraving store in Philadelphia in 1795. By 1804 she had moved to Boston. Descamps is the first glass decorator in America known to have run a shop with several artisans. As she notified the public in 1800, she was now "assisted by several persons whom she [had] successfully enabled to be proficient in that art."[47]

When the fine table glass industry became firmly established in the nineteenth century and a market was created for expensive decorated glass, a few of the larger glassworks included decorating shops. In 1826 the Pittsburgh firm of Bakewell, Page, and Bakewell, for example, employed among sixty-one hands twelve who "constantly" engraved and ornamented glass. It was reported that New England Glass Company had "an establishment for *Cutting Glass*, in all its variety, operated by Steam Power and conducted by experienced European Glass Cutters, of the first character for workmanship in their profession" (figs. 9, 10). Before 1840, however, most of the fancy cut and engraved glass in America emanated from independent cutting enterprises. Joseph Bag-

---

[47] *Pennsylvania Packet* (June 25, 1795); *Aurora* (Philadelphia) (April 4, 1800).

Figure 8. Blown and engraved glass goblet made for George Jacob Schley by John Frederick Amelung, New Bremen Glassmanufactory. Frederick County, Md., probably 1791–93. H. 11⅞". (Winterthur 59.47.)

gott and Edward Yates in New York, Robert Smith in Charleston, and Henry Tingle of Baltimore all operated large glass-cutting factories. Fourteen members of Tingle's Baltimore Cut Glass Works marched in the Fourth of July parade in 1826, each of whom "bore in his hands a piece of BALTIMORE CUT-GLASS, the beauty and richness of which elicited general admiration."[48]

Perhaps the best-known glass cutter was George Dummer who, after learning his trade in Albany, opened a retail glass shop in New York City where he decorated and sold glass. He then started a glass-

---

[48] Pittsburgh City Directory, 1826, p. 70; *Commercial Gazette* (Boston) (April 13, 1818) as quoted in Wilson, *Glass and Glassmaking*, p. 230; *Baltimore American* (July 7, 1828).

Figure 9. Blown, cut, and engraved presentation vase, New England Glass Co. East Cambridge, Mass., 1843. H. 13⅜". (Metropolitan Museum of Art, Purchase, Robert G. Goelet and Mr. and Mrs. William H. Hernstadt gifts, 1980.)

works in Jersey City where he manufactured glass of all types, from "rich cut" to pressed utilitarian wares. His success prompted him to undertake the manufacture of fine pottery, and he opened the Jersey City Porcelain Works. His prominence in manufacturing gave him a certain stature in the community, and between 1826 and 1830 he was president of Jersey City. His portrait, painted by Waldo and Jewett and now owned by Newark Museum, is one of the few known likenesses of an American glassmaker.

Research of American glass cutters is somewhat hampered because *glass cutter* describes both those highly skilled craftsmen who executed ornamental designs upon glass as well as those workers of low skill employed in window-glass factories to cut the finished cylinders or crowns into panes of the desired size. All window-glass factories had "cutting shops" where this activity took place.

Figure 10.   Detail of engraved view of vase in figure 9, showing factory buildings.

Figure 11.   Blown-molded calabash bottle commemorating the visit to America of Hungarian patriot Louis Kossuth, Millford Glass Works. Millford, N.J., 1850–60. H. 10½". (Winterthur 73.429.2.)

Figure 12.   Detail of bottom of bottle in figure 11 showing name of Philadelphia moldmaker Philip Doflein and his address, "N[or]TH 5T[h] ST. [No.] 84."

Blown-glass windows and bottles continued to be the mainstay of the glass industry in the nineteenth century. Mechanized processes for their production were introduced only in this century. The table glass industry, however, was revolutionized by 1830, first with the improvement of full-size molds into which the gaffer blew his gather and then with the invention of mechanical pressing where the role of the glassblower was eliminated entirely.[49] Here the size, shape, and pattern of the object were determined by the skill of the moldmaker, not the glassmaker. Little is known of the glass moldmakers. The name of one, Philip Doflein, appears in glass, molded in relief in the bottom of an 1850s bottle (figs. 11, 12).

[49] See Kenneth M. Wilson, "American Contributions to the Development of Pressed Glass," in *Technological Innovation and the Decorative Arts*, ed. Ian M. G. Quimby and Polly Anne Earl (Charlottesville: University Press of Virginia, 1974), pp. 167–206.

Still, throughout the nineteenth century, glassblowing traditions were kept alive in America. Although the growth of technical knowledge may have diminished some of the mystery of the ancient craft, the glassblower remained a craftsman set apart. From sand and ashes he created transparent articles of utility and beauty, articles that were at once fragile and enduring. The epitaph on the tombstone of Chelmsford glassblower John Joseph Stickelmire, who died of "dropsy by intemperance" in 1814, suggests something of the way in which glassmakers may have viewed themselves and their art. It seems a fitting end to this discussion.

> This verse reminds the heedless as they pass
> That life's a fragile drop of un[an]nealed glass
> The slightest wound ensures a fatal burst
> And the frail fabric shivers into dust.
> So he whom in his art could none surpass
> Is now himself reduced to broken glass.
> But from the grave, and fining pot of man
> From scandiver and glass galls pursed again
> New mixed and fashioned by almighty power
> Shall rise a firmer fabric than before.

The Business of Potting, 1780–1840
Susan H. Myers

The American pottery industry underwent a transformation between the end of the revolutionary war and about 1840. At the beginning of the period the average pottery manufacturer was—as had been true since the early seventeenth century—a master craftsman producing household red earthenware by traditional handcraft methods with the assistance of a small work force. By 1840 such traditional potteries were in decline, challenged by the more sophisticated products of a new ceramics industry. Changes in technology, more complex raw materials, new forms of business organization, and a diminished role for the craftsman accompanied the introduction of the new wares. Some of these changes occurred slowly in the course of expanding production of such things as household stoneware which retained many ties with the traditional handcraft. Other changes came abruptly, particularly with the manufacture of refined molded earthenware. Fineware enterprises required more capital and involved greater risk. Bearing little resemblance to red earthenware potteries, usually they were initiated by an entrepreneur who, although he might take an active role in the business, was not a potter but hired skilled workers, commonly from England or the Continent, to produce the ware.

There was little development in the American ceramics industry in the years immediately following the end of the Revolution. The general economic depression and an excess of imported goods temporarily created an unfavorable atmosphere for expansion. By the 1790s, with improved economic conditions encouraged by America's greater commercial role during the Napoleonic Wars, there were signs of renewed activity in the ceramics industry. While the early tariffs were for the most part intended to produce revenue rather than to protect nascent industries, some interests saw them as an aid in the development of domestic manufactures and as a means of adding economic independence to political independence. The development of American industry was encouraged as well by societies of mechanics and tradesmen. One of these, the Pennsylvania Society for the Encouragement of Manufactures and the Useful Arts, in 1792 offered awards for "the best specimen of [Pennsylvania, New Jersey, or Delaware] Earthenware or Pottery, approaching nearest to Queen's Ware, or, the Nottingham or Delf Ware, of the marketable value of fifty dollars" and for "the best specimen of Stone Ware, or that kind of Earthen Ware which is glazed with Salt, of the marketable value of 50 dollars."[1] Although some wares of these types were being made in America by 1800, success in the potting business would for some years remain concentrated on the red earthenware manufacturer who operated very much in the traditional manner of his colonial counterparts.

The diary of Concord, New Hampshire, potter Daniel Clark, covering the years 1789 to 1828, reveals a great deal about the conservative business of making earthenware in early nineteenth-century New England.[2] It also suggests the nature of many small potteries located in inland communities far from the major urban centers of the East Coast. In time-honored fashion, Daniel was trained in the shop of his father, Peter Clark, in Lyndeboro, New Hampshire. As the third among four sons learning the potter's trade, he could not expect to succeed to the management of the family works. This may explain his move to nearby Concord in 1792 to establish his own manufactory. Since the city had no pottery at the time, Clark thought—correctly—that he would find a good, noncompetitive market. Concord, established in the 1720s, was a promising location. It became the state capital in 1808, and completion of the Middlesex Canal in 1815 stimulated its growth by providing

[1] *New Jersey Journal and Political Intelligencer* (Elizabeth) (January 25, 1792).

[2] Daniel Clark diary, 1789–1828, New Hampshire Historical Society, Concord. I am indebted to the historical society for allowing me to study a copy of their recent transcription of the Clark diary. Although the diary covers the period 1789 to 1828, it has been analyzed only for the years 1794 through 1825 when entries appear to be most complete. Except where otherwise noted, data concerning Clark is derived from that analysis.

a water route between Concord and Boston via the Merrimack River. Although Clark did not long remain the only potter in the area, he was quite successful (fig. 1).[3]

Daniel Clark's yearly potting activities fell into a regular cycle that interlocked with farming. His most invariable crop was hay, some of which he sold and some he kept for his animals. It had a short and early growing season, and its harvest did not interfere with potting. Other crops such as corn, potatoes, and peas were commonly planted in May. The diary indicates that the hay was mowed in July while harvesting of the vegetables rarely is mentioned. Presumably they were grown on a small scale for family use and were not a cash crop.

The materials required to make earthenware are few and easily obtained. Like most earthenware potters, Clark could find both clay and wood to fire the kiln in the immediate vicinity. Working around the farming schedule, clay was dug and carted usually between April and August. Wood most often was cut in March and April and carted the following winter between January and March. The elapsed time between cutting and transporting the wood to the pottery permitted the wood to dry.

The purchase of lead for glazing followed no particular pattern. More difficult to obtain than clay and wood, apparently it was available only in the eastern, more developed areas, and not along the western path where Clark chose to market his ware. The acquisition of lead often required a trip of twenty miles or more, and in one case it was necessary to go as far as Boston, a journey of about sixty miles. Clark purchased lead in whatever form he could get, usually bar or red lead and, occasionally, litharge. In 1814 and 1815, presumably as a result of the diversion of lead to the war effort, he was forced to use lead ore.

Working at a traditional potter's wheel, Clark turned his ware during the summer or early fall and glazed as time permitted. The diary entries for grinding lead are too infrequent to suggest a pattern. The inhalation of toxic lead—one of the earthenware potter's major occupational hazards—is suggested in the diary by Clark's periodic references to "dysentary," "rheumatism in stomack," and "billious chollick." During the last six years of his life he was often sick with "chollick," sometimes for long periods, probably the cumulative effect of many

[3]Lura Woodside Watkins, *Early New England Potters and Their Wares* (Cambridge, Mass.: Harvard University Press, 1950), pp. 120–23.

Figure 1.   Jug attributed to Daniel Clark. Concord, N.H., 1792–1828. Dark-brown-glazed red earthenware; H. 7⅜″. (New Hampshire Historical Society.)

years of exposure to powdered lead.

Formed and glazed ware was fired throughout the year, although it was done most commonly in June. Firing rarely took place in September or October when Clark's time was most heavily devoted to turning. If he was particularly busy, finished ware might wait in the shop for months to be fired. In January 1806, he noted that he had just burned the "20th & last kiln made in 1804," over a year previously.

On the basis of the diary's breakdown of labor, Clark appears to have done a great deal of the work himself, although he did have help of various types. Most assistance came from his brother Benjamin (before 1798), his sons Daniel and Peter, and Samuel Whittemore, a Lyndeboro potter who established his own shop in Concord in 1798 but who continued to work with Clark. Also at the pottery was Peter Flanders, who began as an apprentice in 1795 and stayed with Clark for ten years. One employee worked for him about four years and two others were hired for one year each.[4] The names of various other people appear irregularly in the diary, and often they seem to have been hired to assist only with a specific chore.

Clark family members, as well as Whittemore and his son Peter, are noted in the diary as doing almost all types of work around the pottery—skilled and unskilled. The entries for other workers are limited to peddling ware, cutting and hauling wood, hauling clay, and helping to load the kiln. Flanders, however, must have had experience in other jobs in his ten years with Clark. He learned the business well enough to establish his own pottery in Concord by 1807 (figs. 2, 3). In that year his kiln "fell down in burning," a not uncommon catastrophe. Keyes Powell, mentioned off and on for four years, also may have done more skilled jobs, for the diary indicates that he worked "in the shop."

The interaction of the Clarks and Whittemores in Concord and in Lyndeboro is of interest. Daniel's brothers, his sons, and Daniel himself traveled back and forth between the two family potteries helping each other as needed. Samuel Whittemore, whether living in Lyndeboro or after his move to Concord, helped Clark by, among other things, supervising the firing. The help was reciprocated by Daniel and his sons.

The few diary entries concerning payment of workers indicate no wages greater than $15 per month. Workers were probably paid in kind rather than cash, as in the case of John Libbey who was hired for a year

[4]Watkins, *New England Potters*, pp. 122–26.

at "11.00 pr month in ware, & give in the house rent, & pauster [*sic*] his cow, summer season."

Like most rural craftsmen, Clark was both producer and merchandiser of his earthenware. Insofar as the diary specifies the market to which he sold his pottery, it appears that he concentrated on the Concord area and on the regions to the west where few potteries were established. Even though Concord is on the Merrimack River, there is no reference to transporting goods by boat. Rather, his pots were sledded or carted overland since no water transport could take him to his western markets.

The range of his market rarely exceeded forty miles. The only diary entry that suggests a possible deviation from his usual orientation and range concerned a January 1823 trip to Boston. Noting that two of his workmen bought bar lead there, he also commented that the "Markets [were] Dull."

Little is said in the diary concerning the ways in which Clark was paid for his earthenware. A common method of dealing was barter, and occasional entries refer to that practice. In December 1799 he noted that he "Bot yoke oxen" from William Simpson, "price 40 dols ware"; in April 1803 he "measured & took a deed of Barron hill gave 165 dollars for 18 acres in ware." That some cash did change hands is indicated by at least one partial cash transaction in January 1823 when he "Sold kiln ware to Libbey for $50.00 ½ cash & ½ pro. @ cash price."

With little competition and a growing population Clark's business thrived. Lura Watkins noted that by 1810 his was "the most successful pottery business in New Hampshire." His prosperity is suggested by the building of a new house, a barn, and a shed in 1804 and the subsequent building of a considerably more substantial house in 1810.[5] He made modest investments in the pottery, expanding it as demand grew. During his first year in Lyndeboro he must have worked in an old abandoned pottery, an "old durty shop" by his description, but in 1793 he built himself a new pottery shop and kiln. In July 1806 he had a "stone clay mill" built at a cost of $70; in August 1808 he raised a shed "by the Kiln house"; by May 1815 he had a new lead mill; and in September 1817 he "sett up tub to grind clay." In 1792 and 1800 he bought land from a local family which he used both for digging clay and for haying.

Throughout the period covered by the diary, Clark continued the

---

[5] Watkins, *New England Potters*, pp. 128, 124.

Figure 2. Plate, attributed to Peter Flanders. Concord, N.H., 1807. Clear-glazed red earthenware; Diam. 12″. (New Hampshire Historical Society.)

hand production of household red earthenware of the types common in traditional American potteries. His success never tempted him to try to make the more sophisticated products—stoneware or refined earthenware—that were beginning to be produced elsewhere. His reasons undoubtedly were those of most traditional earthenware potters of the period. The demand from Clark's market was primarily for household utilitarian ware. What demand existed for stoneware or refined tableware could be met by imports from other parts of the country or from England and the Continent. Introduction of the manufacture of either of these products involved different skills and represented a substantial

Figure 3.   Reverse of plate in figure 2.

expense. The more refined wares required different raw materials, forming techniques, and firing methods.

Stoneware, hard and durable, was a better type of pottery for most purposes than the porous and friable earthenware that Clark made. It was, however, made from a type of clay that was far less readily available than the ubiquitous red clay. It also required a somewhat different type of kiln and a higher firing temperature. Unless a pottery was located at the source of clay, the costs of shipping that raw material could be substantial. Before the expansion of overland transportation, location on a major waterway was essential for obtaining clay. In an age of poor overland transportation, Daniel Clark and other inland traditional earthenware potters had no easy access to clay for stoneware. Until national transportation networks improved, they were unlikely to attempt its manufacture. Clark could have brought New Jersey stoneware clay up the coast and along the Merrimack to Concord, but the cost surely would have been prohibitive, preventing him from pricing his wares competitively with imported counterparts.

A few pioneer stoneware manufactories had been established in several East Coast cities before the revolutionary war. After the war, particularly in the early nineteenth century, their numbers grew substantially. A significant phenomenon characterized some of these stoneware ventures. It was the association between an entrepreneur who provided the capital and marketing and a potter, or potters, who provided the expertise needed for production.

An early postwar example is the Boston manufactory established in 1793 by potters Frederick Carpenter and Jonathan Fenton, almost certainly with the financial backing of William Little, a Boston merchant (fig. 4). Little had been importing German and Belgian stoneware via Liverpool for his wholesale firm. Apparently he thought that he could save money by making his own.[6]

Little brought to the business capital, an existing sales network, and an understanding of the market for such products. Without these advantages, it is unlikely that Carpenter and Fenton would have attempted the venture. Although the site had the advantage of a coastal location, it was still a considerable distance from New Jersey clay, and costs for that raw material must have been great.

Precisely how these associations of merchants and potters affected the division of responsibility in the pottery—and the status of the craftsmen—is a matter of conjecture. Presumably Little concerned himself with marketing the products and, perhaps, with the other major "outdoor" activity, getting raw materials. Fenton and Carpenter, who appear to have been trained in the New Haven stoneware pottery of Jacob Fenton, Jonathan's brother, undoubtedly took care of the actual production.[7]

[6] Lura Woodside Watkins, "New Light on Boston Stoneware and Frederick Carpenter," *Antiques* 101, no. 6 (June 1972): 1052–57. Little's decision to establish a stoneware factory no doubt was influenced to some extent by a postwar change in methods of levying freight on goods imported from England. Previously levied on the basis of value, freights now were charged according to weight. Because it is heavy, imported stoneware became more expensive which had the effect of encouraging domestic production.

[7] Watkins, "Boston Stoneware," p. 1052. Other examples of the association of out-

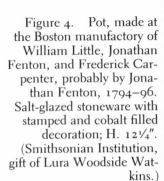

Figure 4.   Pot, made at the Boston manufactory of William Little, Jonathan Fenton, and Frederick Carpenter, probably by Jonathan Fenton, 1794–96. Salt-glazed stoneware with stamped and cobalt filled decoration; H. 12¼". (Smithsonian Institution, gift of Lura Woodside Watkins.)

Not all stoneware ventures were backed by merchants like William Little. William Seaver, an earthenware potter in Taunton, Massachusetts, also began to manufacture stoneware, evidently on his own, in the 1790s. Located on the Taunton River, which gave access to the coastwise trade of southern Rhode Island, Seaver had relatively easy access to New Jersey stoneware clay. His account book for the period from 1791 to 1806 suggests some of the ways in which he was similar to—and different from—his more conservative counterpart Daniel Clark.[8] Both men produced common household forms using traditional hand production methods, but Seaver's business required greater capital investment, and his operating expenses were higher than Clark's. The

---

side entrepreneurs and stoneware potters include a second association in which Frederick Carpenter was the master potter, this time at a Charlestown, Mass., site owned by two nonpotters, Barnabas Edmands and William Burroughs (Watkins, "Boston Stoneware," pp. 1056–57). Entrepreneur Benjamin DuVal operated Richmond Stoneware Manufactory in Richmond, Va., in 1811, although the names of his potters are not known (Bradford L. Rauschenberg, " 'B. DuVal & Co / Richmond': A Newly Discovered Pottery," *Journal of Early Southern Decorative Arts* 4, no. 1 [May 1978]: 45–75).

[8] William Seaver account book, 1779–1811, Old Colony Historical Society, Taunton, Mass. Unless otherwise noted, statements concerning Seaver's pottery are derived from an analysis of the diary for the years 1791–1806, which appear to be complete.

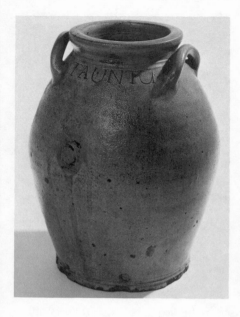

Figure 5.   Pot, inscribed
TAUNTON / POT and
attributed to William
Seaver. Taunton, Mass.,
1799–1815. Salt-glazed
stoneware; H. 11¾″. (Cur-
rier Gallery of Art.)

manufacture of stoneware forced Seaver to deal with the larger economic community to develop a degree of interdependence absent in the
more self-sufficient Clark manufactory.

Seaver shipped his stoneware clay up the Taunton River from South
Amboy, although probably he also used some local clay. It was not an
uncommon practice among New England stoneware potters to stretch
the expensive Jersey clay by mixing it with some of the local red earthenware. Seaver is said to have owned his own small vessel, the *Sam
Adams*, in which he transported the clay. Salt for glazing was acquired
in several different places. He once mentioned buying it in Providence
and another time in Boston. The only piece of stoneware attributed to
Seaver has no ornamentation (fig. 5), but it seems likely that the "paint"
listed in the accounts was cobalt for decorating. There is no indication
of where it was obtained. Rather than gather his own wood for fuel, as
Clark did, Seaver purchased or bartered for what was needed.[9]

[9] Watkins, *New England Potters*, p. 82. Stoneware usually was glazed by throwing
salt into the kiln during the firing. A vitrified and hard glazed surface was formed by a
combination of the sodium in the salt and the silica in the clay.

Seaver probably did not make stoneware in an extensive way until 1799 when he began building a new kiln representing a considerable investment of time and money. The "Company Account" from March through July of that year contains repeated entries mentioning such activities as "Lying Stone [presumably for the foundation] in kiln," and "work half Day on kiln" by Seaver and two hired workers. Time and money were devoted to "geting Stone in Lighter," to "getting out Stone," and to the purchase of bricks, probably refractory bricks capable of withstanding the high and fluctuating temperatures present in firing stoneware. By 1800 Seaver was selling stoneware in volume, which led to a change in his merchandising methods. Of the fifty-six individuals who bought pottery from him between 1791 and 1804, only eleven bought goods worth more than £1 at a time, and only two customers bought on what could be called a large scale. Simon and Enos Burt, merchants and probably importers, were the major purchasers of Seaver's stoneware. In sales of stoneware to the Burts, Seaver wholesaled his ware at half price, something he had never done with his earthenware.

Accounts usually were paid by barter, although occasional cash sales were made. The range of Seaver's market and his methods of transporting goods are not explained in the account book. Watkins stated that he sent ware to New London (roughly 80 miles by water) and to New York (roughly 200 miles by water).[10]

Like most traditional craftsmen, Seaver did not rely exclusively on pottery for his livelihood, although it was his main source of income. He also sold wooden heels and bartered with various farm products and services. Obviously an educated man, he also provided schooling for some of the local children. This is indicated in his account book by such charges as "Schooling Charles and Salley 4½ month 0-10-8" and "Schooling your Daughter Polley 3 months 0-7-3." In 1799, however, as he embarked on his stoneware venture, he sold his "right in the School house" for $3 and gave up that occupation.

As transportation improved and the population expanded in the first quarter of the nineteenth century, more and more stoneware potteries were established, especially in the Middle Atlantic and northeastern states. Jefferson's 1807 embargo, the subsequent nonimportation acts, and the doubling of import duties during the War of 1812, stimulated the stoneware industry as it did domestic industries generally. In

[10] Watkins, *New England Potters*, p. 82.

the face of these restrictions, capital previously directed primarily toward commerce was increasingly invested in manufacturing ventures.

William Myers, a Baltimore china and glass merchant, illustrated this phenomenon. Myers was able to maintain a stock of imported goods during the immediate prewar years. By June 1812, however, undoubtedly feeling the pinch, he turned his attention and capital to domestic manufacturing. He had, he announced, "purchased of Mr. James Johnson, his well known Manufactory of Stone Ware . . . [and intended to carry] on business on a more extensive plan." As late as October of that year, he could still provide "a handsome assortment of [imported] Queen's and Glass Ware, which he [would] put up at the lowest prices." But by February he had "disposed of his stock of *China, Glass*, and *Queens*' Ware" and announced his intention "to devote his whole attention to his manufactory of *Stone-ware*." Like Little, Myers was not a craftsman but a merchant who saw the enterprise as a good investment. Also like Little, he had an established sales network for marketing his ware. His June 1812 announcement of the purchase of the pottery indicated that "the Factory will be conducted under the immediate care of Mr. Johnson, (the former proprietor) whom he has engaged for that purpose." By October he had "engaged Mr. Remmey, from New York, to superintend the Factory." Henry Remmey was the grandson of German immigrant John Remmey (Johannes Remmi), one of the first stoneware potters in America.[11]

The postwar depression had a limiting effect on the stoneware industry, but it soon flourished again. By this time the industry was established on a solid footing, and it could withstand such economic fluctuations.

The expansion of the manufacture of stoneware was an event of some importance in the history of American ceramics. It suggests a growing sophistication in the industry. The necessary location of stoneware potteries on major water or overland routes for shipping in clay also provided access to more distant markets, offering the opportunity to expand production and to interact with a wider economic community than did most earthenware potteries.

Stoneware potteries generally were larger than their earthenware counterparts and the value of their output greater. The 1820 Census of

[11]*American and Commerical Daily Advertiser* (Baltimore) (June 2, October 13, 1812; February 5, 1813); John N. Pearce, "The Early Baltimore Potters and Their Wares, 1763–1850" (M.A. thesis, University of Delaware, 1959), pp. 44–47.

Manufactures provides a basis for comparing the two types of potteries. An analysis of the returns for Pennsylvania, New York, and Connecticut shows that the annual output of common redware potteries in those states averaged around $1,260, while that of stoneware manufactories averaged $3,560. The difference—almost three times as much—reflects the larger volume of output and the higher prices for comparable items in stoneware. The Seaver account book, where it is specific enough to allow such comparison, shows that prices for stoneware were about double those for the same items in earthenware. A difference is apparent in the average number of workers: 2.12 in an earthenware pottery and 6.10 in a stoneware pottery. Differences in capital investment are dramatically illustrated in the data which show an average of $817 for earthenware potteries and $4,335 for stoneware potteries. In other words, a stoneware pottery required an investment five times as great as an earthenware pottery. [12]

The merchants who backed some of the stoneware manufactories of the period stimulated the industry by providing it with capital for ventures that might never have gotten started without them. As suggested by the Boston example, they also introduced a different form of work organization. As financial backers, and sometimes as active participants in the management of the business, they took over roles formerly held by the master potter. In doing this, they eroded the independent position previously held by master craftsmen in more traditional potteries.

Enthusiasm for the manufacture of a ceramic ware more refined than common earthenware and stoneware grew during the 1790s and in the following decades. As noted above, in 1792 the Pennsylvania Society for the Encouragement of Manufactures and Useful Arts placed "the best specimen of Earthenware or Pottery, approaching nearest to Queen's Ware" top on a list of desirable manufactures. Occasional advertisements from people like J. Mouchet who announced his "New Manufactory of yellow or cream ware" in 1798 indicate that attempts were indeed under way. [13] Not until the War of 1812, however, did the same factors that stimulated development in the stoneware industry—

---

[12] Bureau of the Census, "Record of the 1820 Census of Manufactures, Schedules for Pennsylvania, New York, and Connecticut," Record Group 29, National Archives, Washington, D.C. (microfilm); Seaver account book.

[13] *New Jersey Journal and Political Intelligencer* (January 25, 1792); *Greenleaf's New Daily Advertiser* (New York) (March 1, 1798) as quoted in Alfred Coxe Prime, *The Arts and Crafts in Philadelphia, Maryland, and South Carolina, 1786–1800: Gleanings from Newspapers*, 2d ser. (Topsfield, Mass.: Walpole Society, 1932), p. 148.

Figure 6. Teapot, marked JOHN. GRIFFITH / TH / [ELIZA-BETHT]OWN / N.J. 1820(?)–24. Black-glazed red earthenware; H. 6⅜″. (Yale University Art Gallery: Photo, E. Irving Blomstrann.)

availability of capital, scarcity of imported ware, and doubled tariff rates—combine to create an economic atmosphere sympathetic to even limited success in American refined tableware production.

In responding to the new market for domestic tableware, manufactories adopted varying degrees of sophistication. Traditional potteries in Pennsylvania and New Jersey began a considerable production of red, brown, and black coffeeware and, particularly, teaware made from the common red clay and lead glaze familiar for generations (fig. 6). Made from the same materials, the teaware was a natural outgrowth of traditional manufacture. It required no large capital investment and, consequently, no outside financial backing.[14] Although not a radically different or more complex product, these tewares were viewed by potters and consumers as distinct from coarse earthenware. Philadelphia

---

[14] Susan H. Myers, *Handcraft to Industry: Philadelphia Ceramics in the First Half of the Nineteenth Century* (Washington, D.C.: Smithsonian Institution Press, 1980), pp. 12–13, 18–19, 46.

potter Abraham Miller noted in 1820 that his pottery had for the last ten or twelve years made "Black & brown tea pots and a great variety of other articles, known in commerce, by the terms black and brown *china*." These he distinguished from his "common coarse earthen ware." His "china" was, he claimed, "esteemed as highly as the European articles of which they are an imitation." "Black glazed TEA POTS" of "American Manufacture" were offered for sale in Boston in 1812, and ten crates of "Jersey Teapots . . . of an excellent quality" were auctioned in 1816 at Hartford.[15] The brown-glazed teapot shown in J. L. Krimmel's 1813 painting *The Quilting Frolic* may be an example of American red-bodied teaware of the war period (fig. 7).

Other potteries made teaware and tableware more closely resembling imported light-bodied earthenware. These products represent a more radical departure from traditional patterns than the black-glazed teaware. Philadelphia, long a center of American pottery manufacture, was the logical place for the most concentrated effort to make the new type of ware. Between 1807 and 1817 four Philadelphia potteries advertised that they had begun production of what may have been a true "queensware" using light-colored clay.

Only one of the four refined-ware manufactories was established by a local potter. Daniel Freytag, whose family earthenware pottery was in operation by 1794, is noted in the 1811 city directory as a maker of "a finer quality of ware, than has been heretofore manufactured in the United States. This ware is made of various colours, and embellished with gold or silver; exports annually to foreign countries, about 500 dolls." Nothing further is known of Freytag's fineware.[16] The other three manufactories were established through the joint efforts of an entrepreneur and a master potter.

Archibald Binny and James Ronaldson, Philadelphia typefounders, by 1807 had combined with "A PERSON, who [had] been bred in Britain to the POTTERY BUSINESS, in all its branches, with the express view of establishing that important Manufacture in Philadel-

[15] "1820 Census of Manufactures, Schedules for Pennsylvania"; *Columbian Centinel* (Boston) (February 5, 1812); *Connecticut Courant* (Hartford) (September 3, 1816) as quoted in Helen McKearin, notes, Joseph Downs Manuscript and Microfilm Collection 69 x 208.3, Winterthur Museum Library.

[16] James Hardie, *The Philadelphia Directory and Register* (Philadelphia: Printed by Jacob Johnson, 1794); *Census Directory for 1811* (Philadelphia: Printed by Jane Aitken, 1811).

Figure 7.   John Lewis Krimmel, *The Quilting Frolic* (detail). Pennsylvania, 1813. Oil on canvas; H. 167⁄8″, W. 223⁄8″. (Winterthur Museum.)

phia." The typefoundry was itself a joint effort by Ronaldson as financial backer and Binny as tradesman. For the pottery business, the master craftsman was Alexander Trotter, a potter in Philadelphia by 1808 and noted as an associate of Binny and Ronaldson in an 1812 indenture for an apprentice in the pottery works.[17]

Trading under the name Columbian Pottery, in 1808 the firm advertised "Red-tea pots, coffee pots and sugar boxes" which, no doubt, were very like the ware made in traditional earthenware manufactories. They also made a yellow teaware and coffeeware that could have been a coarse red clay with a yellow glaze but which, more likely, was made from a yellow or buff clay covered with a clear glaze. Binny and Ronaldson also made a white-bodied ware—the ultimate goal in refined earthenware production. In 1807, they had advertised in Savannah for white clay "free from all ferruginous or irony matter, as the presence of iron totally unfits them for the uses for which they are intended, and all those which assume a reddish color when burnt will not answer, as the purest white is desired." Their ultimate success at whiteware production is evidenced by an 1813 newspaper notice announcing, "their new manufactory of White Queensware will be ready for delivery in all May." The same advertisement offered for sale "American Manufactured Queensware . . . less than half the price of the cheapest imported Liverpool Queensware." Clearly a lesser quality product than "White Queensware," presumably this was yellowware or redware.[18]

John Mullowny opened a queensware manufactory in Philadelphia in 1810 of which he was the "proprietor" and "Mr. James Charleton (an englishman by birth) the manufacturer." Mullowny advertised in that year that he made "Red, Yellow, and Black Coffee Pots, Tea Pots, Pitchers, etc, etc," all of which could have been made from red clay. By 1812 he may have introduced a more refined yellow or white clay body because he dropped the above description and noted that he was making "new and handsome patterns . . . much improved in fashion, neatness and utility . . . [and] much reduced in weight."[19]

The Mullowny manufactory appears to have been taken over after

[17] *Savannah Public Intelligencer* (Georgia) (September 8, 1807); *Philadelphia: Three Centuries of American Art* (Philadelphia: Philadelphia Museum of Art, 1976), pp. 237–39; James Robinson, *The Philadelphia Directory for 1808* (Philadelphia, n.d.); Guardians of the Poor, Indentures, May 18, 1812, Inventory 35.133, Archives of the City and County of Philadelphia.

[18] *Virginia Argus* (Richmond) (November 25, 1808); *Savannah Public Intelligencer* (September 8, 1807); *Relfs Philadelphia Gazette and Daily Advertiser* (April 27, 1813).

[19] John Mullowny to James Madison, October 26, 1810, James Madison Papers, Library of Congress, Washington, D.C. (hereafter cited as JMP); *Aurora General Advertiser* (Philadelphia) (May 19, 1810, February 10, 1812).

Figure 8.   Pitcher,
attributed to David Seixas.
Philadelphia, 1816(?)–22.
Green-glazed white ear-
thenware; H. 9¼".
(Museum of the City of
New York, gift of Mrs.
Louis J. Reckford.)

his death in 1815 by David Seixas, the son of a well-known New York
rabbi. The pottery was one among many varied enterprises in which
Seixas was involved during his life. Seixas himself was not a potter. A
Baltimore newspaper described him as among those "many persons
stimulated by a desire somewhat connected with patriotic views of national
independence, [who] have retired from mercantile pursuits, and applied
their ingenuity and pecuniary means to mechanical arts." Like Binny
and Ronaldson, Seixas succeeded in making a white-bodied ware. The
same newspaper article is filled with praise for what is called "the only
white ware pottery in the United States."[20] A press-molded pitcher with
a portrait medallion of David's father, Gershom Mendes Seixas, almost
certainly was produced at the Seixas manufactory (fig. 8). It is made
from a white clay and covered with a green glaze on which traces of
gilding can be seen.

Other war-period efforts to make refined earthenware include those
of Thomas Vickers and Son in Chester County, Pennsylvania, who
advertised in 1809 that they had made "a flattering essay towards the
establishment of a Queens Ware Manufactory"; Crockery Ware Cor-

[20] *Niles Weekly Register* (Baltimore) (November 1, 1817). Although the location of
Seixas's factory was noted only as "near this city," logically it would have been at Philadelphia (see Myers, *Handcraft to Industry*, pp. 8–10).

poration, which made refined earthenware in Vermont in 1813; and Englishman William Jackson, who undertook fineware production in Saugus, Massachusetts, in 1811.[21]

The absence of a counterpart to the rich Daniel Clark diary makes impossible a detailed comparison of these refined-ware manufactories with traditional earthenware potteries. Enough information does exist, however, to suggest significant ways in which they differ. The investment of outside capital appears to have been essential to the success of the refined-ware potteries in this period. As with the stoneware ventures, outside capital brought to the manufactories a change in the role of the master craftsman. Indeed, Mullowny had specifically drawn a distinction between himself as the "proprietor" and James Charlton as the "manufacturer."[22] How work, authority, and responsibility were divided is unknown, but this type of association, by definition, meant that the master potters had less autonomy than traditional earthenware potters operating their own shops. Although highly skilled, they did not share the position of Clark who was both proprietor and manufacturer, owned his own shop, and controlled all aspects of production and marketing.

A further and very significant difference lay in the national origins of some of the master potters in these ventures. The known examples of stoneware potteries in which an outside entrepreneur was involved suggest that craftsmen generally came from the ranks of traditional potters working in America. In the few war-period refined earthenware manufactories for which data exists, on the other hand, at least two and probably more of the master potters came from England where they had acquired skills in methods of production unknown among traditional American potters. It was this pattern that became commonplace in such ventures in the next two decades.

There is evidence that sometimes Americans were trained in the skills required in such potteries. John Mullowny noted in 1810 that his manufactory would "be extended as soon as workmen [could] be obtained or boys taught the art of manufacturing as in England." Whether he intended to take these boys from traditional potteries or from among

---

[21] *Pennsylvania Herald and Eastern Intelligencer* (February 22, 1809) as cited in Edwin AtLee Barber, *The Pottery and Porcelain of the United States* (3d ed., rev. and enl.; New York: G. P. Putnam's Sons, 1909), p. 437; Watkins, *New England Potters*, pp. 115, 72–73.

[22] Mullowny to Madison, October 26, 1810, JMP.

the ranks of untrained individuals seeking apprenticeships is not known. *Niles Weekly Register* in 1817 made a point of noting that "no foreigner has ever had any concern, or superintendence or employ in his [David Seixas's] manufactory." The comment suggests that this was a rare rather than a commonplace phenomenon. [23]

Refined-ware manufacture required more complex raw materials, a more sophisticated technology, and greater knowledge and skill on the part of the potters. While simple red clay, lead, and sand sufficed for earthenware production, and clay, salt, and cobalt were the basic ingredients of stoneware, whiteware production was more complex. In addition to suitable clay, Seixas used flint (in the clay body and the glaze), lead oxide (in the glaze), other "metalic oxides [for underglaze colors]— zinc for straw yellow, cobalt for blue, iron for red, chromate for green . . . [and] coloured glasses . . . melted on the ware in an enamel kiln." [24]

Most traditional earthenware and stoneware potters of the period brought clay to the pottery, cleaned it by hand, and mixed it in the pug mill. Sometimes it was also set aside to age before it was ready for use. By contrast Seixas's clay was prepared by the following complex process:

The clay is copiously diffused in water and passed through fine lawn sieves to detach the larger particles of sand, &c.

The flint . . . is exposed to a strong heat, and is suddenly plunged into cold water. By frequent repetition of calcination and refrigeration, whiteness and friability ensue. It is then ground to powder finer than super fine flour, so perfectly impalpable that it will remain many hours suspended in water, it is then subjected to a purification to extract the small portion of oxide of iron it usually contains.

It is then mixed by measure with the purified liquid clay . . . and the mixture poured into vats, the solids in time subside—the water is run off—the residuum further exposed to the solar heat until the remaining water has evaporated to suit it for forming into the required vessels. [25]

Forming technology likewise was more complex in refined-ware potteries. John Mullowny advertised in 1812 that he was lathe turning (decorating or refining the shape of an unfired piece by applying a sharp tool to its surface as it turned on a horizontal lathe) and press molding (forming by pressing slabs of clay into a mold). The latter process was

---

[23] Mullowny to Madison, October 26, 1810, JMP; *Niles Weekly Register* (November 1, 1817).

[24] *Niles Weekly Register* (November 1, 1817).

[25] *Niles Weekly Register* (November 1, 1817).

the more significant, allowing for speed and repetition in the production of relatively complex relief-molded ware. David Seixas also made press-molded ware, and it is very likely that the process was in use elsewhere. Press molding contributed to the declining status of the hand-craftman because little skill was required in the actual molding once the master mold had been created.[26]

During the depression following the War of 1812 many American potteries closed, particularly the budding fineware ventures. The reopening of American ports brought a great influx of imported ceramics, and the ending of the doubled tariff in February 1816 took from domestic producers the protection that was critical to their survival.

As the industry revived in the 1820s, expansion occurred in some established traditional potteries, but it was characterized by a conservatism undoubtedly born of the hard times of the preceding decade. Black-glazed coffeeware and teaware survived the depression and continued to be good, solid, salable products. Probably marketed primarily to those lower in the social strata, by the 1820s black-glazed ware was a great market success. In 1824, the Franklin Institute in Philadelphia noted, "our Potters have discovered the Art of making it [Red & Black glazed Teapots, Coffeepots & other Articles of the same description] equally good, if not superior to the Article imported, & rendered it at a price equally low, it has finally excluded the imported Article from the American market." Even if this was an exaggeration, it is certain that the volume of output was great. When New Jersey potter Edward Griffith died in 1820, the inventory in his shop included 1,796 dozen "Prest Tea Pots" and first- and second-quality "Common Black Tea pots" valued at a total of $2,009.56. Coffeepots, apparently a minor product, numbered only 14 dozen at a value of $31.50. John Griffith, his successor in the teapot and coffeepot manufactory, died in 1824 leaving the considerable value of $5,465.40 worth of "Tea Pots on hand" (see fig. 6).[27]

Another "safe" product was refractory ware for use in homes and by the nation's growing industries. In the 1820s, 1830s, and 1840s,

---

[26] *Aurora General Advertiser* (February 10, 1812); Myers, *Handcraft to Industry*, pp. 7–10.
[27] "Report of the Committee on Earthenware" (first annual exhibition of Franklin Institute, 1824), Franklin Institute Archives, Philadelphia; Wills 11255G (1820) and 11568G (1824), Wills and Inventories, Bureau of Archives and History, New Jersey State Library, Trenton.

potters commonly added to their production firebrick and tile which could be used for such things as liners for domestic heating stoves and industrial boiler settings and furnace linings. Small ceramic cooking furnaces, presumably made from the same refractory clay, experienced a period of popularity, and many potters made these simple devices (fig. 9). Varying in size, the furnaces were used for cooking or laundering in summer when it became uncomfortably hot to perform these jobs inside at a large fireplace or stove. In the 1830s, stoneware for use by the chemical industry began to be produced (fig. 10).[28]

More speculative were the renewed efforts at refined-ware production during the 1820s. Developments during this and the following decade laid the groundwork for its manufacture in this country. The association of entrepreneur and potter continued to be critical to development as did the employment of foreign skilled workers. Success was enhanced by the formation of corporations. Not unknown before the Revolution, the incorporated business had advantages over single ownership or a partnership, and it fostered the general trend toward outside investment in the ceramics industry. In the post-Revolutionary period, state chartering of companies became a common means of encouraging what governments perceived to be projects in the public interest. Although these charters were granted primarily for internal improvements, some manufactures also received them.

The most successful incorporation in the American ceramics industry before 1840 was that of the American Pottery Manufacturing Company. The company grew out of the pottery established in 1828 by David and J. Henderson in the old Jersey City works of Jersey Porcelain and Earthenware Company, which itself had been incorporated in 1825. David Henderson took over the major role in the pottery, and, in January 1833, he "and all and every person, or persons, who may become subscribers, . . . [were] constituted a body politic and corporate, by the name of 'The American Pottery Manufacturing Company' [soon changed to American Pottery Company], for the purpose of manufacturing the various kinds of Pottery, at the works already erected."[29]

States could grant wide and varying privileges to corporations, but

[28] Myers, *Handcraft to Industry*, pp. 20–22.

[29] Lura Woodside Watkins, "Henderson of Jersey City and His Pitchers," *Antiques* 50, no. 6 (December 1946): 388–92; State of New Jersey, "An Act to Incorporate 'The American Pottery Manufacturing Company' " (1833), Smithsonian Institution Collection of Business Americana, Washington, D.C.

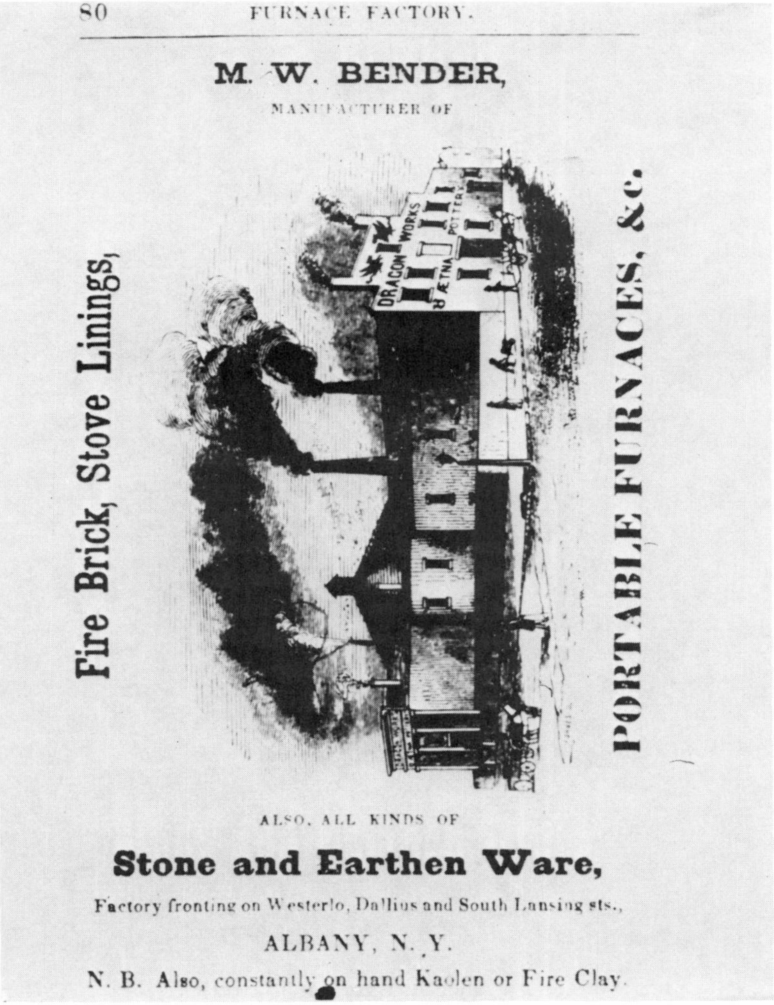

Figure 9. Advertisement of M. W. Bender in *Hunt's Albany Commercial Directory for 1848–9*, comp. William Hunt (Albany: By the compiler, 1848).

Figure 10. Vessel for chemical use, marked H[ENRY] NASH. /
UTICA. Utica, N.Y., 1837–39. Salt-glazed stoneware; H. 17½". (Photo,
Smithsonian Institution.)

even in the basic form assigned the American Pottery Manufacturing
Company, an incorporated business offered inducements to invest scarce
capital funds in high-risk ventures. Corporations could issue their secu-
rities in face values low enough to encourage many small investors. The
Jersey City enterprise was to have a capital stock of $75,000 which was
to be "divided into seven hundred and fifty shares of one hundred dollars each." Strict regulation by the chartering state also guaranteed that
at least minimum standards of business management would be met.
The limitation of liability to the assets of the company had, by this time,
become the rule unless otherwise stipulated in the charter.[30]

Incorporation was important to the future success of the business.
It was chartered just in time to help the company over the economically
difficult years of the mid and late 1830s. Over the next twenty years the
company was reasonably prosperous. By 1849 the factory employed about
sixty people and produced nearly $40,000 in ware annually.[31]

Henderson almost certainly was not a potter. Rather, he provided
capital and management to several different ventures during his lifetime. One of these, the Adirondack Iron and Steel Company, of which
he was part owner, absorbed much of his time during the 1840s, although
he appears to have retained ownership of the pottery until he died in
1845. After his death the pottery continued to operate under different
ownership.[32]

Technical expertise at the Henderson factory was supplied by skilled
workmen such as Englishmen James Bennett (1834), Daniel Greatbach
(by 1839), and James Carr (1844). Many of Henderson's imported skilled
workers later established potteries of their own on this side of the Atlantic.[33]

The products of the American Pottery Manufacturing Company
were innovative to an extent unimaginable in conservative traditional
manufactories. The Hendersons' first product, exhibited at the Franklin
Institute in 1830 and advertised in a "List of Prices" of the same year,
was "flint stoneware" (figs. 11, 12). The term here refers to a refined

[30] State of New Jersey, "Act to Incorporate."
[31] *Directory of Jersey City, Harsimus and Pavonia for 1849–50* (Jersey City: John H.
Voorhees, 1849).
[32] Bruce Seely, "The Adirondack Iron and Steel Company Survey" (Paper prepared
for the Historic American Engineering Record, Washington, D.C., 1978), chap. 3, pp.
1–14.
[33] Barber, *Pottery and Porcelain*, p. 179; Watkins, "Henderson of Jersey City," p.
391.

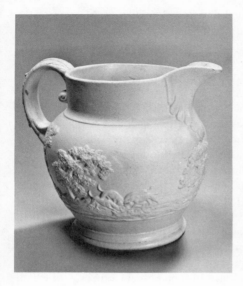

Figure 11.   Pitcher, D. &
J. Henderson. Jersey City,
N.J., 1828–30. Stoneware;
H. 7½". (Collection of
Newark Museum: Photo,
Stephen C. Germany.)

Figure 12.   Detail of base of pitcher in figure 11 showing mark HEN-
DERSON'S / FLINT STONEWARE / MANUFACTORY, / JERSEY
CITY.

Figure 13. Teapot, marked American Pottery Co. / Jersey City, N.J. Ca. 1840. Blue "sponged" decoration on white earthenware; H. 5¼". (Brooklyn Museum, gift of Mrs. Franklin Chace.)

molded stoneware in styles currently popular in England, as distinguished from common household stoneware. Flint provides whiteness, strength, and freedom from warping to an earthenware or stoneware body. Also in 1830, the pottery exhibited at the American Institute in New York "cane colored earthenware" as well as flint stoneware. They soon turned entirely to earthenware, including whiteware, rather than stoneware production (fig. 13).[34]

In 1833, perhaps stimulated by the act of incorporation of that year, the company exhibited an impressive list of products at the Franklin Institute. Their "Queensware . . . consisting of cream couloured ware;

[34] *Address of the Committee on Premiums and Exhibitions of the Franklin Institute of the State of Pennsylvania* (Philadelphia: Printed by J. Harding, 1830), p. 3; *Antiques* 26, no. 3 (September 1934): 109.

Figure 14.   Plate, marked American Pottery Co. / Canova / Jersey City.
1833–40. Blue transfer-printed white earthenware; Diam. 9⅛". (Brooklyn Museum.)

painted, moco, and printed ware" were judged "but a slight shade inferiour to the imported article." Appearing only in the judges' notes and not in their abbreviated published comments, the reference to "printed ware" is of particular interest. The process of transfer printing copperplate engravings on ceramic ware had been in use in England since the mid eighteenth century. The company has been acknowledged for the first successful use of the process in America, but it had been thought that this occurred around 1839 or 1840 (fig. 14). The Franklin Institute

Figure 15.   Teapots, American Pottery Co. Jersey City, N.J., 1835–45. Buff-yellow earthenware with clear glaze (yellowware) and with mottled brown glaze (Rockingham ware); H. 3⅝" and 4⅜". (Smithsonian Institution, John Paul Remensnyder Collection.)

reference shows its use as early as 1833. Perhaps the technique was introduced by David Henderson himself. His interest in the graphic arts is revealed in an 1824 patent that he received for a lithographic process. [35]

Products available from the factory in 1833 are listed in an advertisement of their New York agent, George Tingle, who stated, "The American Pottery Manufacturing Company . . . works are in full operation, in the manufacture of C. C. dipt, painted and edged Earthenware, which they offer for sale, in connection with a full assortment of Printed China and Glass Ware, . . . Just received from the Factory, a fresh supply of the celebrated fire-proof Yellow Nappies and Pie Dishes. Also, an assortment of Stone Pitchers, variously ornamented: Spittoons, Tea Tubs, &c." The reference to "Printed China" is unfortunately ambiguous. It could have been imported. What ultimately proved to be their most reliable products were relief-molded yellowware and "Rockingham," or mottled brown-glazed, ware (fig. 15). Yellowware and

[35] "Report of the Committee on China Glass & Earthenware" (eighth annual exhibition of Franklin Institute, 1833), Franklin Institute Archives; Patent Office, *A List of Patents Granted by the United States from April 10, 1790, to December 31, 1836* (Washington, D.C., 1872), p. 273.

Rockingham ware would become the most successful refined wares in American factories up to the Civil War.[36]

Among the other fineware ventures established in the pre-1840 period was the Horner and Shirley pottery in New Brunswick, New Jersey, which exhibited flint stoneware at the Franklin Institute in 1831. Shirley may have been William W. Shirley, an English potter who had been an incorporator and director of the factory for the unsuccessful Jersey Porcelain and Earthenware Company. It probably was this pottery that advertised in 1831 for "an active man with a small Capital, say 1,500 to 2,000 dollars, . . . [to be] a Partner in the improved Flint Stone Ware Factory, New Brunswick, . . . a person who can advance an equal capital to that now employed." No knowledge of pottery manufacture was specified; rather, "he would be preferred if acquainted with the selling and management of the finished goods, to keep the books, and to attend to all outdoor business."[37]

Another fineware venture of the period, and one about which little is known, is the Salamander Works, originally established in New York City as a firebrick manufactory. The company was making refined ware by 1835 when it exhibited "a fine specimen of flint stone ware" at the American Institute. An 1837 handbill (fig. 16) lists some of their wares, including an "antique" pitcher with strainer (fig. 17).[38]

Although the East Coast cities offered factories the advantage of access to raw materials (particularly from New Jersey, Pennsylvania, and Delaware), large markets, and good transportation, they had the disadvantage of competition from imported ceramics with a well-developed merchandising system. In the 1820s and 1830s several fineware ventures were established along the Ohio River where there was access to clay and good transportation by water. A further advantage was the abundance of coal, a more efficient fuel than wood for firing kilns. Imported refined ware was also less abundant, and the market consequently less competitive.

A series of fineware potteries involving English potter Jabez Vodrey operated in Pittsburgh, Louisville, and Troy, Indiana, between 1827

[36] *National Intelligencer* (Washington, D.C.) (July 16, 1833).

[37] *Address of the Committee on Premiums and Exhibitions of the Franklin Institute of the State of Pennsylvania* (Philadelphia: Printed by J. Harding, 1831), p. 7; Arthur W. Clement, *Our Pioneer Potters* (York, Pa: Maple Press Co., 1947), pp. 67–68; *Daily Chronicle* (Philadelphia) (July 2, 1831).

[38] "List of Premiums Awarded by the Managers of the 8th Annual Fair of the American Institute," *Journal of the American Institute* 1, no. 2 (November 1835): 80.

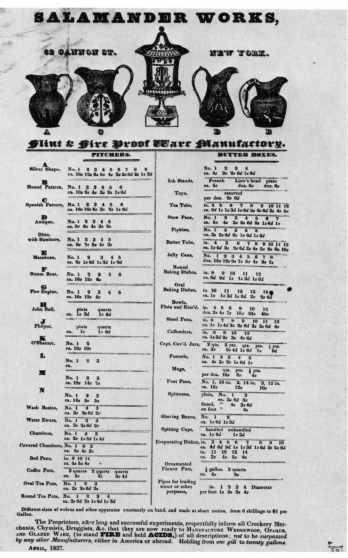

Figure 16. Advertising handbill, Salamander Works. New York, 1837. (New-York Historical Society, Bella Landauer Collection.)

Figure 17.   "Antique" pitcher, marked Salamander / Works / New-York / 1. New York, ca. 1837. Buff-yellow earthenware with mottled-brown, Rockingham, glaze; H. 11¼". (Smithsonian Institution.)

and 1847. Vodrey's diary, which includes scattered entries before 1840, and related papers have been preserved in the Vodrey family and provide information about these early midwestern fineware ventures.[39]

Vodrey and, apparently, William Frost emigrated in 1827 from Staffordshire to Pittsburgh where they began the manufacture of refined ware. The men seem to have been brought to the city by William Price, a Pittsburgh entrepreneur involved in glass manufacturing and brass and iron founding as well as pottery making. According to a brief history, published in 1879, Price had made tobacco pipes from local white clay and "was led to suppose good earthenware could be made from the same material." His interest in this manufacture led him—during a trip to England in search of glassblowers—to visit Staffordshire where he convinced Vodrey and Frost to come to Pittsburgh, bringing with them "the necessary tools and machinery to enter upon the manufacture of

[39] I am indebted to J. Garrison and Diana Stradling for directing me to the Vodrey family materials and to William H. Vodrey for allowing me to study them. They are now in the possession of the descendants of William H. Vodrey in East Liverpool, Ohio. The diary is being prepared by the Stradlings and J. Jefferson Miller for publication by the American Ceramic Circle.

white ware." Whether this is true, and, if true, whether any formal business arrangement was involved, is not known. An 1830 letter from Price to Vodrey indicates that, at the least, the men had been friends in Pittsburgh.[40]

A yellowware pitcher in the collection of Historical Society of Western Pennsylvania further suggests a connection between Price and the pottery (figs. 18, 19). Inscribed "Friendships Gift to Wm Price" and dated 1828, the pitcher almost certainly is of local manufacture and quite probably was made by Vodrey and Frost. Although it is in the English style, the pitcher lacks the refinement one expects of a piece special-ordered from England. It is unlikely, in any case, that such a celebratory piece would have been made in common yellowware rather than whiteware. The method of decoration—painting in cobalt under the glaze—is a very simple and unsophisticated one and would have been a logical choice in such a fledgling manufactory. The likelihood that Vodrey and Frost made the pitcher is reinforced by the 1879 history. "The wife of Jabez Vodrey," it notes, "was the 'decorator' of the establishment, and would, when desired, put the names of purchasers on their dishes. She used blue for this work. Mr. Hatfield resided near the pottery, which stood on an acre of ground owned by Mr. Price, near Fifth and Marion streets. In his possession is a covered dish, on the top of which is this inscription, 'E. Hatfield, February, 1829'; this article having been made for his wife. A granddaughter of Mr. Price has a pitcher made by the firm and presented to him, with a similar inscription applied by Mrs. Vodrey. It was made in 1828."[41]

Also painted on the Price pitcher are various scenes relating to his life in Pittsburgh. On one side is a glass furnace and "Fort Pitt Glass Works." Price was briefly involved in that glassworks along with Robert Curling, a former potmaker and clerk at the Bakewell glassworks. A cannon and various hollowware items seen near the furnace suggest Price's brass- and iron-founding interests. On the opposite side of the pitcher is the inscription "Round House" and a drawing of Price's house which was fashioned after the Pittsburgh Episcopal Round Church,

[40] Jabez Vodrey diary, February 25, 1860; "51 Years Ago in East Liverpool, O, As Recorded by D. B. Martin, Editor 1878" (newspaper article from an unidentified source); W. Price to Vodrey, February 19, 1830, Vodrey Family Papers (hereafter cited as VFP); "The First Western Pottery," *Brick, Pottery, and Glass Journal* 6, no. 8 (August 1879): 89.

[41] "First Western Pottery," p. 89.

Figure 18. Pitcher, attributed to Jabez Vodrey and William Frost. Pittsburgh, 1828. Yellowware with painted underglaze blue decoration; H. 7". (Historical Society of Western Pennsylvania.)

Figure 19. Side view of pitcher in figure 18.

actually an octagonal brick structure. It has been suggested that the pitcher was presented to Price by his colleagues at the glassworks.[42] In light of the connection between Price and Vodrey, however, it may have been made as a gift from the potter to the man who, the year before, had brought him to Pittsburgh.

[42]"Collector's Notes," *Antiques* 93, no. 2 (February 1968): 246; Lowell Innes, *Pittsburgh Glass, 1797–1891: A History and Guide for Collectors* (Boston: Houghton Mifflin Co., 1976), pp. 17–19, 34.

The move of Vodrey and, apparently, Frost to Louisville within only a few years of their arrival in Pittsburgh has been attributed to the unsuitability of the local clay for fineware manufacture. It is also possible that they were attracted by the offer of capital by the Lewis Pottery Company, incorporated in 1829 by five businessmen.[43]

An 1832 agreement concerning ownership of the pottery property allows a rare look at the breakdown of responsibilities in a fineware manufactory of this early period. Most of the incorporators presumably provided financial support only. One of them, however, Louisville merchant Jacob Lewis, was the business manager of the pottery. His responsibilities included getting raw materials, making sales, and keeping the books.[44] David Henderson, as manager of the American Pottery Company in Jersey City, probably played a role very like that of Lewis. There is no evidence that either man was a potter; rather, they managed the financial affairs of the business, leaving the actual production to others.

The two principals in the production process of the Louisville factory were Jabez Vodrey, described as a "turner of fine ware," and another Staffordshire potter, George Nixon, a "fine ware thrower." They were responsible only for making the ware and superintending the factory. The 1832 agreement stipulated that bills were to be made out to "Lewis, Vodery [sic] & Nixon" and the ware marked "in like manner." It called for "each party," apparently referring to the three men, "to draw an equal amount of Money every Saturday night, after meeting the running expenses of the week."[45]

Another fineware manufactory, the Indiana Pottery Company, was incorporated near Troy, a town on the Ohio River west of Louisville, in January 1837. Among the partners were Jacob Lewis, from the Louisville corporation; Samuel Casseday, a Louisville earthenware importer; and Reuben Bates, a Troy merchant who contributed land to the venture. James Clews, from the famous Staffordshire family of whiteware manufacturers, held three shares and, presumably, superin-

---

[43] Frank Stefano, Jr., "James Clews, Nineteenth-Century Potter," *Antiques* 105, no. 3 (March 1974): 553.

[44] Agreement between Vodrey, George Nixon, and Jacob Lewis, agent for John Shallcross and guardian for Jane, Alice, and Thomas D. Lewis, June 18, 1832, VFP.

[45] Agreement between Vodrey, Nixon, and Lewis, VFP. *Turning* as used here and as commonly used among refined-ware potters refers to lathe turning (see p. 227) and should not be confused with Daniel Clark's or some other American potters' use of the term to mean "throwing," or forming ware on a potter's wheel.

tended the factory.[46] He brought many English workers into the factory and appears to have had every expectation of success. His efforts ended in failure, however, probably because he could not find suitable clay or because he could not work with the unfamiliar clay that he did find. An 1839 letter written by Lewis to Vodrey refers deprecatingly to "Clews & his mud digers . . . [who thought] that any dirt [would] do to make ware for this country."[47]

Clews had left the manufactory by 1839, in which year Vodrey and an associate, John Hutchinson, leased from the Indiana Pottery Company "the Pottery Establishment, with part of the lands and tenements belonging and pertaining thereto . . . near the Town of Troy." The pottery was fully appointed, for the two men were "loaned or hired . . . tools, Saggers, moulds, blocks, wheels and implements of every description" as well as the pottery buildings. The company retained the right to develop for commercial use the marl, clay, and coal on the property, permitting Vodrey and Hutchinson to use them only for pottery making. They were also allowed "coal for their use in their families." The company likewise retained the right to "erect buildings thereon or to manufacture fire or clay Brick." The two men were directed that the property was leased "for the purpose of Manufacturing the ware for which the establishment was made and for no other purpose whatever."[48]

The indenture for the lease suggests that the Indiana Pottery Company had given serious consideration to the question of using foreign versus native workers in the pottery. Indeed, the document suggests that the company saw the presence of Vodrey and Hutchinson only as a means of training Americans to carry on the pottery after the two-year term of the rental expired. The two men were required to keep and train twelve apprentices who had to be "native born American." This not only suggests a patriotic desire to use an American labor force but also may indicate a disenchantment with foreign workmen. Interestingly, sometime before 1832, Benjamin Tucker, father of Philadelphia porcelain manufacturer William Ellis Tucker, had counseled Jacob Lewis: "the enterprising genius of Americans, if they are called in, at a proper age, will furnish you with equally excellent, and much more confiden-

[46] Stefano, "James Clews," pp. 553–55; Barber, *Pottery and Porcelain*, p. 159.
[47] Stefano, "James Clews," p. 554; Lewis to Vodrey, May 1, 1839, VFP.
[48] Indiana Pottery Company and Jabez Vodrey and John Hutchinson, indenture, March 12, 1839, VFP.

tial work men than you can generally speaking, obtain from Europe. Some of the apprentices that my son has brought up under his own hand fully verify this statement. The hostility and intrigue which many of his [William Ellis Tucker's] foreign workmen displayed, proved highly injurious to his interests. . . . A few good European workmen you will necessarily want in order to instruct American youths."[49]

The indenture signed by Vodrey and Hutchinson stipulated the jobs that apprentices were to learn and reveals something of the technology in use and the degree of job specialization. It noted,

of the twelve American apprentices named, the Second parties are only bound to take in Six immediately or during the Spring, One of which is to be put at throwing, two at turning and three at flat and hollow pressing and Squeesing. One of these last to be learned to handle [presumably to apply handles], the other Six apprentices to be taken in and put to work One Year from this time at the same branches, unless the contracting parties mutually agree to learn them Some other branches. Again the parties of the Second part engage to select and Keep a smart inteligent boy at the buisket & Gloss Kilns and to instruct him as far as practicable in the art of Burning.[50]

Throwing, the dominant method of forming in red earthenware and stoneware potteries, was to be learned by only two apprentices, while six of the twelve apprentices learned press molding. Lathe turning, rarely found in other than fineware manufactories during this period, was to be taught to four boys.

The indenture suggests a degree of task specialization unknown in traditional potteries. Unlike Daniel Clark's sons and his apprentice, Peter Flanders, who worked at all or most of the jobs in the pottery, these apprentices were expected to learn only certain aspects of production. There is no suggestion that they should be trained in jobs other than those specifically noted.

Whatever the company's plans may have been for the "Americanization" of the factory, Vodrey stayed in Troy until 1847 when he moved to East Liverpool, Ohio. There a pottery had been established in 1839 by English potter James Bennett with financial assistance from one Anthony Kearns. By the time Vodrey arrived, several other potteries

[49] Benjamin Tucker to Lewis, n.d., Benjamin Tucker letter books, 1830–31, Philadelphia Museum of Art (hereafter cited as PMA) (microfilm, Archives of American Art, Smithsonian Institution, Washington, D.C.).

[50] Indiana Pottery and Vodrey and Hutchinson, indenture, VFP.

were in operation in this small town that was in the process of becoming a major center for American ceramics production.[51]

The manufacture of porcelain—the most difficult and the most valued of all ceramics—achieved little success in America before 1840. Before the Revolution, Bonnin and Morris briefly made porcelain in Philadelphia in 1771 and 1772. In New York, Henry Mead was making porcelain by 1818 as evidenced by his 1824 newspaper notice that he had "expended a large sum of money and six years of perseverance" in the manufacture in that city. He also indicated that he was seeking public support for his manufactory, noting that he found "himself compelled to abandon the object, for the want of sufficient funds." The pottery apparently closed soon thereafter.[52]

The Jersey Pottery and Porcelain Works of Jersey City, established in 1825, by the next year had located "the materials both for the body . . . and for the glazing . . . in the United States" and they had induced "skillful and experienced workmen . . . to come over from France." When the company exhibited its porcelain at the Franklin Institute in 1826, the judges gave it reserved praise in their published notes. The manuscript version of their report, however, reveals their more candid opinion that the product "abounds in faults." Boston Porcelain and Glass Company and the Monkton Argile Company in Vermont briefly attempted porcelain manufacture during the War of 1812.[53]

The only venture to achieve any degree of success was that of William Ellis Tucker whose factory operated in Philadelphia between 1826 and 1838, but it too was always in financial difficulty. Following the familiar pattern, Tucker was the proprietor but not himself a potter. He is said to have hired an Englishman, John Basten, as foreman of the works. His other workmen were of English, French, and American origin. It was William's father, Benjamin Tucker, who had advised Jacob Lewis to train native workers for his pottery.[54] William's brother Thomas

<hr/>

[51] Barber, *Pottery and Porcelain*, pp. 161, 192.
[52] *Gazette and Advertiser* (Alexandria, Va.) (November 4, 1824).
[53] *Phoenix Gazette* (Alexandria, Va.) (July 31, 1825); "Abstract of the Report of the Committee on Premiums and Exhibition on the Subject of the Third Annual Exhibition [1826]," *Franklin Journal and American Mechanics' Magazine* 2, no. 5 (November 1826): 264; "Report of Committee on Pottery" (third annual exhibition of Franklin Institute, 1826), Franklin Institute Archives; Watkins, *New England Potters*, p. 41; John Murry to Abijah Bigelow, Joseph Downs Manuscript and Microfilm Collection 63 x 107, Winterthur Museum Library.
[54] Barber, *Pottery and Porcelain*, pp. 130–35, 151–53.

served an apprenticeship at the factory and eventually became its manager and chief decorator.

William Tucker devoted much effort to technical questions concerning the clay, glaze, and enamel colors. Henry Mead, a New York physician and a partner in the Mead and Beekman chemical business, probably played a similar role in his porcelain manufactory. Such technical questions were particularly critical in a porcelain works. Although materials for porcelain production were available in America, they were entirely new to potters and proved difficult to work with. Tucker's father complained of "foreign substances in our American materials, that, at a high temperature form new chemical combinations, which destroy either the beauty or the texture of the ware." [55]

Because porcelain was fired to a very high temperature, decoration applied under the glaze had to be executed with a coloring agent that could withstand the heat. Unable to master this problem, Tucker decorated all his porcelain in colors that were applied over the high-fired glaze. The piece then was refired at a low temperature to fix the colors. Good underglaze decoration was not perfected in America until several decades after Tucker's manufactory closed.

William Tucker was also concerned with finding sufficient capital and raw materials and with marketing the ware. These efforts were often shared with his father who was not only an investor but also a constant—and not always welcome—"guiding influence" in the business. [56]

The actual work of forming, decorating, and firing the ware was the province of his skilled workers. Thomas Tucker's formula and price book indicates that they were paid by the piece for turning, painting, burnishing, and making saggers (protective cases within which the ware was fired). [57]

Although the Tucker factory produced creditable copies of currently fashionable French and English porcelain (figs. 20, 21), the business was not a financial success. The reason lay to some extent in the national economic difficulties of the 1830s, but their business practices may also have been a factor.

[55] *Longworth's American Almanac, New-York Register, and City Directory* (New York: David Longworth, 1812); Benjamin Tucker to Isaac C. and Hannah Jones, February 16, 1827, Benjamin Tucker letter books, 1823–29, PMA.

[56] Benjamin Tucker letter books, 1823–29, 1830–31, PMA.

[57] "Prices for Burnishing . . . Making Sagers . . . Turning . . . Painting," September 26, 1832, Thomas Tucker formula and price book, PMA.

Figure 20.   Vase, William Ellis Tucker or successor. Philadelphia, 1825–38. Porcelain with polychrome and gilt decoration; H. 11⅞″. (Winterthur Museum.)

The possibility of incorporating the business—as other potteries were doing—must have occurred to the Tuckers, but they chose instead to rely for capital funds on partnerships and on pleas to the federal and state governments for subsidies. The firm was finally incorporated as the American Porcelain Company in 1835, two years after William's

Figure 21. Tea and coffee service, William Ellis Tucker or successor. Philadelphia, 1825–38. Porcelain with gilt decoration; H. (coffeepot) 9⅝". (Winterthur Museum, gift of Philip Hammerslough.)

death, but the company was never actually formed. Tucker's first two partnerships were failures, neither lasting more than a year; the third, with Joseph Hemphill, provided badly needed capital, but only in the amount of $7,000. In their letters to President Jackson and to the Congress, the Tuckers had requested $20,000 and $40,000 respectively in return for "a complete and perfect Knowledge of every branch of [our] business in the formation of American Porcelain, so that the discovery shall for ever be secured to the country." Neither request met with success.[58]

In marketing their ware, the Tuckers again showed an independent or, perhaps, provincial outlook that must have worked against their business. Phillip Curtis's study of the Tucker works reveals almost no advertising in Philadelphia newspapers. Indeed, one of Tucker's contemporaries noted that the porcelain works needed "the bell and the speaking trumpet. It is [in] vain that he makes the most splendid ware

[58] Phillip H. Curtis, "Tucker Porcelain, 1826–1838: A Re-Appraisal" (M.A. thesis, University of Delaware, 1972), pp. 15–24; William Ellis Tucker to the president of the United States, March 3, 1830, Benjamin Tucker letter books, 1830–31, PMA.

in the world, unless he lets the public know it."[59]

By 1840 the American ceramics industry had polarized into roughly three avenues of development, each illustrating a different response to economic and industrial changes. At one end of the spectrum were redware potters who conservatively adhered to tradition as had Daniel Clark in Concord. They were a dying phenomenon, especially in large cities, but would continue to exist in diminishing numbers in rural areas and small towns for many decades.

Other potters found the changing economic climate conducive to the introduction of new products. The most widespread choice was stoneware which, before the Revolution, had almost all been imported. More complex and expensive, but still sharing many of the characteristics of redware production, stoneware manufacture for the most part brought with it changes of an evolutionary nature. They grew out of the American pottery traditions in an essentially nondisruptive way. Technology and raw materials were altered to some degree, a larger work force usually was employed, and potters operated within a wider economic community. In some stoneware manufactories, like that of William Seaver, the master potter himself provided the requisite capital and took the risks of this new endeavor. Others involved outside entrepreneurs who made possible ventures requiring capital beyond the means of most potters. Such infusions of capital also altered the independent status of master craftsmen.

Very different in almost every respect from redware or stoneware potteries were the refined-ware manufactories established in America before 1840. Dramatically different in raw materials, technology, and work organization, they almost always were initiated by outside entrepreneurs. They shared with stoneware manufactories of similar organizational structure a diminished role for master potters. Significantly, however, most master craftsmen in the early fineware manufactories were not traditional American potters but skilled foreign workers trained largely in the British factories that provided the model emulated on this side of the Atlantic.

Before 1840 fineware manufactories probably had little impact on American potters. Not only were they quite different from traditional potteries; they were also few in number and had not yet concentrated

[59]Curtis, "Tucker Porcelain," p. 62; *Poulson's American Daily Advertiser* (Philadelphia) (January 24, 1831).

in such highly visible centers as those that later developed at East Liverpool, Ohio, and Trenton, New Jersey. Potters located near the fineware works or in large urban areas must have been aware of their existence, and perhaps they could see their significance for the future. More than likely, however, most potters viewed fineware manufacture as distinctly separate from their own interests and concerns.

The Transmission of Skill in the Shoe Industry: Family to Factory Training in Lynn, Massachusetts
William H. Mulligan, Jr.

It is probably fair to say that until quite recently the shoe industry had been largely ignored by scholars interested in the transition from craft to factory modes of production. Largely because it was the earliest to enter this process the textile industry has attracted the greatest amount of scholarly attention. The history of the industrial revolution, in both Great Britain and the United States, has been the history of the textile industry. While in England the mechanization of textile production displaced skilled workers, profoundly changing their lives, it is not at all clear that such was the case in the United States. The shoe industry, however, is an excellent arena within which to study this important transition. For about 100 years, roughly between the 1750s and 1850s, American shoemakers produced large quantities of shoes for sale throughout the country and the West Indies entirely by hand. Over this long period these artisans developed a strong sense of craft pride and identity and passed their skills and traditions from generation to generation. The transmission of skill is an essential part of any artisan community, and the skill needed to make a pair of shoes by hand took years to acquire. In those communities that were heavily or, in some cases, almost exclusively involved in shoe production, learning how to make shoes was part of growing up for most youngsters. Obituaries of nineteenth-century residents of Lynn, Massachusetts, often mention that the deceased had entered a ten-footer, as the front-yard workshops were called, between the ages of ten and fourteen as was "the custom at that time" or "as everyone did."[1] With the mechanization of the shoe industry, beginning in 1850, this long period of training became obsolete; it was replaced by a short period of training as an operator of a specific machine. This paper will examine the ways in which shoe workers were trained in Lynn during the handicraft period and after machinery was introduced as part of the larger transformation of American industrial life from an artisan to a factory system.

Lynn was the largest, in terms of shoe production, of a number of nineteenth-century shoe towns. Like the other shoe towns of Massachusetts, Lynn was dominated by its major industry which shaped the character of the community. The town had begun to emerge as a major center of the industry after 1750, and it was the nation's leading producer of women's shoes by 1800, a specialization it maintained until the 1920s when the industry declined. It was also a center for innovation both in materials for shoes—morocco was first used in Lynn—and in machinery; nearly all of the machines that transformed shoe production were either invented or introduced in the town.[2]

Shoemaking had a long history in Lynn. The first shoemakers, Henry Elwell and Philip Kirkland, settled in the community during the 1630s. By the time of the American Revolution Lynn was firmly established as a leading center of the industry, and it was beginning to become involved in the world market. Early in the development of the industry Lynn specialized in women's shoes. Largely because the material used for the uppers of women's shoes was lighter than that used in men's shoes, women and children became involved in the shoe industry in Lynn much earlier and in greater numbers than in the other Massachusetts shoe towns. By 1800 the family was the basic unit of work in the town, with mother and daughters "binding" the shoes (that is, sewing the uppers together) and father and sons "making" the shoes (that is, attaching soles and heels to the bound uppers).[3]

[1] These obituaries are in *The Register of Lynn Historical Society, Lynn, Massachusetts*, vols. 1–22 (1897–1918/21).

[2] The most convenient overview of the history of the shoe industry remains Blanche E. Hazard, *The Organization of the Boot and Shoe Industry in Massachusetts before 1879* (Cambridge, Mass.: Harvard University Press, 1921).

[3] Hazard, *Boot and Shoe Industry*; see also Alonzo Lewis, *History of Lynn* (Boston, 1829), and subsequent editions by James R. Newhall.

The hand skills of the adults in the family were essential elements in the manufacture of shoes and were the basis of the entire way of life of the cordwainers of Lynn. While the shoe manufacturers tried to increase both production and their own control over the process by the division of labor, they enjoyed only limited success. The way shoes were made remained essentially the same in 1850 as it had been 50 or even 100 years earlier, despite a tremendous expansion of the market in both size and scope. The independent position of the skilled cordwainer ended only with the total mechanization of the industry which occurred rapidly after 1850.

Hand skills, as either a binder or a cordwainer, were the essential elements underlying the way of life of Lynn's skilled artisans. There were very few other economic opportunities in Lynn and even fewer that offered the prestige and independence of shoemaking. Transmission of this skill was essential to the continuation of the town's economy. Making shoes was an activity in which all elements of the community had an interest, and it was predominantly a function of the family before mechanization.

Clear evidence about how and when young women learned the part of shoemaking that was their sphere is not abundant, but it does exist in sufficient quantity that some definite statements can be made. We know from the descriptions of mothers teaching their daughters "needle skills" that young girls in Lynn learned binding as a most important part of this general package of talents. Binding was the lot of a great number of Lynn's young women, both while they were single and after marriage. Lucy Larcom, poet, factory girl, and shoe binder, described the binders' life in a frequently cited poem entitled "Hannah Binding Shoes."

> Poor lone Hannah,
> Sitting at the window, binding shoes.
> Faded, wrinkled
> Sitting, stitching, in a mournful muse.
> Bright-eyed beauty once was she,
> When the bloom was on the tree:
> Spring and winter
> Hannah's at the window, binding shoes.

. . . .

Twenty winters
Bleach and tear the ragged shore she views.
Twenty seasons:
Never one has brought her any news.
Still her dim eyes silently
Chase the white sails o'er the sea:
Hopeless, faithful
Hannah's at the window, binding shoes.[4]

Fortunately, we know a good deal more about the training of boys from several autobiographies, diaries, and a large number of obituaries. David Newhall Johnson in his autobiographical *Sketches of Lynn* described entering a ten-footer at age ten to learn the shoemaker's art. Ten is the youngest age recorded in any of the sources; fourteen is far more common. Joseph Lye recorded in his diary for December 22, 1817: "This day began to learn my brother Robert to make shoes." Robert Lye was fourteen, and Joseph, while only twenty-five, was the head of the family because his father, who had "learned" him, was dead. John Basset Alley was apprenticed at fourteen and a half and a "jour" at twenty.[5] In account after account the basic story is the same; they left school to learn the shoemaker's art "as was the custom of the times." Formal apprenticeship is occasionally mentioned.[6] John Lewis Loring came to Lynn in 1832 at age fourteen with his mother and was apprenticed to George Atkinson. Formal apprenticeship was generally reserved for those from outside the artisan community, usually boys

[4] David N. Johnson, *Sketches of Lynn; or, The Changes of Fifty Years* (Lynn, 1880), pp. 336–40.
[5] Johnson, *Sketches of Lynn*, p. v; Henry F. Tapley, "An Old New England Town as Seen by Joseph Lye, Cordwainer," in *Register*, 19:42; *Vital Records of Lynn, Massachusetts, to the End of the Year 1849*, vol. 1, *Births* (Salem, Mass.: Essex Institute, 1905).
[6] In this essay the term *formal apprenticeship* is used only in those cases where a youth learned shoemaking from someone to whom he or she was not related. The term *master* has not been used to designate the fully trained craftsman because changes in the organization of work that occurred as the market for Lynn shoes expanded after 1750 made the term anachronistic. Lynn's cordwainers referred to themselves as "jours," an abbreviation or a corruption of the term *journeymen*. The levels within the industry at the height of the putting-out system were, for male workers, bosses, or manufacturers, who owned the raw materials and who controlled access to markets; jours, or cordwainers, fully trained artisans who made shoes; and "boys," who were learning the craft. A number of artisans specialized in cutting and worked in the central shops of the manufacturers after 1830. Women in the industry were almost entirely binders.

either newly arrived in Lynn or whose fathers were dead. There is strong evidence that a formal apprenticeship was less common than the informal method of learning from a father, an older brother, or an uncle. Jacob Meek Lewis was, in many ways, typical of his generation. In his obituary his career summary begins, "left [Lynn Academy] to learn the trade of a shoemaker in his father's ten by twelve shoemaker's shop, according to the custom of those times [late 1830s]." As late as the 1850s it was common for young boys like Luther Johnson and George A. Breed to enter their father's ten-footer after completing a "town school" education. The family played a decisive role even when technical training was received outside the family. In an autobiographical note, William Stone described how he chose where to start his career: "For twenty six years prior to 1840, my grandfather made shoes for Micajah C. Pratt, and my grandmother bound shoes for him the same length of time. . . . In 1854, when I left school, it was natural that I should go into his shop and learn to make shoes."[7] This pattern is clearly reflected in the 1850 census population schedules. Lynn's cordwainers emerge as a very tightly knit group. In households headed by a cordwainer nearly every son over fifteen is also listed as a cordwainer; so are almost all boarders. This suggests that the description of the sturdy cordwainer (secure in his skill, working in his ten-footer surrounded by his sons and fellow jours) that appears in nineteenth-century accounts of the industry is probably accurate.

The location of the ubiquitous ten-footers, as the small workshops of the putting-out era were called, in the yards of the cordwainers' houses reinforced the strong role of the family. Home and workplace were close together, making movement between the two easy and natural. A ten-footer was a small building, about twelve feet square, with work space for five or six workers. Each work space, called a berth in the trade, had a bench, or seat, and was far enough from the others to permit the cordwainer to move his arms freely as he stitched. The men who worked in each ten-footer were called its crew, another reflection of the nautical influence on the argot of the craft.

What did these young men do during the five or six years they spent as the "boy" in a ten-footer learning the gentle craft? Fortunately, while

---

[7] *Register*, 8:56; William Stone, "Lynn and Its Old Time Shoemakers' Shops," in *Register*, 15:84.

there are no detailed accounts of the day-to-day activities of a crew, there are a number of general descriptions from which we can reconstruct the duties of the trainee and the steps through which he learned how to make shoes. The younger boys, those just beginning the long learning process, were often used as errand runners. They were sent to the house to bring out bound uppers or down the block to borrow a particular size and style of last from a nearby crew. One of the boy's first responsibilities was to arrive early, especially during the winter, to start the fire in the shop stove and to prepare the candles that might be needed. One of the first jobs the boy learned was how to prepare wax for the thread. Shoemaker's wax was made from black pitch, a quarter part rosin, and "as much oil as the season requires." The mixture had to be heated in an earthen or iron pot over a slow fire and the ingredients mixed thoroughly together. The whole mass was poured into a tub of cold water (every shop had a tub which also served to soak sole leather) and then kneaded by hand, much like taffy, until it developed the proper consistency. Between errands the boys watched and listened to the men work. Gradually they might be asked to help hold a piece of work and then to do a few stitches or to wax a thread and attach the bristle. During the years of their apprenticeship the boys came to be familiar with the tools in the shoemaker's kit learning what each could and could not do. When the crew felt he was ready the youth made his first pair of shoes, putting together all the knowledge he had been accumulating and practicing. When he was finished the shoes were passed around the shop with each jour examining them closely, checking the stitchwork and, finally, bending the sole to see how tightly it had been sewn. A gap, called a smile, was the telltale sign of poor workmanship. If the shoe held up to all this testing, the young man was ready to begin his career as a jour with his own berth in a ten-footer.[8]

The transition from boy to jour was generally accomplished by age twenty, although men as young as sixteen are referred to as cordwainers in the manuscript census schedules just as the more mature men were. This raises the interesting question of just when people were thought of, and thought of themselves, as full-fledged members of the craft. If

---

[8] Johnson, *Sketches of Lynn*, pp. 27–69; John F. Rees, *The Art and Mystery of a Cordwainer; or, An Essay on the Principles and Practice of Boot and Shoe Making* (London, 1813). I am grateful to Kenneth Carpenter of the Kress Library at Harvard University for calling this item to my attention.

the answers they gave to the census takers are a measure of this—and I think they are—identification as a member of the gentle craft began sometime before one had fully mastered the art. Also, while learning to make a shoe was part of the transition to adulthood, completion of the learning process was not immediately followed by embarking on an independent life either by leaving home or by marriage. These few years between the average age at which young men finished learning their craft and the average age at marriage are intriguing because of the close connection in Lynn between family and work and the place of work in the life cycle. Almost all sons remained at home living, and perhaps working, with their fathers. Almost none of the sons living at home were married, but very few were more than twenty-five years old. Conversely, few boarders were under twenty-five, and while the majority were also single, a larger group were married than was the case among the sons living at home. The family and the household played key roles in the training of young men for their entry into the work force and the community.

The introduction of machinery and the factory system into Lynn between 1852 and 1879 had profound and lasting effects on the process sketched broadly above.[9] The earliest machine to directly affect the hand skills of Lynn's cordwainers and binders was John Brooks Nichols's adaptation in 1851 of the Howe sewing machine to sew the light leathers and heavy cloths used for the uppers of women's shoes. John Wooldredge of Lynn introduced the machine into actual use in the industry the following year, and it was rapidly adopted by other manufacturers in town.[10] Nichols, who had been a cordwainer in Lynn, continued to improve his machine, patenting refinements in 1854 (no. 11,615) and 1855 (no. 12,322). The new machine had several advantages over the hand method of binding, chief among them the evenness of the stitches and the speed at which it operated. Even before the machines were connected to a common power source (the earliest models were powered by a foot treadle), manufacturers and subcontractors brought binders

[9] Two studies that discuss the political and cultural effects of these changes are Alan Dawley, *Class and Community: The Industrial Revolution in Lynn* (Cambridge, Mass.: Harvard University Press, 1976); and Paul G. Faler, *Mechanics and Manufacturers in the Early Industrial Revolution: Lynn, Massachusetts, 1780–1860* (Albany: State University of New York Press, 1981).

[10] Joseph W. Roe, *The Mechanical Equipment*, vol. 9 of *Factory Management Course* (New York: Industrial Extension Institute, 1922), pp. 459–60.

together to work in large, open rooms filled with sewing machines. In these binding sheds work could be supervised closely and workers introduced to factory time and discipline.

The second major machine to be introduced was a stitcher invented by Lyman R. Blake and patented by him in 1860. This machine, along with an entirely new type of shoe to be sewn on it, solved the serious problem of sewing the soles onto the shoes. Sole leather was much heavier than upper leather and had to be sewn on the inside of the shoe as well as from the outside. Gordon McKay, a machinist, bought Blake's patent rights and, with R. H. Mathies, perfected the machine. He patented several refinements of the machine and the special shoe that was sewn on it. He also developed a marketing technique, practiced by McKay Association and its successor, United Shoe Machine Company, of renting the machinery at a low, uniform rate and providing, at minimal or no cost, a full array of support services including training for machine operatives.[11] Blake himself worked for McKay for a number of years training operatives on the McKay Stitcher. The rental system, which kept overhead very low, made the machinery developed by McKay Association and other shoe machinery firms more attractive and affordable for even the smallest shoe factory. It also greatly accelerated McKay's penetration of the industry at every level. A direct result of the mechanization of the industry was the rapid obsolescence of the skills of the city's cordwainers and the end of their way of life.

Two other branches of the industry resisted mechanization somewhat longer. Cutting, which had moved into the central shops during the 1830s, saw the introduction of paper and then tin patterns which standardized sizes and styles before dies and presses were developed that could cut leather without stretching or otherwise damaging it. The final aspect of the industry to be mechanized was lasting, the process of attaching the bound upper to a wooden form shaped roughly like a human foot. Long after the other major (and an incredible number of minor) divisions of the production process had been fully mechanized and brought into the factory, lasting remained handwork. A number of lasting machines had been patented but none had proved successful in

---

[11] William S. Brewster, *USM Corporation: Our First Seventy Five Years*, Newcomen Society in North America Publication, vol. 989 (1974); Roe, *Mechanical Equipment*; *Dictionary of American Biography*, s.v. "Lyman R. Blake" and "Gordon McKay"; Hazard, *Boot and Shoe Industry*, pp. 121–22.

actual operation. In 1883 Jan Ernst Matzeliger patented his "hand-process" lasting machine.[12] The machine was successful and hand lasting disappeared.

The transformation of shoemaking, from a handicraft practiced by skilled artisans in small workshops to an industry where every process was divided and subdivided into simple tasks done on separate machines in a well-organized factory, occurred very quickly. In 1850 shoes were still being made by hand; even as the Civil War broke out machinery was limited to binding. Yet by 1879 the last of the central shops putting out work to workers in the ten-footers had closed; the factory system was solidly entrenched.

An important, but easily overlooked, aspect of the process of mechanization was the centralizing role of McKay and his firm, McKay Association. McKay not only controlled Blake's patent and his own for the refinements he and Mathies developed, but he also offered manufacturers a growing variety of machines and services: sewing machines for binding, assistance in designing the factory, instructors to train the work force, and repair and maintenance of the machinery—all for a small royalty per pair of shoes. This package made the machinery attractive and affordable and contributed to the speed with which it drove out hand labor from industrial production.

These changes affected the whole relationship between the family and work, but nothing was altered more completely than the transmission of skills. First, of course, the machines made the hand skills that cordwainers and binders had spent years acquiring and developing totally irrelevant to the job of producing shoes. In testimony before the Massachusetts Bureau of Labor Statistics, many shoemakers and manufacturers described the process of mechanization and its destructive impact on the way of life in Lynn and other shoe towns.[13] According to all accounts McKay's representatives could train the entire work force of a factory in two days. The key function of training was removed from the family and taken over by the manufacturers of shoe machinery. In 1919 the Lynn Chamber of Commerce set up a trade school to train machine operatives for the city's shoe industry. The various manufacturers sup-

---

[12] Sidney Kaplan, "Jan Ernst Matzeliger and the Making of the Shoe," *Journal of Negro History* 40 (1955): 8–33.

[13] Massachusetts Bureau of Labor Statistics, *Second Annual Report* (Boston, 1871), pp. 93–98; Massachusetts Bureau of Labor Statistics, *Fourth Annual Report* (Boston, 1873), pp. 304–6.

ported the school financially, and it was free to all Lynn residents, just as if it had been part of the city school system. In the space of two generations technical training for full participation in the city's key industry passed from a familial responsibility to a public one. At the same time the nature of that training changed from initiation into a skilled craft to training in machine operation.

The implications of these changes were already clear by 1880 and were reflected in the manuscript census schedules of that year. The clear patterns of the 1850 schedule—a reflection of the neat, orderly process of the life cycle in a traditional society where life proceeded from generation to generation at much the same pace, with much the same rhythm—was gone; it was replaced by a much more complex arrangement showing no relationship among family, skill, age, or stage in the life cycle. The sons of shoe workers were pursuing a wide variety of occupations, as were the boarders in those households that took them in. This change was, at least in part, a reflection of a diversification of Lynn's economy; there were more occupational choices available in 1880 than there had been in 1850. But other changes are evident as well. The single designation, cordwainer, which identified the skilled artisans in 1850, had been replaced by myriad descriptions of functional jobs, an inevitable part of the process of making shoes with machinery in a factory. The new diversity of job descriptions is the clearest reflection of the fragmentation of the cohesive world of family and work the cordwainers had enjoyed for so long.

The preceding is a broad picture of what happened to a group of people who enjoyed a way of life based on a hand skill when the technology that was the basis of that life-style changed and their industry was rapidly mechanized. The shoemakers of Lynn, as a group and as individuals, were rapidly brought into a modern way of life with an entirely different technological foundation. It is this process that is my primary concern in this entire research project.[14] The change from a seemingly orderly, timeless world to a less orderly, time-conscious world is one of the profound changes in all of history. Different groups entered this process, and emerged from it, at different times. The cordwainers of Lynn entered this process relatively late, at a time for which relatively

---

[14]William H. Mulligan, Jr., "The Family and Technological Change: The Shoemakers of Lynn, Massachusetts, during the Transition from Hand to Machine Production, 1850–1880" (Ph.D. diss., Clark University, 1982).

complete records exist, thus allowing a fuller reconstruction of the process generally and of the careers of individuals as well. To understand what happened to Lynn's shoemakers and their world is to gain a better perspective on our own world of rapid technological change.

The broader implications of all of this are related to the changed relationship between work and family life. Unfortunately, it is difficult, and often impossible, to get at the dynamics of family life historically. We know, for example, that Joseph Lye taught his younger brother, Robert, to make shoes and that at that time he was head of his family. In conjunction with an array of other data, that information helps us to understand both the structure and the function of the artisan family in traditional Lynn, but it tells us nothing of how either party looked on their relationship. Who decided that Robert would learn his brother's (and father's) craft? Was Joseph anxious to teach his brother as his father had taught him, or was this an unpleasant duty that had to be done? There is no way to know and little basis for any statement. Joseph's laconic style might be significant if it were not pervasive in his and many other diaries.

The family has proved to be a tenacious institution. Despite periodic predictions of its imminent demise, it retains the same essential structure today that it had many hundreds of years ago. The nuclear household has now been traced far back into the past.[15] The same is true for Lynn. Mechanization did not alter the structure of the family in any significant way. It did, however, profoundly alter the relationship between the family and work and the role the family played in the lives of its members. The relationship between the family and work was not destroyed by the introduction of the factory system, but it was changed. As work was removed from the household, the economic role of the father lost much of its significance; he was no longer the one who taught his sons their trade, who dealt with the boss. Even if he and his sons were together in the factory, his lengthy experience was of little, if any, advantage and not a source of knowledge his sons might seek to draw on. Perhaps in the future we will have data that will allow us to compare the experience of the first generation of factory shoe workers with textile workers. Both Michael Anderson in his study of mid nineteenth-cen-

---

[15] Peter Laslett, *The World We Have Lost: England before the Industrial Age* (1965; rev. ed., New York: Charles Scribner's Sons, 1971); Peter Laslett, ed., *Household and Family in Past Time* (Cambridge: At the University Press, 1973).

tury Preston, England, and Tamara K. Hareven in her study of late nineteenth-, early twentieth-century Manchester, New Hampshire, have demonstrated that the family played a very important role in helping people to find jobs and housing.[16] Hareven has even been able to show the family operating within the factory itself, directing members toward more desirable jobs and departments. So it is clear that work and the family were still closely interconnected fairly late, at least, in the textile industry. The question remains as to whether shoe workers were able to maintain a similar role.

There were (and are) important differences between the relationship of the family to work in traditional, hand-skill societies and in modern, mechanized societies. In Lynn, before mechanization, the family was at the center of an individual's life. They learned the skills with which they would support themselves and later pass on to their children. Their skills allowed artisans a degree of independence. Prominent in diaries and other accounts are days spent at Nahant fishing and picnicking on the beach, working on a garden, or engaging in any of a variety of diversions. The family provided access to all of these benefits by passing on the skills needed to make shoes. As less time was needed to pass on the skills, the nurture of the family, which sustained young people during their training, became less important, and training for the job was taken over by the employers as an "investment." Once the critical function of training in the craft was taken from the family and transferred to the control of the manufacturer, the family's role became secondary, not primary. While the family continued, perhaps, to help individuals find employment and adjust to new surroundings, work now involved machinery, and operating it was a skill taught by the factory owner or his representative.

The full impact of these changes, in both the technology and the organization of work, was profound. Each separate function, once part of a package of skill and inherited knowledge, had become a separate job. The close relationship between craft and all other aspects of life was gone. The household structure of the city no longer reflected this

---

[16] Michael Anderson, *Family Structure in Nineteenth-Century Lancashire* (Cambridge: At the University Press, 1971); Tamara K. Hareven, "The Laborers of Manchester, New Hampshire, 1912–1922: The Role of Family and Ethnicity in Adjustment to Industrial Life," *Labor History* 16 (1975): 249–65; and Tamara K. Hareven, "Family Time and Industrial Time: Family and Work in a Planned Corporation Town, 1900–1924," *Journal of Urban History* 1 (1975): 365–89.

strong identification with craft in 1880. The children of shoe workers did not follow their parents into the trade in anything like the numbers they had before machinery replaced hand skill. In short, the artisan lifestyle and society were gone, swept away by the rush of mechanization. The Massachusetts Bureau of Labor Statistics noted in its report for 1871 that the "use of machinery has virtually swept away the old race of shoemakers who could make up an entire shoe."[17]

At the onset of mechanization the family was still a pervasive institution in the lives of shoemakers, providing many services for its members. It was the prime agency for transmitting the skills needed for full participation in the economic life of the city. As pointed out above, young men and women not only learned their craft in the family but were introduced into the town's major industry through their family as well. As the technological base of that industry changed and became less tied to those hand skills, the role of the family in the lives of individuals began to change. For example, less and less of an individual's work experience took place within a family context as brick factories replaced the ten-footers of the putting-out system. Job training passed from the family to the factory as the machinery manufacturers provided trainers to instruct new operatives. The family remained an important part of people's lives, to be sure, but it was less pervasive.

It is important to keep in mind that while family functions changed in response to changes in the world of work, the structure of the family changed imperceptibly if at all.[18] Structure is quite resilient, and the nuclear family, while certainly not a creation of industrialism, was well suited to the demands of the new economic order. Function, on the other hand, is more fragile because it is not as free from outside influence, involving the family's contact with the wider society. And while cultural tradition is a strong influence on role definition, economic forces outside the family are equally, or almost equally, important, especially as they define possibilities and horizons. This study of the role of the family in training shoemakers is one example of the process of adaptation to a changing environment.

[17] Second Annual Report, p. 242.
[18] See Mulligan, "Family and Technological Change," chaps. 3, 5.

Latrobe, His Craftsmen, and the Corinthian Order of the Hall of Representatives
Charles E. Brownell

In March 1796 the thirty-one-year-old architect and engineer B. Henry Latrobe arrived in Norfolk, Virginia, from England. For the next quarter century, down to his death in 1820, he practiced his two professions in a wide variety of commissions at a wide variety of places, principally in the region from Richmond to Philadelphia along the Atlantic Seaboard, in Pittsburgh, and in New Orleans. His activities involved him in both extensive and diverse relations with craftsmen.

To discuss Latrobe's relations with architectural craftsmen coherently requires drawing upon his oeuvre selectively. His architectural works range from Baltimore's Roman Catholic cathedral and the United States Capitol at one pole, through domestic architecture, to utilitarian

This essay dispenses with footnotes. As to the subject of B. Henry Latrobe and his craftsmen, the principal source of information is the architect's letters and other papers. I have cited relevant Latrobe documents in the text in such form that the interested reader can consult them in the microfiche edition of *The Papers of Benjamin Henry Latrobe*, ed. Thomas E. Jeffrey (Clifton, N.J.: James T. White for the Maryland Historical Society, 1976). Other sources of information on Latrobe's craftsmen (for example, the Washington *National Intelligencer*) are treated comparably. As to other topics, such as the evolution of the Hall of Representatives, the reader will find more extensive information in Charles E. Brownell, *The Architectural Drawings of Benjamin Henry Latrobe*, in *The Papers of Benjamin Henry Latrobe*, ed. Edward C. Carter II et al. (New Haven: Yale University Press, forthcoming).

and industrial buildings at the other pole. But Latrobe made his central contribution in the field of public buildings. Essential to these public buildings and to Latrobe's brand of neoclassicism is the union of Roman inspiration for planning and structure with Greek inspiration for ornamentation. The Roman inspiration reached its finest expression in the monumental all-masonry dome, while the Greek inspiration reached its finest expression in the monumental all-masonry order of columns. Two realizations of a particular Corinthian order, Latrobe's first and second colonnades for the Hall of Representatives (now Statuary Hall) at the national Capitol, stand at the core of his art. Thus the story of how the architect and his craftsmen brought them into being holds special interest in any case. But this story is also exceptionally rich. Elaborately documented, it runs from 1803 to 1817 with one short break. A long and complicated strand, it knots with many others that represent basic kinds of relations between Latrobe and his men. By discussing this subject one can endeavor to sketch out basic issues that belong to the general topic of Latrobe and the men who executed his designs.

This paper will first touch on Latrobe's neoclassicism—represented by the Corinthian order in question—as a brilliant but initially alien intrusion into the architectural world of the young United States. Second, it will review the history of the two colonnades, respectively during Latrobe's first building campaign at the Capitol, or campaign one (1803–12), and his second, or campaign two (1815–17). Third, it will close with some generalizations about Latrobe and his craftsmen.

When Latrobe reached this country in 1796, the craftsman and the gentleman architect largely divided the practice of architecture between them. For their knowledge of architectural possibilities these men relied extensively on a narrow range of commonly limited and outdated books. They made much use of wood and much use of brick but on the whole only a rudimentary use of stone. Into this setting Latrobe carried a conception of architecture almost unknown to his American public.

Latrobe belonged to the mainstream of that classical tradition that stretched behind him back to the rebirth of the Greco-Roman visual arts in the Italian Renaissance. That is, he belonged to a tradition that identified the true architect as a self-conscious artist who must produce wholly unified conceptions based upon and controlled by a broad range of higher learning. As a universal man, Latrobe had intellectual interests that far exceeded the requirements of his profession. Time and again these interests played a part in shaping his architecture; they expanded his power to control his designs in minute and subtle detail. A further point applies to Latrobe's learned art: by the later eighteenth century, its British practitioners had begun to recognize a parallelism between their learned techniques and those of the legal and medical professions, and they had begun to crystallize the concept of architectural professionalism.

Upon his learning rested Latrobe's style. He brought with him to America the most radically advanced kind of architecture possible at the time, the architecture of the second phase of neoclassicism. As a neoclassicist he consciously participated in an international movement that sought to purify the entirety of Western art by restoring the supposed fundamental principles of the arts. Latrobe sought for certain of these principles in Greek architecture, notably the principles governing simplicity in ornament. In particular, he believed that he had abstracted from Greek architecture the principles that should govern the orders of column (elements structural in origin but ordinarily used as decoration outside Greek antiquity). Believing that the Romans had deviated from the pure Greek principles of ornamentation, Latrobe had scant use for the Roman orders. But, on the basis of Roman as well as Greek and other precedents, he devoted himself in civic architecture to the ideal of all-masonry construction, incombustible construction of brick and stone which would challenge the destroying power of time itself. For the orders, the ideal of masonry construction meant stone, and beyond permanence it also meant the beauty of fine stone handsomely wrought.

The two colonnades will illustrate the nature of Latrobe's architecture, but first they demand some attention in their own right. Of the first version no single good likeness survives, but the architect's drawings and remarks permit one to piece together its appearance. The second colonnade still exists, along with a quantity of drawings (for example, fig. 1) and written documentation.

Latrobe used fundamentally the same Corinthian order both times. Both sets of columns measured 26 feet 8 inches in height from base through capital, but the two versions differed in plan, materials, and details. At the outset of his work at the Capitol Latrobe wished to treat the Hall of Representatives as a version of a classical, semicircular theater without a colonnade. President Thomas Jefferson, who acted as both patron and virtual collaborator, insisted that Latrobe approximate the elliptical colonnaded hall that George Washington had approved, and

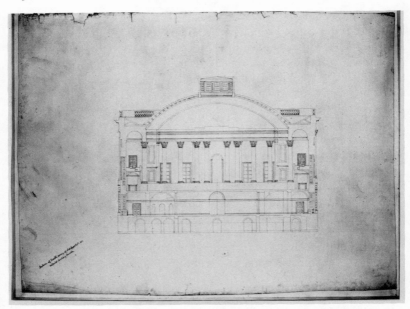

Figure 1.   John H. B. Latrobe, after B. Henry Latrobe, section of south wing, U.S. Capitol, Washington, D.C., looking south. 1817. Pencil and pen-and-ink; H. 21⅝", W. 28¾". (Prints and Photographs Division, Library of Congress.)

Jefferson further wished him to use a highly enriched Roman Corinthian order. Latrobe produced and executed a compromise design that arranged an enriched, Greek-looking Corinthian colonnade around a plan of two semicircles abutting a rectangle. Necessity thrust upon him a far from ideal material, Aquia sandstone from Virginia. (He discussed this stone revealingly in his 1807 American Philosophical Society paper, "An Account of the Freestone Quarries on the Potomac and Rappahannoc Rivers," which drew upon material of August 1806 in his journal and his Sketchbook 9.) He built each of the twenty-four columns from a series of drums and, in order to protect the material, left the lowest portion of the columns unfluted.

After the British ruined the first chamber in 1814, Latrobe revised his scheme for a classical theater to include a highly enriched colonnade. It seems very likely that he added the columns partly in order to lessen the difference between his theater and the hall that Washington had approved. More important, he added the columns because much in the effect of his first colonnade had won him over. This time around, working from a far more satisfactory budget, he chose superior materials. Expressly determined to rival the polychromatic richness of Roman architecture, he selected for the shafts a conglomerate stone that, as a geologist, he had discovered himself—the richly figured Potomac breccia (also called Potomac marble and calico rock). He planned to make each of the twenty-two column shafts a monolith, to polish the stone, to dispense with fluting because the figure in the rock would ornament the shafts sufficiently by itself, and to complete the order with elements of white marble and warm Aquia stone.

Now for a closer look at the two colonnades, concentrating on the essential sameness of the Corinthian order in both. The order in question consists of two primary parts, the post, or column, and its beam, or entablature. The column consists of three secondary parts—base, shaft, and capital—and the entablature also consists of three parts—architrave, frieze, and cornice. In this case there is an extra element on the architecture, a blocking course. Latrobe intended each colonnade to support solid masonry vaulting, which in both instances a president prevented him from using.

Underneath the design of this order lies rich and diverse learning. Even if a full analysis of the subject were not premature, such a commentary would exceed the bounds of the present essay. Instead, two points about the shaft, one about the capital, and two about the cornice must stand in place of a full discussion.

Normally a column shaft diminishes in diameter as it rises. It has become common knowledge that the Greeks and, imitating them, the Romans employed the principle of entasis, or swelling; in other words, they tapered the shaft on a curve. Andrea Palladio discussed entasis in his *Four Books of Architecture* (1570), and it seems likely that his treatment became standard in North America via the Anglo-Palladian builders' manuals of the eighteenth century. But Latrobe subscribed to a substantial body of neoclassical opinion in believing that entasis had originated as a post-Greek corruption and that the Greeks had tapered their columns on a straight line, in effect as fragments of elongated cones. He mentioned his view in a letter of August 5, 1804, to John Lenthall, his second in command at the Capitol.

The shafts of the second colonnade entail a further point. Encouraged by the budget for rebuilding the Capitol, Latrobe determined to compete with the splendor of the polychromatic stonework employed by the Romans themselves. His conception depended upon using shafts of Potomac breccia, a gray stone overall, but one spangled with color. He meant to make each shaft a monolith, its figure unmarred by joints, and thus he contemplated what probably would have been the grandest monolithic order to date in the short history of monumental American masonry construction. And he composed a play of color with this stone, white marble for the bases and capitals and tawny Aquia stone for the entablature. Writing to his friend Robert Goodloe Harper (August 13, 1815), he quoted from the Roman poet Propertius (*Elegies* 2.34.65) to spell out his ambition of challenging Roman colorism: if he overcame official resistance to the breccia, then he could say, "Cedite Romani [Yield to me, Romans]."

For the capitals Jefferson had preferred the Corinthian order of the Temple of Castor and Pollux in Rome. Latrobe, the man who had introduced the Greek orders into American practice at the Bank of Pennsylvania (1799–1801 and later) and the Centre Square Engine House of the Philadelphia Waterworks (1799–1801 and later), had wished to use another Greek order. He gave in to Jefferson's preference for the Corinthian, but with both versions of the colonnade he followed a Greek model for the capital, the model of the Choragic Monument of Lysicrates in Athens (fig. 2). Believing that the United States held no one capable of working the capitals satisfactorily, he had the first set carved in Washington by Giovanni Andrei, an Italian imported for the purpose, and the second set carved in Italy under Andrei's supervision. Finding skilled hands solved one problem but created another, the need to reform minds habituated to the Roman orders. When Latrobe wrote to the commissioners of the public buildings (May 2, 1815) to urge that Andrei accompany the order for the capitals to Italy, he explained:

Mr. Andrei himself, accustomed on his arrival in America to the roman finery of his country, found it very difficult to accomodate [*sic*] his chisel to the simplicity of the Grecian taste which I have labored to introduce into our country,

Figure 2 *(facing page).* Detail of the Corinthian order of the Choragic Monument of Lysicrates, Athens. Late fourth century B.C. From James Stuart and Nicholas Revett, *The Antiquities of Athens*, vol. 1 (London: Printed by John Haberkorn, 1762), chap. 4, pl. 6. (Winterthur Museum Library.)

and which he now infinitely prefers. And unless he remains [in Italy] long enough to get one quarter of a Capital executed as a model, I should despair entirely of the taste in which they would be sent hither.

The cornice presents a twofold issue because it rests on brackets, or modillions. Nothing of the sort supports the cornice of the Choragic Monument of Lysicrates. Apparently Jefferson insisted on this rich treatment, in the manner of the Temple of Castor. In consequence, Latrobe had two problems. First, he had to create a modillioned treatment that would assimilate to the qualities of his Greek order. The second problem is yet more important. Despite all the thought that architects have devoted to the orders in the course of more than two millennia, the orders tend to run into trouble—trouble based on geometry—when they turn corners. Unlike the problem of Doric corners, the difficulty in turning a modillioned Corinthian cornice around more than one angle is no longer well known. The ideal cornice of this sort would obey an intricate set of rules; suffice it here to note three. A column, an element of support, must always have a bracket, likewise an element of support, centered over it. The brackets must alternate regularly with square panels. And the square panels must do the work of turning corners. However Latrobe handled this matter in the first Hall of Representatives, his second cornice turns its compound corners with seemingly effortless regularity, panel alternating with bracket in unbroken sequence, and a panel making each turn. But a comparison of two sheets of Latrobe drawings demonstrates that this treatment did not come easily. In a generally messy early attempt (fig. 3, upper left), the sequence running from left to right breaks off with a panel at the first corner, around which the sequence picks up again with a modillion. This ruptured treatment is simply a confession of embarrassment. An alternative, drawn to a smaller scale at the upper right of the same sheet, tries to turn the corner with three panels in succession and is equally a confession of embarrassment. Only by taking further pains with proportions did Latrobe reach his final, satisfying outcome (fig. 4).

Such, then, was the Corinthian order of the Hall of Representatives, predicated upon the renewal of antique principles and steeped in learning of many kinds. Successful execution of such a design required exact fidelity to the architect's intentions—deviation from those intentions would merely defeat the purpose by mutilating the forms. Given a nation with no established tradition of monumental masonry con-

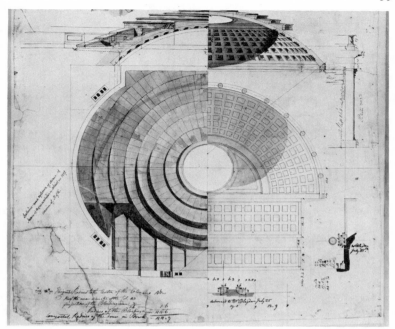

Figure 3. B. Henry Latrobe, studies for south wing, U.S. Capitol, Washington, D.C. 1815. Pencil, pen-and-ink, and watercolor; H. 27⅛″, W. 18⅜″. (Prints and Photographs Division, Library of Congress.)

struction, and given the alienness of Latrobe's architectural elements to the experience of American craftsmen, how did Latrobe fare in building his two colonnades?

The initial period of construction at the Capitol began in 1793 and ended in 1800 (by which time the design had become the hybrid creation of at least three minds, those of William Thornton, Etienne Sulpice Hallet, and Thomas Jefferson). The north, or senate, wing now stood complete, but its monumental sandstone facades concealed defective wooden construction that would decay rapidly. Across the gap for the center, or rotunda, block, the south wing, built still worse, had risen enough above ground level to hold a temporary chamber for the representatives. In this state the Capitol languished until 1803.

In March 1803 Jefferson committed to Latrobe the task of resuming

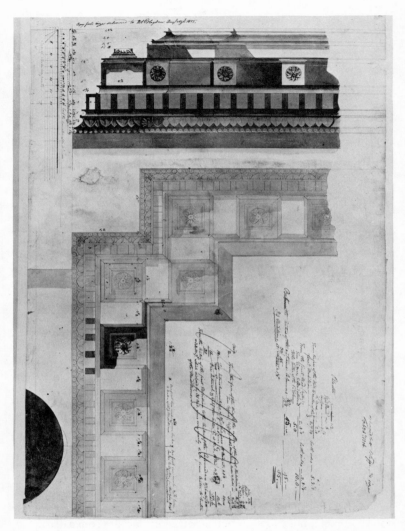

Figure 4.   B. Henry Latrobe, details of cornice of the Hall of Representatives, U.S. Capitol, Washington, D.C. 1815. Pencil, pen-and-ink, and watercolor; H. 18⁷⁄₁₆″, W. 27⅜″. (Prints and Photographs Division, Library of Congress.)

work on the south wing. Latrobe determined to raze the defective construction. He drew up his own astylar theater design as an alternative to the elliptical colonnaded hall laid down on the inherited plans. And he gathered his men. In an often-quoted journal entry of August 12, 1806, the architect discussed the misfortune of those craftsmen who had optimistically thrown their lot in with that of the city of Washington, only to find themselves stranded when the metropolis failed to materialize. Of the men Latrobe found at hand, two merit singling out.

First and foremost comes the English-born carpenter John Lenthall (ca. 1762–1808). Because Jefferson could not offer Latrobe an adequate salary (only $1,700), the architect accepted responsibility for the Capitol on condition that he not move to Washington but instead appoint a clerk of the works to direct operations, with Latrobe exercising control by means of correspondence and visits. In Lenthall he found his clerk. Lenthall remains a somewhat mysterious figure, best known from Latrobe's correspondence with him and from Latrobe's obituary of him in the Washington *National Intelligencer* (September 23, 1808). But three points are clear. First, the technology of raising a masonry structure depended heavily on wooden devices, so that the choice of a carpenter for clerk of the works made excellent sense. But, second, Lenthall was no ordinary carpenter. He brought to his job a variety of experience with mechanical contrivances in English mills, mines, and elsewhere. He had rigorous standards of workmanship. He possessed a good mind, he read eagerly, and Latrobe thought highly enough of his understanding to discuss architectural principles with him. Indeed, the Latrobe letters to Lenthall rival those to Jefferson as revelations of the theoretical ideas that their author did not frequently put into writing. Still more impressive, in a rare instance of confidence in a craftsman's taste, Latrobe permitted Lenthall to make decisions affecting the design of the south wing, principally in the form of adjustments of structural detail. Third, in Lenthall the architect gained a friend and confidant. Lenthall did have a difficult temperament, a matter connected with both his high standards and his physical illnesses. Initially his personality led to trouble with other men on the work force, not with Latrobe.

Fortune also favored Latrobe with the services of George Blagden (d. 1826), the English-born stonemason who supervised the Capitol masons in every period of construction from around 1795 to his death. Writing to the commissioners of the public buildings on August 26, 1815, Latrobe declared, "[Blagden] is deservedly at the head of his art in this country, & I have not seen his superior in Europe." But Blagden would see fit to turn his invaluable expertise against Latrobe during the rebuilding of the Capitol. It is important to note that, unlike Lenthall, Blagden figured prominently in the life of his city. For example, his obituary in the *National Intelligencer* (June 5, 1826) identifies him as an alderman and a director of the Bank of Washington.

A third individual who worked under Latrobe in 1803 had no significant connection with the colonnade of the Hall of Representatives, but he offers a convenient opportunity to mention a significant kind of relation between Latrobe and craftsmen. In three major instances Latrobe gave the son of a building craftsman training that led to a career as an architect and engineer. In 1803 Latrobe's office included an undependable fifteen-year-old pupil, William Strickland (1788–1854), the son of a carpenter and ultimately one of Latrobe's most important successors. In 1799 another carpenter's son, Frederick Graff (1774–1847), had entered the office. A favorite pupil, Graff became not only an eminent engineer but also a significant architect, a role that the Graff papers lately acquired by Winterthur do a good deal to clarify. By late March 1817 Latrobe had taken as a pupil William F. Small (1798–1832), the son of a prominent Baltimore builder and lumber dealer. Small, principally active as an architect, would play a major part in the creation of neoclassical Baltimore.

The year 1803 saw the defective south wing construction removed, and 1804 saw the form of the Hall of Representatives arrived at by way of a succession of compromises between Latrobe and Jefferson. Although Latrobe would not succeed in his wish to raise a brick dome over his colonnade, he preserved the important principle of using only stone for the order. The principle of expedience in respect to both materials and labor—a principle important to Jefferson—threatened Latrobe's principles of permanence and beauty, but he dealt with a series of challenges to his goal. On November 27, 1803, he wrote to Lenthall that he would resign rather than use wooden columns at the president's suggestion and thus "build a temple of disgrace to [himself] & Mr Jefferson." In February 1804 he faced a more general problem that resulted from his inevitable reliance on private quarries. The firm of Cook and Brent attempted to raise the price of Aquia stone. Latrobe outmaneuvered them by reopening the public quarry, but he could not put that quarry on its feet. And he got around Jefferson's suggestion (February 28) of using stuccoed brick column shafts on the example of Palladio. Consulting his own ideas of expedience, Latrobe recommended to Jefferson (March 29) the use of the relatively simple foliate capital of the Tower of the Winds in Athens, a capital that he could have cast in iron— presumably he meant to rely on the privately incorporated rolling and slitting mill that ran on the excess power of the Philadelphia Water- works and in which he had an interest. Jefferson's preference for the Corinthian order killed the possibility. The architect informed the pres- ident (April 29) that casting this more complex order would cost as much as carving it in stone.

A basic problem made itself felt in 1804. Throughout Latrobe's first building campaign at the Capitol, Congress appropriated the funds annually—any year could have been the last. Laborers hired themselves out for the year on January 1; thereafter there were fewer men available, and the available men demanded higher wages. Until each year's appro- priation passed, Latrobe and his quarriers did not know whether to sign on men. Congress did not pass the 1804 appropriation until March 27 (and appropriated only $50,000 for all the public buildings, whereas Latrobe had wished $50,000 for the south wing alone). Off to a bad start, the year did not proceed well. At its end Latrobe could only report (December 1) that he had made a little progress and exceeded his bud- get.

In 1805 Congress appropriated $110,000 for the south wing on January 26 and came up with the unrealistic demand that Latrobe have the wing finished within the year. In this year Latrobe achieved some happy results. On March 6 he wrote Jefferson's old friend Philip Mazzei in Italy to request that Mazzei find him a first-rate Italian ornamental carver with an assistant. Latrobe's search for craftsmen for the Capitol had become international. Mazzei misunderstood, fortunately enough, and as of September 12 wrote of his discoveries, Giuseppe Franzoni (d. 1815), a sculptor, and Giovanni Andrei (1770–1824), the decorative carver that Latrobe had had in mind. On the home front, after paying Lenthall out of his own pocket, in March and April Latrobe finally settled Lenthall's compensation, a retroactive $4 per day plus an office in which the Lenthall family could live.

But the year 1805 did not smile on the south wing and its colon- nade. In Latrobe's report of December 22, he recorded that the men had completed building the cellar, the ground story, and the upper walls and had some of the stone for the colonnade ready for construc- tion. Progress had suffered from a shortage of workmen and trouble in providing stone of a grade appropriate for the interior. As to the workmen, the Capitol had to compete with other construction projects in Washington and Baltimore. Latrobe, who had foreseen the problem for some time, had written Jefferson (August 31) some interesting details. The public buildings in Washington—the Navy Yard, the President's House, and the Treasury fireproof—competed for stonecutters. The Baltimore mason William Steuart had lately visited Washington "for the avowed purpose of enticing away as many of [their] hands as he could," but had failed. Latrobe's best stonecutter had taken with him three or four others to work on the Bank of Columbia in Washington. The architect foresaw that in 1806 the construction of his own cathedral, of Union Bank in Baltimore (by the carpenter-architect Robert Cary Long, Sr.), and of other buildings would draw off men.

Franzoni and Andrei arrived in January 1806. Mazzei's error had provided Latrobe with a sculptor. The architect set Franzoni at work on the great eagle designed for the House frieze and later had him execute reclining allegories of agriculture, art, science, and commerce for the portion of the frieze opposite the eagle. Pleased with his Italians, in a letter of December 19/28, 1806, Latrobe would write Mazzei asking what Franzoni's father would charge to carve fifty Corinthian capitals for the exterior of the main block of the Capitol. But the time had not yet come for such a measure.

A singularly interesting letter of March 3, 1806, from Latrobe to Lenthall discusses the House order. Evidently Latrobe had let Lenthall try his hand at working out the modillions. He accepted his clerk of the work's design over his own tries, although with some reservations, the principal one concerning the corner problem.

On the whole, 1806 went badly. Congress did not make its appropriation until April 21. The House turned to the president to see to the completion of their hall within the year. Jefferson demanded a detailed schedule from Latrobe and regular reports from Lenthall. But that summer the insufficiency of the force of stonecutters put the freestone work further and further behind, and this in turn retarded the carpentry and the plastering. Matters came to a head in July. Authorized by Jefferson (July 1 and 17) to hire additional hands at any cost, Latrobe hunted in Philadelphia and Baltimore. But a large number of Philadelphia stonecutters had moved to Manhattan to work on New York City Hall (a commission that Latrobe had lost in 1802 to Joseph François Mangin and John McComb, Jr.). And when Latrobe's emissary, probably his pupil Robert Mills, reached New York, he found that he had to proceed further north, because a shortage of funds had stopped work on the city hall and the stonecutters had moved on to Albany to work on Philip Hooker's statehouse there. The quest for craftsmen, then, had a national as well as an international character. When Latrobe reported to Jefferson on August 14, the endeavor to sign on stonecutters had not yet proved highly fruitful, but in any case it was now a shortage of stone that held up the work. In the end, the attempt to ready the south wing for an impatient House failed, although the men did finish putting up the colonnade and its wood-framed dome.

Latrobe made two important public statements in November 1806. His annual report justified his expenditure of $134,000 on the south wing, his estimate for completing this project, and it promised completion for 1807. Pointing to the evils of uncertain annual appropriations, his *Private Letter to the . . . Members of Congress* stated that the $250,000 cumulatively appropriated for the public buildings under him would have covered developing the quarries properly, assembling a sufficient force of permanent stonecutters, and, hence, finishing the wing, if he could have counted on this sum from the beginning.

In 1807 Latrobe fulfilled his promise of opening the south wing, in the face of a series of troubles. Despite his explanations of architectural economy, the appropriations bill did not pass until the last day of the session (March 3), and it provided $42,000 rather than the $45,000 that Latrobe had requested for the wing. The July decision to convene Congress in late October, not early December, further curtailed the working time. And a sad complication arose. After Latrobe moved from Philadelphia to Washington in June, relations deteriorated between him and Lenthall, who had become accustomed to supervising the work in his own way. Lenthall's resignation became a possibility. On September 12, the architect wrote Jefferson that he had composed the differences, but he spoke too soon. On October 17, Latrobe held a banquet for the workmen to celebrate the completion of major labors on the south wing. Lenthall sprang an embarrassing surprise on him by deciding at the last moment not to show up, on the grounds that Latrobe had not invited the laborers as well as the craftsmen. And the Latrobe-Lenthall problem continued in 1808.

But the House took possession of its new home on October 26, 1807. It would appear from Latrobe's description of the Hall in the *National Intelligencer* (November 30) that, although the multiple compromises in the architecture still distressed him—here and elsewhere he claimed only the credit of having overcome difficulties—the effect of the colonnade had won him over to no inconsiderable degree. The Hall remained unfinished. For instance, it would take Andrei years to complete the carving of the modillions and the capitals. (In fact, he left the rear faces of the latter unfinished because curtains covered them, according to Latrobe's letter of May 2, 1815, to the commissioners of the public buildings.) And there were problems, which Latrobe acknowledged in his report (March 23, 1808) for 1807: defective acoustics, defective ventilation, defective heating, and a deficit of some $39,000 (for the south wing, out of a deficit of $51,949 for the entire public buildings budget). As to the three former issues, Latrobe ameliorated them. As to the deficit, the House exonerated Latrobe, although a stigma remained. But the deteriorating north wing (with its decaying wooden colonnade in the Senate), almost immediately to undergo reconstruction, as of 1808 had cost roughly $61,000 more than its solid mate to the south.

In Latrobe's report of March 1808 he stated that of the twenty-four columns, only two had their capitals entirely finished, fourteen had merely "bosted," or rough-hewn, capitals, only part of the cornice moldings had reached completion, and Franzoni had not finished the allegories in the frieze, but Franzoni and Andrei now had an American pupil named (David) Somerville. While the House sat, however, Andrei and Franzoni could not work on their respective parts of the order, so during the spring they took on commissions in Baltimore. They worked for Latrobe's friend Maximilian Godefroy on Saint Mary's Chapel, where Latrobe's plasterer, William Foxton, molded and cast Andrei's capitals and corbels, and they collaborated on work for the Union Bank, their tympanum for which survives in the collections of the Peale Museum.

Lenthall's career terminated grimly but swiftly on September 19, 1808, in the newly built Supreme Court chamber in the north wing. Lenthall had redesigned Latrobe's system of vaulting in the interest of saving construction money. When the vault showed signs of failing, Lenthall seems to have lost his judgment and removed the centering— the timber framework used to construct vaulting—in an erratic fashion. His procedure brought the vault down, killing him. Latrobe did not replace his clerk of the works. Instead, he redistributed duties, assumed much of Lenthall's responsibility, and brought his own sixteen-year-old son, Henry Sellon Latrobe, into the office at the outset of 1809.

The story of the first colonnade now winds down. Jefferson, its sponsor, left office in 1809, the last year for major construction in the first campaign. On December 28, 1810, Latrobe reported to President James Madison on progress at the Capitol. Work on the capitals—suspended, of course, during the sessions of the House—had reached the west side of the Hall and there was "far advanced," while only the two capitals at the entry remained untouched. Andrei now had four American pupils. With their aid, Latrobe predicted, the Italian could complete the capitals in another twelve months.

Meanwhile, another Baltimore edifice, Latrobe's cathedral, had become the beneficiary of the craft skills that had accumulated at the Capitol. In 1810 Andrei and his pupils George Henderson, Thomas McIntosh, and David Somerville had undertaken the private project of carving ten white marble capitals for the giant Ionic order within the church. In 1811 the undertaking fell afoul of a misunderstanding and the financial troubles of the patron, the Roman Catholic board of trustees. The carvers proceeded no further than the ornamented necks below the volutes. None of the necks would reach Baltimore before 1817. Not until 1819 would the trustees resolve to accept and pay for the full set, and Latrobe would complete the capitals with volutes cast in metal (apparently bronze) as an economy measure.

Campaign one closed somberly enough. Around July 1, 1811, Latrobe volunteered—in the absence of funding—to remain in office without salary. On June 18, 1812, the United States declared war on Great Britain. An act of July 5 treated Latrobe's position as extinct by twelve months, although the architect directed some work at the Capitol thereafter. In the autumn of 1813 he moved to Pittsburgh to work for Robert Fulton's Ohio Steam Boat Company, a disastrous venture for him. And on August 24, 1814, the British burned as much of the Capitol as they could—much of Latrobe's construction defied them. But in the Hall of Representatives they heaped up the wooden furnishings, added rocket fuel, and lighted the mass. In the sudden and intense heat, the surfaces of the sandstone colonnade expanded and scaled off, leaving a frightful ruin that threatened imminent collapse.

The commission to rebuild the Capitol summoned Latrobe from grim straits in Pittsburgh. In Washington, on April 18, 1815, he accepted his appointment and entered a situation materially unlike the one that he had formerly occupied.

Latrobe had contracted to serve as "Architect or Surveyor of the Capitol"; that is, he had no responsibilities but the Capitol. Congress had appropriated $300,000 for the restoration. This sum, exceeding any architectural budget that Latrobe had ever had, obviated the annual uncertainty of campaign one and permitted him to plan comprehensively. The architect had no Jefferson to support him—or to hinder him. He answered to a bureaucracy, the three commissioners of the public buildings (1815–16), succeeded by the single commissioner of the public buildings (1816–17), four men unqualified to oversee the erection of a public edifice. Under them Latrobe had a minimum of authority.

As to his artisans, Latrobe found himself happily situated. Replying to Jefferson (who had hoped for positions for two of his Charlottesville house joiners), Latrobe declared (July 12/18, 1815) that the commissioners had permitted him to assemble "a corps of Mechanics capable of executing any Work of any degree of difficulty or magnitude." The commissioners had favored those local men of ability who had suffered—and suffered miserably—with the city since the outbreak of the war.

The position of clerk of the works went to Shadrach Davis, a carpenter who had served similarly under Latrobe at the Washington Navy Yard from 1805. Latrobe held a high opinion of Davis's abilities and had declared to Secretary of the Navy Paul Hamilton (July 3, 1812) that "it will not be easy to find such another Foreman of Carpenters & Joiners, as Shadrach Davis." To the Baltimore builder Jacob Small, Jr., Latrobe wrote (June 30, 1816) that Davis "is perfectly master of the whole business of Centers [that is, centering] let them be ever so complicated, & having worked under me for 10 Years he understands me in a moments [sic], & saves me a vast deal of trouble in drawing, by his habitual perception of my intentions. But besides this, his fidelity & integrity cannot be replaced by any superior." The same document notes the attachment of Davis's men to him. One suspects that Davis did suffer from one defect, an imperfect degree of literacy, which may partly account for his obscurity in the general history of Washington.

A second key figure was, of course, George Blagden. Material in the report of the House Committee on the Public Buildings of February 18, 1817, identifies him as "inspector of stone and superintendent of the stone cutters and setters" at both the Capitol and, under James Hoban, the President's House.

And Andrei stood ready, with some of his pupils. Latrobe's letter of May 2, 1815, to the commissioners records that the Italian now had two assistants, McIntosh and Henderson. (When Latrobe drew up a bill for the cathedral necks on November 5, 1817, he identified Henderson and Somerville as then working for Andrei. Thus, at least three of Andrei's pupils had some part to play in campaign two.) As to the other men, although Latrobe had by no means a flawless work force, he could draw upon individuals whom he had accustomed to his wishes over a long period of time.

Won over by his first Hall of Representatives to the idea of a mighty colonnade in the House chamber, in 1815 Latrobe united his order of campaign one with his 1803 notion of a theaterlike hall. The history of the colonnade in campaign two revolved around the superior materials that he now determined to use, particularly for the shafts and the capitals. As of spring 1815, he had in mind employing white marble from Loudoun County, Virginia, for the shafts. On May 2 he wrote the commissioners urging that they send Andrei to Italy to have the capitals worked in marble there under his supervision in the interest of economy, expedience, and quality. In reviving the solution that he had devised for the unexecuted center part of the Capitol in campaign one, Latrobe noted that Jefferson had approved that earlier scheme.

Latrobe secured his wish: Andrei left for Italy in August, and at some point he further received authorization to prepare the Ionic capitals for the Senate there too. In the course of the summer Latrobe learned that the old quarries could no longer provide the best grade of Aquia stone that he had used formerly and that he could not hope to quarry the Loudoun County white marble. But the potential of Potomac breccia for sumptuously varicolored, monolithic shafts had seized his imagination, as witness the already quoted letter of August 13 to Robert Goodloe Harper. A tale of mighty exertion begins here.

In 1815 the men removed the ruins of the first colonnade. As of July 18 Latrobe informed the commissioners that better wages elsewhere in the District of Columbia were luring his hands away. The commissioners agreed to competitive pay the next day, but they and their architect had not seen the last of labor problems, which included a stonecutters' strike in late August.

Confronted with competition from other public buildings in Washington and Baltimore—the latter group included Robert Mills's Washington Monument, Godefroy's Battle Monument, and Latrobe and

Godefroy's exchange—Latrobe proposed to the commissioners (January 23, 1816) that they import French stonecutters for the Capitol. On February 1 the commissioners acquiesced, but the plan somehow died.

March 1816 brought Latrobe humiliation. The commissioners first extracted from their architect his admission that his position depended on obedience to them, and subsequently they fired an indeterminate number of workers. Latrobe pleaded for the men and against this inroad on the Capitol's resources, but he pleaded fruitlessly. After all this ugliness, he repeatedly acknowledged that the system under which he worked vested no authority in him.

That spring was otherwise eventful. On a quarry trip of March 11–25 Latrobe decided in favor of the breccia shafts. On April 10, arguing for his choice, he informed the commissioners that he could have breccia monoliths ready for August 1817, the earliest that he could plan to set the House entablature. The contract for this stone went neglected, however. Congress ousted the three commissioners and replaced their positions with a single post, filled by Col. Samuel Lane in May. Meanwhile, and ominously, whereas the completed capitals ought to have left Italy on April 1, they did not, nor did any word of them reach Washington then.

Two developments in June 1816 have a place here. On June 2 Latrobe wrote to Samuel Clapham, the owner of the land on the Potomac in Montgomery County, Maryland, and Loudoun County, Virginia, where the breccia deposit lay, that Commissioner Lane had made some kind of contract with a quarrier named John Hartnet (or Hartnett) to quarry the stone. About Hartnet one knows very little other than that he had lately arrived from England and that Latrobe had confidence in him. In the same month Lane misguidedly decided to dismiss Shadrach Davis, a disaster that Latrobe labored to forestall. He went so far as to solicit his friend and Lane's contact Jacob Small (who had contracted to build the Baltimore Exchange and whose son William would shortly become a Latrobe pupil) to send the commissioner a carefully calculated letter, for which Latrobe supplied the model (June 30). Davis kept his place—this time.

In the ensuing months, Latrobe's initially good relations with Lane began to go bad, and Hartnet encountered a series of costly failures at the quarry. But as of November 3, when Latrobe reported on the subject to Lane, the architect believed that Hartnet could provide monoliths for some if not all of the House shafts (that is, the remainder would

have to be constructed from multiple drums) and advised Lane to contract for breccia columns and pilasters for the Senate apartments. On
November 28 Latrobe wrote in his report for 1816 that he expected the
first piece of breccia, a block for one of the antas, or pilasters, within a
few days. Via Andrei the year netted him two more Italians, Giuseppe
Franzoni's sculptor-brother Carlo (1786–1819) and the ornamental carver
Francesco Iardella. When Latrobe wrote to Lane on December 3 he
said of the House and Senate capitals only that he expected them on
the first public ship from the Mediterranean.

The first block of breccia reached Washington, and, in response to
the curiosity that it excited, Latrobe wrote an account of it, with a slight
notice of the quarrying enterprise, which appeared in the *National
Intelligencer* (January 24, 1817). Immediately after a visit to Hartnet,
he wrote to Lane a more detailed account of the quarry (January 31).
On February 1, Lane informed the House Committee on the Public
Buildings that obstacles to supplying the breccia, an endeavor that now
looked less promising, and the mysterious absence of the Italian capitals
retarded the work on the Hall of Representatives. By now, Latrobe found
it a misery to work under Lane. Hartnet's financial means had begun
to ebb perilously; Latrobe had already involved his own resources in the
attempt to keep the quarrier from going under. The architect hoped to
win the support of the next president for the breccia, and on February
28 he wrote to the man on whom he pinned his hope.

On March 3, 1817, Congress appropriated an additional $100,000
for the public buildings; on March 4 James Monroe, a president determined to expedite the completion of the Capitol, took office. Monroe
judiciously resorted to Brig. Gen. Joseph G. Swift, head of the Corps
of Engineers, and Lt. Col. George Bomford of the Ordnance Department, for architectural counsel. Swift, Bomford, and Latrobe, all former members of the extinct United States Military Philosophical Society,
worked together well, even congenially. And Lane's star sank.

An undercurrent of the preceding year, a set of challenges to Latrobe's
competence, now reached the surface. The early history of the problem
is unclear, but apparently Blagden played a leading role in the formu-
lation of the challenges. Broadly, the contentions stated that Latrobe's
proposed north and south wings would collapse. In a related but distinguishable set of issues, the case ran that the breccia could not be wrought
and polished nor could breccia columns support even their own weight.
(A Latrobe letter of March 26, 1806, to Bishop John Carroll regarding

an analogous challenge to his fifth design for the Baltimore Cathedral makes clear his opinion of artisans who opposed rule of thumb to the scientific calculations of an architect.) The two military engineers altogether vindicated Latrobe's ability as a structural engineer. But Monroe, following their recommendation, vetoed the masonry domes for the House and Senate in the interest of expedience, to Latrobe's pain. Even so the architect would look with gratitude upon the president (who interested himself so far as to visit the breccia quarries with Latrobe, Swift, and Bomford) for saving the breccia columns.

Now, with Swift and Bomford's advice and Monroe's support, came a phase of boldly scaled measures. A conference of president, engineers, and architect of March 21, 1817, resulted in the decision to send the quarrier employed for the national arsenals, with all the men he could hire, to Hartnet. Latrobe, reporting to the latter on the meeting, exuberantly declared, "in fact, you are to have all America to help you, if necessary." After the trip to the quarry Swift and Bomford made recommendations to Monroe (March 31). Among other points, they advised hiring a hundred good men and a leader in New York or Boston, they outlined a system for federal operation of the breccia quarry, and for that quarry they advised hiring not only the available men in the district and Maryland but also thirty to forty quarrymen and twenty stonecutters in Philadelphia and a like contingent in New York. Swift, shortly to depart for New York State to oversee the provision of stone for the Senate orders per these recommendations, would handle the latter. They also advised that Latrobe hire draftsmen (long a sore point with him and now an urgent matter), and this measure gave him William F. Small. Swift and Bomford thought that the new program could ready the Capitol for the House and the Senate by the end of the year.

Spring rolled into summer. At some point arrangements secured American marble bases and upper cinctures (the ornamental element between the shaft and the capital) for the House columns. On June 28 Latrobe informed Jefferson that nine unpolished drums of breccia, enough for three columns, had reached the Capitol, where work proceeded at maximum intensity, while a hundred men now labored in the breccia quarry. On July 24 he shared with Jefferson the bad news that the collapse of the locks on the lower Potomac Canal forced the breccia now to come overland. On August 12 he wrote Jefferson exultantly over the future of the breccia, but he still had only nine drums and these not yet finished. By September 26 an order had gone out for fifteen marble polishers from Philadelphia.

Before the summer ended, Latrobe had fallen into Monroe's disfavor and Lane had gained ground. Friends of Charles Bulfinch, the gentleman architect turned professional, had begun fostering the idea of replacing Latrobe, Lane, or both men with him, while artisan-builders had started eyeing Latrobe's position. In September, learning that the wings could not go into use that year, Monroe—so Latrobe believed—angrily put the blame on him. At the end of October Lane decided to transfer Davis to the President's House and bring the clerk of the works there to the Capitol, apparently owing—like the firing of the men in March 1816—to the machinations of Latrobe's incompetent foreman of the carpenters. On October 31, after Latrobe opposed the transfer, Lane wrote him an authoritarian letter directing him to mind his own business. Latrobe's current work on the Baltimore Exchange became a bigger and bigger bone of contention between him and the commissioner. At last finding his position intolerable, the architect resigned on November 20.

Bulfinch succeeded Latrobe and executed his designs for the south and north wings with a high degree of fidelity. By the time that Bulfinch took over early in 1818, the long-awaited House and Senate capitals had reached Washington. On November 21 of that year Bulfinch reported that the House colonnade had gone into place and he had the wooden dome over it in hand. The House and the Senate took possession of their new apartments at the end of 1819. Expenses had far exceeded Latrobe's calculations. Thus, on December 20, 1819, Lane informed the House that, because of the painful disappointments at the quarry, the House shafts had cost not the $1,550 apiece estimated by Latrobe but something like $5,000.

What of the results of all the labor? One can fault the execution of the second colonnade. For example, the Italian capitals suffer from a degree of stiffness. A close look at the shafts reveals the evidence of the struggle with the stone. Thus, the joints between drums fail to align from column to column, and inserted patches compensate for the fragments of breccia that broke off during fabrication. Indeed, one wonders what Latrobe would have made of the finesse of garden-variety classical masonry buildings erected about a century after his time, when American architects could rely on a major industry for elements worked of

Figure 5.　B. Henry Latrobe, Statuary Hall (old Hall of Representatives), U.S. Capitol, Washington, D.C. 1815–19, with later alterations. From Glenn Brown, *History of the United States Capitol*, vol. 1 (Washington, D.C.: Government Printing Office, 1900), pl. 101. (Winterthur Museum Library.)

stone. Nonetheless, in the old Hall of Representatives, today's Statuary Hall (fig. 5), Latrobe's mighty conception transcends its imperfect execution as well as the drastically altered state of the room, and the hall ranks as a genuinely great neoclassical interior.

Latrobe's kind of architecture, initially a novelty in the United States, in essence depended on the detailed working out of a unified conception within a single, learned mind, the mind of the architect. But to migrate from mind to matter, or rather from the architect's drawings to brick, stone, timber, and metal, the design required the labors of craftsmen. One can make nine points here about Latrobe in relation to his artisans in the United States.

1. Latrobe repeatedly found the kind of craftsman that he needed at hand, even in the field of monumental masonry construction. While his conception of all-masonry construction was novel to Americans around 1800, the nation had begun to grope toward a grand civic architecture before his arrival. Practitioners of relevant crafts—Lenthall and Blagden can stand for the group—thus stood ready for Latrobe.

2. But circumstance did not uniformly meet Latrobe's needs, conspicuously at the Capitol. Building this grandest of Latrobe's architectural works required national measures, measures national both in the geographic sense (for instance, the hunts for men in 1806 and 1817) and in the sense of federal facilities (as witness the role of the Washington Navy Yard, the parts played by army personnel in 1817, and the federal takeover of the breccia quarry). Building the Capitol further required international measures in the case of the most important class of ornamental carving, the capitals of the most enriched interior orders.

3. Latrobe wrote to his brother Christian Ignatius (November 4, 1804), "[I have] to make the Men who are to execute, as well as [make] the designs of my works. Now and then indeed I pick up a ready made English artisan, the rest I manufacture out of American Carpenters, who, to do them justice are incomparable Jacks of all trades." He shaped his men to suit his special requirements, men such as Andrei, and Lenthall—Latrobe's expositions of theory to him seem germane to this issue—and Davis, whose responsiveness to the architect's wishes represents the desired result. Latrobe's labors further extended to numberless humble names that history has lost.

4. Latrobe reshaped craftsmen, but in the case of an artisan such as Blagden or Andrei or Davis, he valued the mastery of craft intricacies that the individual had developed on his own. When Latrobe had such a man in his service, he had an expert whom he could consult about such technical matters as estimates or problems of execution.

5. In rare instances Latrobe had an artisan on whom he could rely to make decisions affecting his design. That is, he actually relinquished his otherwise absolute control over the unity of his conception by permitting such a man to decide on the form of some detail. In this small class of men Lenthall stands preeminent.

6. Time and again Latrobe's role as an architect set him in opposition to artisans, both to individuals and to the class, particularly for two reasons. First, on the strength of tradition these men claimed the lion's share of building opportunities. Second, in repeated cases they

presumed—often successfully—to interfere with the execution of Latrobe's designs, as Blagden did in campaign two.

7. It was not Latrobe and his patrons alone who profited from the skills of his men. The Baltimore works of Andrei in 1808 may stand as cases in point. The extent of this is hard to calculate until one assembles more information on such subjects as the activities of Latrobe's artisans and the careers of Andrei's pupils.

8. In three instances, all important, Latrobe initiated the sons of artisans—Graff, Strickland, Small—into the ranks of his two professions, architecture and engineering.

9. In Latrobe's greatest stone buildings—the Bank of Pennsylvania, the Capitol, the Baltimore Cathedral—one can recognize shortcomings in the masonry work. These very shortcomings, standing as they do at the outset of monumental stone architecture in the United States, tell how grand a task Latrobe set himself and his men.

The Moravian Craftsman in Eighteenth-Century North Carolina
Paula Welshimer Locklair

After traveling through woods for many days, the sight of this little settlement of Moravians is highly curious and interesting. Between 200 and 300 persons of this sect here assembled live in brotherly love and set a laudable example of industry, unfortunately too little observed and followed in this part of the country. Every man follows some occupation; every woman is engaged in some feminine work. . . . I found every one hard at work; such a scene of industry, perhaps, exists no where in so small a place.[1]

This 1790 description of the Moravian town of Salem, North Carolina, from the journal of William Loughton Smith expresses the admiration felt by many eighteenth-century visitors to Salem (fig. 1). The Moravians' dedication to an exemplary life was not only admirable but also successful. They aspired to perfection, and although their continual efforts to attain it—efforts evident in their religion, economy, and society in general—were often hindered by unforeseen obstacles, their strength of character and spirit prevailed. The community prospered and grew.

Craftsmen in Salem worked diligently at their trades, but much of their time was also devoted to church services, council meetings, and

[1] *Journal of William Loughton Smith, 1790–1791*, ed. Albert Matthews (Cambridge: At the University Press, 1917), p. 73.

Figure 1.   Ludwig Gottfried von Redeken, A *View of Salem in N. Carolina*, 1787. Watercolor on paper; H. 10¼", W. 16¼". (Old Salem, Inc.)

their families. The Moravian craftsman was not an independent agent. At all times he was held accountable for his behavior and was expected to accept the respect as well as the responsibilities he merited. It is important to emphasize that no more or less was required from the craftsman than from any other member of a Moravian community. When a craftsman or anyone else in eighteenth-century America said that he lived in Salem he was revealing a dedication to a way of life focused on Christian principles which were established by the church and which directed a person's religious, economic, and social affairs. As part of a community so centrally influenced, the craftsman produced artifacts that embody the values of Moravian culture. My study, then, is not so much concerned with the art or the artifact as it is with defining some of the elements of a developing culture that directly affected the craftsman.

To begin this investigation we must look at who the North Carolina Moravians were. The idea to involve the Unity of Brethren—*Unitas Fratrum*, commonly called the Moravians—in the colonization of a portion of North Carolina originated with a British nobleman, John, Lord Carteret, Earl Granville, who was heir to one of the eight lords proprietors from whom Carolina received its founding charter. Granville, who admired the Moravians' industry and stability, offered their leaders in London the opportunity to purchase some of his land in North Carolina if they would settle there. In the fall of 1752, August Gottlieb Spangenberg, the leader of the Unity in America, set out for Carolina with his surveying party on a mission to choose a tract of land. Fortunately for us, he kept a detailed diary of this strenuous and enlightening venture. The entry for January 8, 1753, records, "Towards the end of the year we came into this neighborhood and found a 'body of land' which is probably the best left in North Carolina." They bought this tract of 98,985 acres from Lord Granville. But Spangenberg also noted with dismay and surprise, "Trade and business are poor in North Carolina. . . . Almost nobody has a trade. In Edenton I saw one smith, one cobbler, and one tailor at work. . . . whether there are others I do not know."[2] Edenton at that time was the largest city in North Carolina. The startling dearth of craftsmen certainly challenged the ambition of this exploring party and encouraged them to proceed with their plans to establish an organized and productive trade center.

Interspersed throughout Spangenberg's diary are detailed observations of springs and available pasture land as well as potential mill sites and other geographical features, which leave the reader with a vivid image of this uninhabited wilderness. From reading discussions and descriptions contained in other early Moravian documents, it becomes clear that only through continuing faith, untiring efforts, and detailed planning was this group able to develop not only its theocratic society but also a reputation for excellent craftsmanship.

On November 17, 1753, the first pioneering band of fifteen Moravian men from Pennsylvania arrived in the newly acquired land they called Wachovia and began the arduous task of founding a settlement, which they named Bethabara (Hebrew for "House of Passage"). Since maximum production would be required from a minimum number of dedicated workers, these men had been carefully selected according to their abilities and skills. Most of them were multitalented, like Henrich Feldhausen, for example, who was thirty-eight and a shoemaker, carpenter, millwright, cooper, sievemaker, turner, and farmer. It was fortunate that the Brethren anticipated their remote situation realistically

---

[2] Adelaide L. Fries, *Records of the Moravians in North Carolina*, 6 vols. (Raleigh: North Carolina Historical Commission, 1922–43), 1:59, 38–39.

and supplied themselves with capable craftsmen because, in the absence of stores and trading posts, they had "to manufacture all . . . household furnishings, which otherwise could be bought and time saved thereby."[3]

Gradually the frontier settlement of Bethabara grew as more land was cleared and cultivated. As additional people were needed and as sufficient accommodations became ready for them, more brave souls were sent from Pennsylvania. This increased the population of the "Oeconomie"—the housekeeping system in which an individual's private property remained his own, but income from the land, farm products, and industries automatically became part of a common fund, and life's necessities, such as food and housing, were supplied to all. As success encouraged independence of families, the Oeconomie gradually dissolved. There can be no question that the Moravians' isolation inspired self-sufficiency. By meeting their needs as best they could, they learned a new kind of respect for their past training, acquired an appreciation for the life they had left in Pennsylvania, and developed a patience that was continually tested.

Although by 1780 there were six Moravian congregations in Wachovia, the producing craftsmen lived and worked primarily in the three earliest settlements of Bethabara (1753), Bethania (1759), and Salem (1771). Most of what we now know about Bethabara comes from two sources, the written records and the gleanings from an extensive archaeological excavation that took place in 1964. There also remain a few pieces of furniture attributed to this early period (figs. 2, 3, 4) as well as an outstanding collection of pottery from the shop of master potter Gottfried Aust. It is obvious from the records that the people of Bethabara were interested first and foremost in providing themselves with the basic necessities and what few comforts they could manage. But the Moravians were not an aesthetically plain or dull people. They enjoyed, for example, Brother Aust's colorful glazes and slip decoration (fig. 5) as well as what decoration their short supply of tools and manpower would allow in the production of furniture (figs. 6, 7). Special interest in more sophisticated products is evident as early as February 1755 when records reveal that a turning lathe was made.[4]

The bedstead, both a necessity and a comfort, is the first specific

[3] Fries, *Records*, 1:73; August Gottlieb Spangenberg to the Brethren in Bethabara, North Carolina, June 29, 1755, Archives of the Moravian Church in America, Southern Province, Winston-Salem (hereafter cited as AMCA).

[4] Fries, *Records*, 1:124.

Figure 2.   Schrank. Bethabara or Bethania, 1760–80. Yellow pine with "Spanish brown" paint (paint restored); H. 90⅜″, W. 72¾″, D. 26⅜″. (Old Salem, Inc.)

Figure 3.   Corner cupboard. Bethabara or Salem, 1760–76. Yellow pine with blue and orange paint (paint restored); H. 82⅝", D. 33". (Wachovia Historical Society.)

Figure 4. Table. Bethabara, 1753–60. Walnut; L. 52⅝⁄₁₆″, H. 29″, W. 32″. (Old Salem, Inc.)

furniture form mentioned as being made in Wachovia (fig. 8). In June 1755 an anonymous Bethabara diarist noted the need for bedsteads: "we held a conference as to the best and cheapest and most satisfactory way to make bedsteads," and he continued a week later: "We put all the Brethren to work making bedsteads, and completed as many as we need, that is twenty-three."[5] These were built for the newly completed Single Brothers House. Such diary references suggest not only the importance of the bedsteads but also the makers' sense of success at the completion of the project.

The Moravians' success was not just luck. Throughout the records one is aware that a method was developing to deal with life and its demands: a problem or a need would be identified, discussion would follow, and finally, if possible, some action would be taken to resolve the situation. Procrastinating or ignoring a problem was simply never allowed. Community pride and a sense of history, even in those early days, are consistently apparent. Accomplishments were frequently noted, as when the same Bethabara diarist recorded in September 1755 that

[5] Fries, *Records*, 1:131–32.

Figure 5.   Plate, attributed to Gottfried Aust. Bethabara, ca. 1780.
Green, brown, and red slip over a white slip wash; Diam. 13⁹⁄₁₆″. (Old
Salem, Inc.)

"Work at the mill continues. Today the frame was raised, and we sang
several verses to the Saviour as we laid the foundations of this building
in His name, placing our names under the sill at the south-east corner."[6] The practice of singing hymns of praise and thanksgiving during
the raising of a building continued for many years among the Moravians. To hear the songs and witness the solemn, grateful mood of the
working men laboring in the quiet of the wilderness must have been a
moving experience.

[6]Fries, *Records*, 1:137.

Figure 6. Table. Bethabara or Salem, 1760–70. Walnut with poplar and yellow pine secondary woods; L. 47⅞″, H. 28½″, W. 27⅞″. (Old Salem, Inc.)

After the Brothers had completed the primary structures necessary to sustain life, they began to add buildings to house some of the trades. In November 1755 the craftsmen began to furnish "their quarters in the small houses with tables, chairs, and benches, arranging them to suit their trades." With working areas established, more organized production could begin. We also know that Aust "made a small oven and burned some earthen-ware" in April 1756, and in August of the same year "Br. Aust burned earthenware in his new kiln for the first time, and was pleased with it." The Brothers' joy was increased a month later with Aust's next success: "Br. Aust burned pottery for the second time, the glazing did well, and so the great need is at last relieved."[7] It took time to establish the trades, but the production of necessary household items was always very important (fig. 9), and through intense perseverance, the quantity and variety of Bethabara output increased.

November 1756 was another important month for the artisans because "The new joiner's shop was finished on the 26th. . . . Ceilings

[7] Fries, *Records*, 1:147, 158, 159, 172.

Figure 7.   Side chair.
Salem, 1770–75. Walnut;
H. 41⅛", W. 18¾", seat
height 17". (Old Salem,
Inc.)

were placed in the kitchen, pottery, and Brothers House. Br. Aust burned
stove tiles, and when they were ready he set up stoves in the Gemein
Haus and the Brothers House, probably the first in Carolina" (fig. 10).[8]
It is not only we who are impressed with these early accomplishments
and "firsts," so were the Brothers themselves. Today we analyze Moravian tile stoves primarily for their aesthetic qualities, but surely for the
Brethren it was more important that Aust had helped to solve a critical
heating problem.

By the end of 1759 the settlement at Bethabara had made great
strides; an admirable example had been set for those who were to come

[8] Fries, *Records*, 1:161.

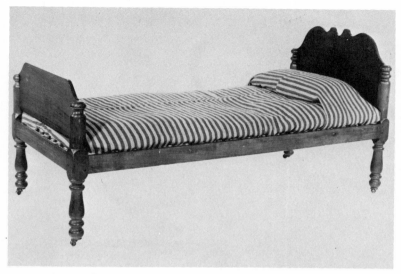

Figure 8.   Bed. Wachovia area, possibly Salem, 1765–80. Walnut; L. 71⅛″, H. 35⅜″, W. 32¾″. (Wachovia Historical Society.)

later. With a population of only seventy-three, the Brethren were justified in feeling pride in their successes. "In addition to the ordinary work of each day on the farm and in the trades we have cleared 60 acres of land this year; have built a house for those who look after the cows, also a large shed, a new smithy, a new house at the tanyard, a laboratory for the doctor, a new wash-house for the Single Brethren." There were thirty-eight Single Brothers, ten married men, and one widower in this small population; thus over half of the citizenry were able-bodied and skilled men. Although personal letters and the church records reveal the hardships and often the homesickness felt by the Brethren, they managed to maintain themselves. Their spirit, by and large, was undaunted as "All went again contentedly and cheerfully to work."[9]

In 1768 Frederic William Marshall, administrator of Wachovia, wrote to the Unity Board in Herrnhut, Saxony, declaring of Bethabara that "in this land, and so far from the sea, there is [no other town] like it." But Bethabara was primarily agricultural, while the Brethren's pur-

[9] Fries, *Records*, 1:208, 246.

Figure 9.   Water jug, Gottfried Aust pottery site. Bethabara, ca. 1765. Black glaze on interior and shoulder; H. 11⅜". (Old Salem, Inc.)

pose in coming to North Carolina had been to establish a permanent town that could supply manufactured goods to fellow Moravians and to trade with their neighbors. This was to be the function of Salem, as Marshall outlined in 1768 when he wrote to Herrnhut that the settlement was "intended not so much for farming as for the various businesses; and for the Choir Houses and other establishments, and for the supervision of all Wachovia." Unlike the country congregations of Bethabara and Bethania, Salem was to be a congregation town, which "differ[ed] from other Congregations in that it [was] more like one family, where the religious and material condition of each member [was] known in detail."[10]

[10] Fries, *Records*, 2:605, 606, 1:313.

Figure 10 *(facing page)*.   Tile stove, attributed to Gottfried Aust or Rudolph Christ. Bethabara, ca. 1780. Unglazed and finished with stove black; H. 59", W. 17¾", D. 43⁵⁄₁₆". (Old Salem, Inc.)

Because of a multitude of delays and hindrances beyond the Brothers' control, the site for Salem had not been chosen until 1765, and construction, according to a definite town plan, had not begun until 1766. But the Moravians were intensely aware of the passage of time and of the possibility that others might open stores and operate trades that would preempt their market. Finally in 1772, after six years of clearing land for planting crops, chopping out streets, and constructing buildings, the town of Salem was ready for habitation.

The organization of the religious and financial aspects of church affairs that had been predetermined for Bethabara were appropriately adjusted for Salem. The craftsmen and all other members of the society were subject to the same rules as established by a management hierarchy which systematically directed all aspects of life in Moravian communities. The Unity Elders Conference in Herrnhut directed the affairs of all congregations around the world through local administrators. There were four principal governing boards at Salem: the Elders Conference, the *Aufseher Collegium* (Board of Overseers), the Greater Helpers Conference, and the Congregation Council. Each consisted of a leader and board members.

The Elders Conference was concerned primarily with spiritual supervision, passing on all applications for reception into the congregation and for confirmation, administering church discipline, and establishing religious services. Only the elders could put a question to the lot, which was a method by which important community matters were decided. Only one of three answers was possible: *ja, nein,* or a blank. The Aufseher Collegium supervised the material welfare of the community and in particular regulated the finances of the Community Diacony (a term defined later), and supervised the trades, the professions, and all commerce in Salem. The Greater Helpers Conference had no executive powers, but was to act as the "eyes" of the congregation, thereby keeping the other boards informed of matters needing their attention. The Congregation Council dealt mainly with issues that affected all members of the community. It met upon request of the Elders Conference and the Aufseher Collegium or if five Brothers made a written request for a meeting.

Women served along with the men on all boards except the Aufseher Collegium, an indication of the high degree of equality between the sexes. However, the husband's professional standing in the town seems to have directly affected that of his wife, as shown by an Elders

Conference that recorded: "That Sr. Aust is a member of the congregation council is not to be questioned, since her husband is a master."[11]

Except for the Congregation Council, all boards met on a regular basis, generally once a week, some first thing in the morning and some in the early evening. Each kept accurate minutes, and it is largely due to these extraordinary published volumes that we have such varied and precise information about the Moravians in Wachovia.

In addition to the governing boards, there were three business organizations called diaconies: Congregation, Single Brothers, and Single Sisters. Each had its own overseer and internal hierarchy, and each operated its own businesses. The Congregation Diacony, representing the whole community, operated the pottery, store, tavern, red tannery, and mill. It required these businesses to present a yearly inventory, which would then be compared year by year. Because of these accounts we know a great deal about the materials and tools used by the craftsmen. The inventory also originally served to distinguish between tools and materials owned by the diaconies and those owned by the craftsmen. In order to organize such matters further each adult in Salem was encouraged to write a will specifying the disposal of his possessions.

The Single Brothers Diacony operated the slaughterhouse, the brewery and distillery, a plantation, and the trades in the Single Brothers House and Workshop (fig. 11). The Single Sisters Diacony (fig. 12) was not quite so clearly defined in terms of actual producing industries, but the Sisters generated income by weaving, knitting, spinning, glovemaking, and laundering; and they received wages for working in private households and gardens. One of their most important functions, however, was providing teachers for the Little Girls School, begun in 1772. The Aufseher Collegium emphasized in 1786 that "It must be expressly understood that the Single Sisters shall not lose the spirit of service for the other Choirs, especially in families and at harvest time."[12] Each person, craftsman and noncraftsman alike, was a member of a "choir." In all Moravian congregation towns the people were divided for religious training and interests into choirs by age, sex, and marital status: married people, single men, single women, widows, widowers, older girls, older boys, and children.

[11] Edmund Schwarze, Elders Conference, June 28, 1780 (unpublished translations made for Old Salem, Inc.), AMCA.

[12] Erika Huber, Aufseher Collegium, April 6, 1786 (unpublished translations made for Old Salem, Inc.), AMCA.

Figure 11.   Single Brothers House, 1769 with 1786 addition, and Single Brothers Workshop, 1771; reconstructed. Winston-Salem. (Old Salem, Inc.)

In a diacony there could be only one master of each trade or business, thus eliminating competition and friction. As the Salem trades were getting under way in 1772, the Helpers Conference clearly stated that "In a Gemein Ort [Congregation Town] no one can start a business, open a store, or begin a profession, until the Congregation has recognized and installed him as a Master-workman. If a business, store, or profession is already being carried on in the town all other Brethren who wish to work in it, whether they come from Europe or Pennsylvania, or grow up here, shall be considered as journeymen under the Master-workman, and shall be personally responsible to him." But the basic and most important reason for anyone to become a resident of a Gemein Ort was "a special call from the Lord to live in that place." After one felt such a call he would be received into the congregation upon signing the "Brotherly Agreement" and promising willingness to abide by the "Rules and Regulations" drawn up by the General Synod in Herrnhut. According to these rules, the "Master-workmen must give Bond that they will not treat their apprentices in any manner contrary

Figure 12. Single Sisters House, 1786 with 1819 addition. Winston-Salem. (Old Salem, Inc.)

to the Congregation Rules."[13] Many craftsmen happily joined the Moravians, but others sometimes found life too restricted and left.

Boys were bound into a seven-year apprenticeship when they were about fourteen. However, if a boy demonstrated little aptitude or liking for a craft, he could change trades and try to find a more suitable one. By the time he was indentured, he had already attended Salem Boys School for about eight years. Therefore, by the age of apprenticeship, he had completed a well-rounded curriculum, which included arithmetic, English, surveying, history, and geography. Once apprenticed, he moved into the Single Brothers House, where he lived until he married, at which time he built or purchased his own home. The church leased the land, but any improvements made were the owner's. Also, when a master craftsman married, and the shop was moved out of the Single Brothers House, he was allowed a shop sign giving his name and profession and perhaps displaying a sample or a picture of the finished goods. At the time of his marriage he was released from his debts in

[13] Fries, *Records*, 2:724, 725, 726.

order that the Sister would not be entering into poverty.

Respect for a master's position and authority was expected from the journeymen and apprentices. "[They] must stand in proper subordination to their masters, and no journeyman much less apprentice, leaves his work or remains away from work whenever he pleases." The "greatest duty" of the trade master was to supervise apprentices and journeymen and keep them "industriously" at work so that they did not "just hang around all day." A journeyman or an apprentice was not to take on new work without the direction of the master, since this would foster too great a sense of independence, which might cause a "terrible disorder."[14]

In principle, the Moravians did not believe in slavery. Blacks were neither taken into a craftsman's shop nor taught a trade, although occasionally several worked in the community as day laborers or perhaps in service at the tavern. The paucity of black labor surprised two men from Virginia, who spent a day in Salem in 1773. "Among other questions they asked how many negroes we had? Answer, two. They were the more surprised to find that white people had done so much work."[15]

Even before the establishment of Salem and the new organization of trades offered by the facilities in the Single Brothers House and the diacony system, the Moravians' purpose—to rear and train their boys to be responsible members of society—had been well known. The English rector of Braunschweig on the Cape Fear River asked the Moravians to take care of his son, as he, the father, was returning to England. "The Reason I choose to have him brought up under this Care is, that I look upon them to be a sober, pious and exemplary prudent society of Christians, who will bring him up in a laudable and virtuous Education and some Profession."[16]

Order in all aspects of life was important in a Moravian community. The Moravians believed that an organized and orderly life was more productive and, therefore, of higher quality than a life left to chance. Punctuality was stressed: the boys were expected to be at work by a certain time each day, to take only a reasonable amount of time for meals, and never to leave their work until the shop was closed. The master decided the working hours by taking into consideration the

---

[14] Edmund Schwarze, Helpers Conference, October 12, 1772, AMCA; Huber, Aufseher Collegium, September 20, 1775, October 12, 1772.

[15] Fries, *Records*, 2:788.

[16] Fries, *Records*, 1:244.

demands of the trade and the strength of the apprentice, the master often becoming personally involved in the welfare of his helpers. Some masters relaxed their shop rules by the 1780s and permitted the boys to leave early on Saturday (which, as the Sabbath, was already a slightly shortened workday). The Aufseher Collegium, however, recommended that such leniency be stopped.[17]

In 1774 an agreement was made guaranteeing a set salary for trade masters who worked for the diaconies. The journeymen were usually paid a weekly wage. In 1775 a "Trade Conference" was held to discuss salaries and wages more fully and to encourage close contact among the tradesmen. At this conference it was also resolved that some more or less seasonal trades—such as those of the carpenter and the mason—would be paid accordingly; the daily wage for the long summer day was to be more than for a short winter day. This arrangement also applied to the master joiner when he worked by the day. By 1780 the Elders Conference had decided that masters who had accounts with the Congregation Diacony would receive 6 percent of the profit of the shop, and those who had been especially diligent during the year would receive a bonus. Later it was also decided to encourage the journeymen and apprentices a bit more, so a loyal and diligent boy received a bonus or a gift.[18]

Many craftsmen suffered financial difficulties through the years, but apparently the strain was particularly severe for some in 1774, as the Elders Conference that year admonished each person serving in a Congregation Diacony trade to take only what had been assigned to him, "otherwise it is sinning."[19] But a craftsman could make an honest appeal for an increase in wages and dire circumstances would be considered, the Brethren believing it always best to avoid debt.

The Moravian communities were automatically set apart from other towns of the southern colonies, not only because of their remote locations but also because of the laws established by their governing body, the church. The Brethren, specifically the Trade Conference, tried to enforce the insular regulations, but conditions were changing and influ-

[17] Huber, Aufseher Collegium, September 25, 1787.

[18] Schwarze, Helpers Conference, November 14, 1774 (set salary agreement); Fries, *Records*, 2:899 (seasonal salaries); Schwarze, Elders Conference, October 11, 1780 (masters' percentage of profit); Erika Huber, Congregation Council, November 7, 1793, AMCA (journeyman and apprentice bonuses).

[19] Schwarze, Elders Conference, July 19, 1774.

ences from the outside were becoming stronger. Consequently, in 1777, the Elders Conference had to face infiltrations and deal with infractions. The elders were "anxious that [their] Brethren might not be torn out of the congregation-plan into a world-conforming way of life." They admonished the Brethren not to stray away from "correct congregation principles."[20]

Occasionally a master would request permission to take a "stranger" into his shop for a time. Usually this was not permitted, because it was feared that these outsiders would have a bad effect on the community's young people, infecting them with worldly rather than worshipful motives for production. The Aufseher Collegium was worried, declaring, "Our Brothers and Sisters must never disregard the principles [which explain] why we are together in this community. All our Brothers should go after their profession as if it were done for the Lord and his sake."[21] The spirit in which a product was crafted was as important as the product itself.

Repeatedly in the records there are discussions about wages, bonuses, and individual master-apprentice and master-diacony conflicts. Most seem to have been resolved with little difficulty. Probably one of the most surprising and distressing events, however, took place in April 1778. The congregation at large and the older members of the Single Brothers Diacony in particular were extremely dismayed when a strike took place among their young apprentices. The dispute was over a wage supplement and the amount to be paid for dinner in the Single Brothers House. The young men "calmly walked away from their work, their leaders looking on sadly," but the next day all returned repentant. The elders decided to "let patience and sympathy have way instead of strict Church discipline." Nevertheless, the offenders were not permitted to attend church services in which the kiss of peace was given. In the eyes of the elders they were rebelling against "Leaders and Conferences which the Lord had approved as constituted authority."[22] No observance of a "wrong" could be ignored, and according to the rules, all were bound in charity to confront an errant Brother with his error.

Although every effort was made to establish and maintain a stable economy, there were often times when Salem was in great need of

[20] Schwarze, Elders Conference, July 19, 1774.
[21] Huber, Aufseher Collegium, October 27, 1795.
[22] Schwarze, Elders Conference, April 3, 1778.

importing master workmen who had the "pilgrim spirit." In Salem there was no lack of work, and the wages were said to be higher than those in Europe. At various times the Moravians in Salem negotiated with Unity officials in Europe for additional craftsmen. For example, in 1786 the Single Brothers were willing to finance the journey to America of a shoemaker, a linen weaver, a tailor, a cook, and a housekeeper. There was also plenty of work for a clockmaker, a silversmith, a cooper, and a pewterer, they explained, but these men would have to bear their own expenses. In that year they did not need a tinsmith, a bookbinder, a glazier, or a painter (whose work was done by the cabinetmaker). They also did not advise the elderly or married people with several children to come. The Brethren examined their needs and were selective about the choices they made. [23]

Frederic Marshall quite candidly enumerated some of the difficulties that would confront a craftsman once he had decided to commit himself to be "faithful, industrious, economical, and obedient to the rules of the congregation." Marshall wrote that one "must think of the large outlay for travel expenses, the difficulty of language, the establishing or taking over of a trade, the thought of marrying before circumstances warrant it, the shortage of family houses which sometimes exists, the expense of building suitable houses, and especially that there is no fund to cover all this except the industry and economy of the Brother himself." [24]

After a Brother arrived in Salem, he not only was responsible for the success of his trade but also had responsibilities to the church, to his peers, and to his family, responsibilities so closely intertwined with his trade that they are hardly distinguishable from it. Like any member of the community, the newly arrived craftsman was assigned to the choir appropriate to his sex, age, and marital status. Each choir had its own responsibilities, meetings, and festival days, and in the cases of the Single Brothers and Single Sisters in Salem, its own choir house where members lived and worked together. The strict order was firm but fair, making life productive and rewarding.

Each choir usually had several religious services each day—morning, noon, and evening—which all choir members were expected to attend. These were "special meetings for edification . . . yea, it is cus-

---

[23] Fries, *Records*, 5:2147.
[24] Fries, *Records*, 5:2147.

tomary for each Choir to begin and to conclude the Day with appearing fellowshiply before the Lord to implore His blessing." During a week there were often additional services, such as lovefeasts, weddings, funerals, and special choir services. Saturday afternoon was held as the Sabbath, for a rest from daily toil, and appropriate services were conducted. The Unity Constitution established the ideal order of the religious services; if all of these services had been held on a regular basis in Wachovia, the Sunday church services would have been almost continual: 8 A.M., litany; 10 A.M., the preaching; 2 P.M., the children's meeting and doctrinal text; 3 P.M., the married people's service; 5 P.M., the liturgical meeting of the Communicants and a song service; toward night, an entire congregation meeting; and at 9 P.M., the evening blessing of the whole congregation.[25] Such services were vitally important elements in the structure of the craftsman's life, and much of his time each day was spent in some kind of religious activities.

Allowances were sometimes made for very inclement weather, during which services were canceled. Seasonal changes also affected them; one record notes: "The winter order of services began today, that is, a service at twilight, before supper, and singstunde at half-past eight when the weather permits." The *Singstunde* was an important—relaxing, yet inspiring—song service which all were encouraged to attend. It was held early enough in the evening so that the "elderly Brethren who [were] tired from the day's work and [could not] keep awake till nine o'clock" could participate.[26]

The lovefeast, a gathering for worship, fellowship, and the sharing of a simple meal, symbolized the unity of secular and religious life in Moravian communities. The lovefeast was held for many reasons, and occasionally there was one specifically for the masters in the workshops of the Congregation Diacony and for Single Brothers, who "were encouraged to thankfulness for the blessing of God on [their] trade during the past year."[27] As they were blessed, they were in turn expected to contribute to the work of the church in foreign missions and missions among the American Indians. Also, each person contributed a certain amount for the lovefeast, and all members of the community over sixteen years of age made contributions to the Poor Fund. These funds

[25] Fries, *Records*, 3:1006, 1010–11.
[26] Fries, *Records*, 5:2056, 3:778.
[27] Fries, *Records*, 5:2086.

were available to help not only the poor of Salem, but also, upon occasion, beggars who would come to town seeking help.

The members of the congregation also donated funds to projects that affected the entire community, such as the new clock tower built in 1780. They also contributed according to their means to the "collections for the Heathen, for the Children, and for the poor of the Unity . . . and [for] arrangements made to cover the cost of copying and sending the *Gemein Nachrichten*," a newsletter written weekly in Herrnhut and sent periodically to all the Moravian provinces, where it was copied and sent to individual towns. This was an important means by which the Moravians kept abreast of the situation of the Brethren. "In our isolation the Gemein Nachrichten have been a blessed means of keeping in touch with our dear Brethren and Sisters."[28]

In Wachovia not only were the Moravians interested in their own settlements throughout the world, but they were also anxious for news of America at large. By 1772 they were receiving the Wilmington, North Carolina, newspaper—one copy each for the store, the Single Brothers House, and the tavern.[29]

Much correspondence was exchanged between the Wachovia and Pennsylvania settlements—not a casual activity, since one had to plan well ahead to have letters ready for transporting. As one Brother noted, "I am writing this in advance because in harvest time there is little travel, and opportunities to send letters come only unexpectedly and go just as quickly." The Brethren were always very anxious to receive any news of their friends and loved ones in America and abroad: "With regard to having news," one wrote, "we must learn to wait and even when all patience is at an end, still learn to wait." The postal service would not be improved until the 1790s, when a post rider would make a stop in Salem every fourteen days.[30] This not only made general communications easier and more frequent but also facilitated the ordering of materials for the craftsman.

By 1762 there was such success in some areas of production that it became necessary to establish reliable trade patterns with other cities. Accordingly, trade was established between Salem and Charleston, South

[28] Fries, *Records*, 4:1586, 2:661, 5:2166.
[29] Fries, *Records*, 2:706.
[30] Frederic William Marshall to Johannes Ettwein, June 29, 1787; John Daniel Koehler to Ettwein, April 20, 1788; Moravian Archives, Bethlehem, Pa. Fries, *Records*, 5:2349.

Carolina, and with Petersburg, Virginia. In addition to the already established trade with the Philadelphia Moravian settlements, Charleston and Petersburg became the primary trade centers for Wachovia. Even before Salem became a center of production, Bethabara had been exporting whatever products it could. For example, in March 1763 one wagon was sent to Charleston with 3,000 pounds of deer hides, 80 pounds of beaver pelts, and 120 pounds of butter. At that time the best prices were to be found in Charleston. The trades producing household goods in 1763, however, were barely manufacturing enough for the use of the local inhabitants. "The pottery is best and brings in something. . . . The gun-smith trade makes great talk but has turned out only two guns since I am here. . . . Hardly anything has come out of the cabinet-making trade."[31] From these meager beginnings the Moravians persevered to become acknowledged as the leading craftsmen in interior North Carolina.

A reason for new hope was the opening of roads in 1770 from Salem to Cross Creek and to Salisbury, which allowed trade to begin with neighboring settlements. The prospering of this small group caused neighbors to try "to ruin [their] commerce and draw people away from [them]," but that year they "had more than ever coming to buy." By the eve of the Revolution, Salem had soundly established its reputation as the largest trade center in interior North Carolina. The quality of Salem products was held in great esteem, as attested to in September 1775 when, at the Provincial Congress in Hillsboro, North Carolina, the encouragement of domestic industry was discussed. "Premiums were offered for certain goods if made in this country, for instance linen, woolen cloth, iron for needles, knitting needles, and so on. One man in Congress wanted to debar the *Moravians*, for they would win all premiums, but . . . his suggestion was not accepted."[32]

The demand for products was often greater than the supply. Accounts of the pottery sales provide the most vivid evidence of the importance of Salem trades:

Such a crowd gathered that the street from the tavern to the blacksmith shop was so full of people and horses that it was difficult to pass through. The potter-

[31] Abraham Van Gammern to Nathanael Seidel, March 9, 1763, Moravian Archives, Bethlehem, Pa.
[32] Fries, *Records*, 1:397, 2:883.

shop was kept closed, and the persons who had ordered pottery, had paid for it in butter, and had received tickets, were served through the window. Col. Armstrong did good services, threatening the people with his drawn sword if they did not keep quiet; and for a wonder they were still, for there were not as many pieces of pottery in the shop as there were people outside.[33]

This encounter was in 1778, when the pacifist Moravians often found themselves overrun by American and sometimes British troops. In that same year the Moravians unanimously declared, "We Brethren do not bear arms, and we neither will do personal service in the army nor enlist others to do it; but we will not refuse to bear our share of the burden of the land in these disturbed times if reasonable demands are made."[34] In order to be exempt from military duty, many Single Brothers were required to pay fines. The Brethren also curtailed production in some trades such as gunsmithing, which could have had military applications. The hopeful attitude of the Brethren prevailed during these turbulent years despite a shortage of money. Although people were not buying and tradesmen often had to settle for items of poor quality, the Brothers and Sisters were urged not to fret over the war conditions. Nevertheless, the cost of almost everything rose so drastically that in spite of their care the Congregation and Choir diaconies suffered heavy financial losses.

The Moravians of Wachovia in general, and the residents of Salem in particular, were a cosmopolitan society. Their roots reached to many parts of Europe. Their personal education and industrial training were varied. The society was an amalgamation of personalities and people with a broad spectrum of skills. Accepting in common the same purposes and goals, they contributed to the church, their trades, and their society in individual ways. Their collective reason for being in Salem was summed up by Frederic Marshall, who, contemplating the move from Bethabara to Salem in 1771, wrote: "The present building of Salem is an extraordinary affair, which I would not have undertaken had not the Saviour Himself ordered it. I verily believe that the rich city of London could not do that which we must accomplish,—move the entire town and its businesses to another place."[35]

[33] Fries, *Records*, 3:1231.
[34] Fries, *Records*, 3:1231.
[35] Fries, *Records*, 2:618

This faith in their own ability was shared by all. There was never any doubt that a central town—Salem—would be established, would grow, and would prove to be the commercial and religious success that they anticipated. Their united and individual efforts resulted in a society where excellence in workmanship was second only to worship.

Craft Processes and Images: Visual Sources for the Study of the Craftsman
Jonathan Fairbanks

Visual sources for the study of craftsmen are as numerous as they are diverse. Countless images of craftsmen and their wares can be found in broadsides, trade cards and catalogues, billheads, dictionaries, directories, newspapers, journals, and other printed or engraved advertising sources. Such pictorial materials, together with paintings, drawings, and photographs, form our historic image of the early American craftsman. They provide background for interpretive programs and restorations at historic villages and museums. While this essay will not serve as a catalogue or survey of these various pictorial sources, it will offer thoughts on some problems encountered when one makes scholarly use of them.

A potter, a broommaker, and a candlemaker are only three of many craftsmen at Old Sturbridge Village, Massachusetts, who reenact the work routines of early American craftsmen. Historic craft demonstrators who perform these roles at early sites and open-air museum reconstructions create the most direct impression the public has of the historic craftsman at work. Members of the professional staff of craftspeople at Colonial Williamsburg or Plimoth Plantation are artisans whose insights, skill, and work routines have become familiar to thousands through films and sightseers' photographs. Such accomplished contemporary craft demonstrators are important interpreters of history, who share their work experiences and research based on their knowledge of the limitations imposed by old tools, early methods of fabrication, and the use of traditional materials. Educational slide sets sold at Colonial Williamsburg show the operations of the gunsmith shop, the Geddy silversmith shop, and the Anthony Hay cabinetmaker's shop. The legend on one of the slides showing the master printer notes that he uses eleven distinct hand operations to print a single sheet. Such a note attempts to convey a sense of craft process. Demonstrations by craftsmen actually operating their shops have enormous impact on the public. Living craft reconstructions may constitute the public's single most important exposure to historic craft practices. Better than any pictorial sources, the *well-researched* craft demonstration is perhaps the best way to understand the whole spirit and process of early craftsmanship.

Related to the crafts practiced in historical villages and museum reconstructions are crafts surviving from a bygone era. Sometimes an elderly craftsman can be found who works in traditional ways with old-fashioned tools. These individuals are often studied by younger craftsmen who want to understand the roots of their discipline. Although unorthodox and not always reliable as research sources, these traditional craftsmen can provide insights into tools and techniques that have survived over many generations. Craftsmen's work patterns and perceptions of their techniques are accessible through oral history as well as through observation. By persuading veteran craftsmen to explain their crafts, the folklorist or novice craftsman is able to study master craft practices and gain insight into the past. In this process of extrapolating backward in time, one must take care to sort fact from fiction. It is important to identify which generation added what techniques in the evolution of craft processes. For example, Brother Delmar Wilson, a Shaker, began to make traditional crafts in the late nineteenth century and continued working into the twentieth. Significantly, however, Brother Wilson was not strictly a handcraftman in the accepted sense of the Shaker tradition. He developed a highly technical machine shop which speedily produced Shaker boxes for sale until his death around 1960.[1] Many highly varnished boxes found in prominent collections of early Shaker artifacts were made by Brother Wilson. His are considered the lightest and strongest of all Shaker boxes.

Those who learn their business through apprenticeship (watching and imitating a master) are one kind of contemporary craftsman; another

[1] Rob Emlen, assistant curator, Rhode Island Historical Society, supplied information about Brother Delmar Wilson.

Figure 1.   Sam Maloof. Alta Loma, Calif., 1981. (Photo, Jonathan Pollock.)

relies less on traditional training and is largely self-taught. Yet both groups of contemporary craftsmen normally turn to modern machine tools and manufacturing techniques to facilitate production.

An example of a self-taught, innovative modern craftsman is furniture designer and maker Sam Maloof of Alta Loma, California (fig. 1). He started his career designing and making furniture for himself and his wife in the 1940s. Finding that many others wanted to purchase his works, he gave up employment as a graphic designer to produce furniture full time, becoming an internationally recognized leader in the new crafts movement. Although he respects the past, and his work shows the influence of traditional forms, Maloof does not consciously imitate any traditional style. Technologically, he is fully equipped as a contemporary craftsman with a power machine shop; but spiritually he has

Figure 2. Harold Ionson. Westwood, Mass., 1981. (Photo, courtesy Harold Ionson.)

rebelled against machine-made objects and dull factory-produced furniture. Although he sensibly makes good use of modern power tools, his furniture is not a factory product. Each piece is individually constructed, personally finished, and sold directly to the customer. Sales are made as they were in the eighteenth century—furniture "bespoke for" by the individual client.

In contrast, the second category of modern craftsman is represented by cabinetmaker Harold L. Ionson (fig. 2), who was employed in the late 1940s by Irving and Casson, the venerable Boston and Cambridge furniture company that began in the nineteenth century and went out of business in the early 1970s. In his own words, Ionson was used as a "human machine for production" in the Irving and Casson workshop. Today, he makes furniture in his own shop located behind his home in Westwood, Massachusetts. His work is modeled after examples of neoclassical furniture made by the early nineteenth-century Boston cabinetmaker Thomas Seymour (1771–1842). Although Ionson relishes hand-planed boards, hand-cut dovetails, and other historical joinery details, he is no slavish copyist. Rather, he makes what he calls "improvements" on Seymour's designs by modifying certain construction features of the original furniture.

Both Maloof and Ionson have small shops. Both produce limited quantities of highly specialized furniture and have a deep affection for and understanding of fine tools and excellent workmanship. Competitive in today's market, their products rival commercial cabinetmaking. Not surprisingly, when these two craftsmen were introduced to one another in 1979, they responded sympathetically, displaying a sincere regard for each other's accomplishments and approaches to their craft.[2]

Pictures of these two craftsmen in their shops present a basic problem encountered when pictorial sources are used for interpretive purposes. The layouts of their shops and the step-by-step processes followed in their production routines can hardly be explained through the static medium of still photography. With this in mind, one can better understand the interpretive limits imposed by such famous images as John Singleton Copley's portrait (ca. 1770) of Paul Revere (see Schlereth, fig. 1). Posed with teapot in hand and with some of the tools of his profession spread before him on a table, Copley's Revere is a rare and compelling eighteenth-century image of an American craftsman planning his work. Few paintings or prints of American craftsmen depicted with the implements of their trade exist from the pre-Revolutionary period, and none is known that documents shop interiors. Copley's painting, then, is an extraordinary record of a young goldsmith. Deliberately arresting and thought-provoking, it nevertheless has all the limitations of a single composed image. It can only hint at processes. It does not explain the steps involved in silversmithing and engraving.

Tracing simple construction from beginning to end makes quickly apparent the difficulty of capturing a process in paint, with a camera, or by other means. Sometimes such pictorial limitations can be purposely overlooked when a single splendid image presents itself, like

[2] For Maloof, see John Dreyfuss, "The California Home of Sam and Alfreda Maloof," *American Craft* 41, no. 5 (October–November 1981): 4–8; Robert L. Breeden et al., eds., *The Craftsman in America* (Washington, D.C.: National Geographic Society, 1975), pp. 39, 41; and John Makepeace, *The Art of Making Furniture* (New York: Sterling Publishing Co., 1981), pp. 34–35. For Ionson, see Rick Mastelli, "In Search of Period Furniture Makers: What They Do about What the Old Guys Did," *Fine Woodworking*, no. 23 (July–August 1980): 32–40.

a

Figure 3.   State Parlor Frame shop, Roxbury, Mass., 1980: *a*, loading area; *b*, storage and shipping area; *c*, milling or planing area; *d*, ripping the lumber to widths; *e*, squaring off lengths; *f*, boring machine; *g*, band sawing; *h*, carving; *i*, sanding; *j*, turning; *k*, job assembly; *l*, finished chair frames stacked for shipping. (Photos, Jonathan Fairbanks.)

Copley's Revere, which shows one craftsman at work. Nevertheless, the single image cannot tell the whole story. By attentively studying living craftsmen at work in their shops, one can better realize the problems of using pictorial sources to document craft routines. Consider a modern chair shop in Roxbury, Massachusetts. State Parlor Frame Company produces commercial frames for upholstered easy chairs and couches, which interior decorators and upholsterers buy to provide clients with furniture in Queen Anne and Chippendale styles. It is a production shop but does not rely on—or even own—a moving conveyor belt. The manufacturing techniques employed at the shop are not much different from those used by inexpensive furniture factories in the second half of the nineteenth century. There are only a few modern improvements: electrical power sources, high-speed tools, and electric lighting. Employing seven men, the shop is owned by three members of the Winer family, who do all of the skilled work themselves. Figure 3 illus-

b

c

d

e

f

g

h

i

j

k

l

trates—really only hints at—the steps involved in producing a frame for
a wing chair.

The illustrations cannot tell us everything about the organization
of the Winers' shop. An interview with the owners revealed that they
do not have a precise term to describe each step in the assembly process,
but they do share a sense of mutual understanding about what needs to
be done. Masses of (interchangeable) parts are made by one man or a
team of men who then move on to another work area of the shop,
bringing with them necessary parts for the next operation. Thus, while
the shop has no moving assembly line requiring constant attention by
employees doing the same job year in and year out, it does use some of
the techniques of the modern factory. Work is subdivided and assigned
to individuals as separate tasks, and assembly operations are simplified
down to their most basic steps. However, there is flexibility and variety
for the worker because those who make the parts may also assemble

them. Every piece of furniture made in the seventeenth, eighteenth, or nineteenth centuries, no matter how it was fastened together—joined, framed, dovetailed, doweled, or screwed together—went through similar steps in the manufacturing process.

From these illustrations and the interview, the problems involved in isolating complex craft processes or even suggesting the appearance of an active shop in a single engraving, painting, drawing, or photograph become apparent. The illustrators of Denis Diderot's *Encyclopédie* had a formidable task before them when they sought to picture craftsmanship in eighteenth-century Europe. Even modern motion pictures fail to convey completely a schematic sense of craft processes. The necessary delays and repeated actions for curing, setting, coloring, and finishing most products escape the edited film. The spatial organization of a shop and its appearance of activity change constantly during the frantic moments of peak production. The intrusion of an artist or a photographer interferes with routine procedures, and the act of picturemaking itself, like the writing of history, is selective.

With these warnings about the limitations of pictorial documents in mind, let us consider some historical images of early craftsmen to determine what they can tell us about the nature of certain crafts. Fifth-dynasty stone carvings from the tomb of Ti, in Saggara, near Cairo, Egypt, shows men shaping wood, about 2494–2435 B.C. (fig. 4). The image of the carving is difficult to interpret without knowing the meaning of the hieroglyphics or looking at a genuine piece of early Egyptian furniture. The hieroglyphics explain that the craftsmen are smoothing a bed of ebony, sawing wood, and drilling a hole in a chest. Recent research indicates that the round legs characteristic of early Egyptian furniture were fashioned by rasping round sticks. That this was a common production process is apparent from examining heartwood at the core of Egyptian furniture legs. To shape a leg the artisan held the wood vertically with the aid of a hand pad and manipulated it with a rasplike device made of punched copper sheeting attached to a stick. The arrangement of this vertically held wood stock prefigured the design of the turning lathe. Although the Egyptians knew how to use a bow drill, they failed to convert it for use as a lathe, preferring to shape furniture legs in their traditional time-consuming way because plentiful and cheap labor was available to execute such painstaking hand-shaping procedures. There was no demand for a labor-saving lathe, a machine that did not come into use until the eighth century B.C. Even so, this most

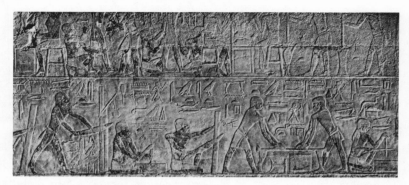

Figure 4.   Relief carving. Egypt, fifth century B.C. From Georg Stein-
dorf, *Das Grab Des Ti* (Leipzig: J. C. Hinrichs'sche Buchhandlung,
1913), pl. 133 (detail). (Museum of Fine Arts, Boston.)

basic tool of the wood craftsman was not recorded pictorially until 330–
300 B.C., on a tomb of Petosiri in the cemetery of Hermopolis. At least
no pictures of lathes earlier than this survive.[3]

   To leap from the ancient world to the early Renaissance in the
Netherlands, we may consider a famous image of Joseph and his carpenter's tools represented in *The Merode Altarpiece* (fig. 5), completed
by Robert Campin about 1428 and now owned by the Cloisters in New
York City.[4] The tools painted on the right section of the triptych are
convincingly real—they seem to have been observed from life and
therefore present a useful record of fifteenth-century tool forms. But,
even so, their selection is symbolic, like other elements in the triptych,

   [3] A translation of the hieroglyphics by Edward Brovarski, assistant curator of the
Egyptian Department, Museum of Fine Arts, Boston, describes the activities of the three
craft groups as follows: "Sawing with a saw, . . . smoothing a bed of ebony by the polisher
of the mortuary estate, . . . drilling a chest by a carpenter." The figures in the upper
register illustrate the process of making sculpture. Fred Lucas (revised by J. R. Harris),
Ancient Egyptian Materials and Industries (London: Edward Arnold, 1962), pp. 448–
54, shows that the basic tools for Egyptian woodworking included adzes, axes, chisels,
reamers, saws, bow drills, polishing blocks, and wooden mallets. Other useful books
about ancient craft methods and tools include Hollis S. Baker, *Furniture in the Ancient
World: Origins and Evolution, 3100–475 B.C.* (New York: Macmillan Publishing Co.,
1966); and W. M. Flinders Petrie, *Tools and Weapons* (London: British School of
Archaeology in Egypt, 1917).
   [4] Erwin Panofsky, *Early Netherlandish Painting*, vol. 2 (Cambridge, Mass.: Harvard
University Press, 1953), pl. 91.

Figure 5.   Robert Campin, *The Merode Altarpiece*. Ca. 1428 (detail of right panel). Oil on wood. (Metropolitan Museum of Art, Cloisters Collection, New York.)

and they probably do not represent a full range of carpenter's equipment.

A more complete assortment of woodworker's tools is found in Moxon's *Mechanick Exercises*, first published in London in 1679. It is the earliest illustrated book in the English language that explains craft processes and tools in an orderly fashion (fig. 6). The book was probably of little use to seventeenth-century craftsmen, who had produced elaborate workmanship for generations without the aid of printed pictures or instruction books. Moreover, the usefulness of the plates for understanding the process of craftsmanship is fairly limited; the illustrations

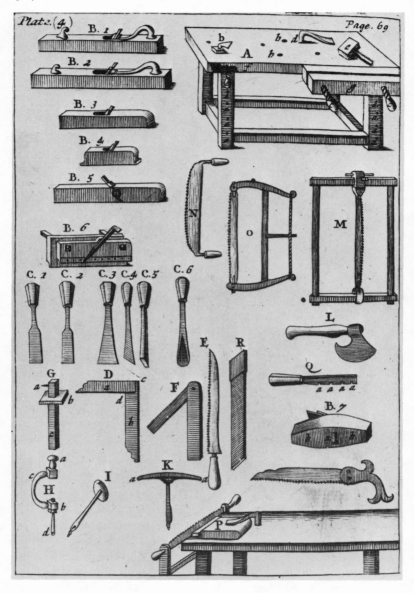

would hardly have served as an instructive guide to anyone who had even rudimentary experience in shop practice. But *Mechanick Exercises* does help the modern scholar to identify terms associated with tools, and, in its own time, the book did serve an important purpose. Without its standardization of terms and illustrated plates, there would have been no way for widespread craft industries to develop since it would have been impossible to purchase reliably through agents parts and tools sight unseen.

In the eighteenth century, to satisfy further the need for standardization, Diderot and other encyclopedists were instrumental in cataloguing and publishing in systematic order the tools and working procedures of craftsmen at labor. The famous illustrations from Diderot are too well known to discuss at length. However, it should be observed that in many of his plates several craft activities or different sequential steps in the assembly process are pictured in a single image, as if they were occurring simultaneously. Potentially misleading for the modern viewer, this was actually a conventional graphic device used for the sake of economy. It was a standard practice readily understood by most contemporary viewers.

Making intelligent use of such pictorial sources as Andre-Jacob Roubo's great work, *L'art du Menuisier* (1769–75), Diderot's *Encyclopédie* (1751–65), illustrated trade catalogues, and such modern books as Charles Hummel's *With Hammer in Hand* (1968), the student of early industrial history may gain a fair notion of actual craft processes now largely things of the past.[5] In the case of Hummel's book, which catalogues and discusses the Dominy shops and tools at Winterthur

[5] Andre-Jacob Roubo, *L'art du Menuisier*, 3 vols. (Paris: L. F. Delatour, 1769–75); Denis Diderot, ed., *Encyclopédie, ou dictionnaire raisonné des sciences, des arts, et des metiers*, 17 vols. (Paris: Briasson, 1751–65). Charles F. Hummel, *With Hammer in Hand: The Dominy Craftsmen of East Hampton, New York* (Charlottesville: University Press of Virginia, 1968), sets high standards for American studies in systematic analyses of tools used by the Dominy family of craftsmen in their eighteenth- and nineteenth-century East Hampton, Long Island, shops. Worth noting also is Paul B. Kebabian and William C. Lipke, eds., *Tools and Technologies: America's Wooden Age* (Burlington: University of Vermont, 1979), which deals with woodworking methods and tools from both historical and contemporary viewpoints.

Figure 6 *(facing page)*.   Joiner's tools. From Joseph Moxon, *Mechanick Exercises; or, The Doctrine of Handy-works* (London: Printed for D. Midwinter and T. Leigh, 1703), pl. 4. (Winterthur Museum Library.)

Museum, there is the rare advantage of being able to study woodworking and clockmaking tools of the eighteenth and nineteenth centuries from a single, well-preserved historical site. One can move from the book to the museum display and even see the tools in actual use.

No better opportunity is provided for understanding the nature of tools than from live demonstrations. Through these, the craftsman's shop gains a dynamic character: chips of wood fly, templates guide scribed lines, planes reveal the elegance of freshly shaped wood. Sharp-edged tools are beautiful in themselves, but even more so when put to use making something fine under an intelligent hand. The word *craftsmanship* takes on a special meaning for the observer of craft processes. No written description or two-dimensional image can do justice to the actual experience of making a deftly riven piece of oak or a beautifully mitered, mortised, tenoned, pegged, or bent piece of wood. The sensations of touch and smell cannot be fully and finally conveyed with words or pictures. These senses crave exposure to the bench, where multiple parts come together systematically in an environment that, to a passing observer, may seem only chaotic.

Lest we retreat entirely into romantic nostalgia for the good old days of handcraftmanship, it must be observed that fine craftsmen are the first to welcome labor-saving devices into their shops. They especially desire to use those machines that help systematize and increase production. English ceramic entrepreneur Josiah Wedgwood (1730–95) was distinguished in the eighteenth century for his perfection of efficient production methods. In 1790, 178 men, women, and children at his Etruria works were arranged in a protomodern production line. All but five of these laborers had specialized tasks to perform. The pottery at Etruria moved continuously from hand to hand and person to person, a procedure that replaced the traditional method in which the potter moved from piece to piece. Through this basic change in work habits, production was increased immensely and the quality of workmanship was improved.

In 1866 Eliza Meteyard wrote an illustrated history of Wedgwood's life that, unfortunately, failed to represent accurately the factory in its heyday of productivity. The book's illustrator, identified only as Mr. Pearson, depicted the throwing room at Etruria as it was supposed to have appeared in June 1769 when Wedgwood and his friends came riding into the new factory and summarily threw six vases, to the cheers of admiring visitors. What the illustrator depicted was a conventional

Figure 7. [Mr. Pearson], *Throwing Room, Ornamental Works, Etruria*. From Eliza Meteyard, *The Life of Josiah Wedgwood*, vol. 2 (London: Hurst and Blackett, 1866), p. 111.

small-scale pottery shop hardly big enough to have produced the quantity of goods Wedgwood regularly displayed for sale in London (fig. 7). Meteyard's biography of Wedgwood and the illustrations it contains fail to note the single most important innovation of the Wedgwood pottery operation, the assembly line, which, of course, had a profound impact upon other crafts at the turn of the century.[6]

The successful craftsman-entrepreneur of the nineteenth century

[6] Eliza Meteyard, *The Life of Josiah Wedgwood*, 2 vols. (London: Hurst and Blackett, 1865–66). I am indebted to Gale Andrews Trechsel, assistant director, Birmingham (Alabama) Museum of Arts, for the Wedgwood references.

Figure 8.   Billhead, R. Gleason and Sons. Dorchester, Mass., 1870s.
(Museum of Fine Arts, Boston.)

usually had his home, office, and factory close together, as illustrated
in a late nineteenth-century woodcut of a billhead for Britannia-metal
manufacturer and pewterer Roswell Gleason (1799–1887) of Dorchester, Massachusetts (fig. 8). The office and factory were owned and managed by Gleason, whose home was no more than a block or two away.
The buildings still survive, although vastly altered in appearance. Daily
surveillance of the factory to insure that production levels were being
maintained was essential to the success of manufacturers like Gleason,
whose small tinsmith's shop had rapidly evolved into a successful metal-
working factory. Significantly, then, it was not until assembly-line production became commonplace that manufacturers could afford the luxury
of offices and homes far removed from factory sites. The assembly-line
method of production made it possible to measure with some accuracy
and without continued observation the failure of any single person to
keep pace.[7]

Productive and cheap labor was one important ingredient of success; another was proximity to cheap transport for raw materials and
distribution of products. An 1820 New York advertisement for Thomas
Ash, a fancy and Windsor chair manufacturer, illustrates his shop near
a wharf (fig. 9). Whether the engraving represents a real or an idealized
relationship of shop and wharf is unimportant. The message of the image
is clear: transportation and profitable manufacturing enterprises go hand
in hand.

[7] Many of my thoughts on craft processes derive from Melvin Kranzberg and Joseph
Gies, *By the Sweat of Thy Brow: Work in the Western World* (New York: G. P. Putnam's
Sons, 1975), a study of the social issues of craft, work, and the production process.

Figure 9. Advertisement for Thomas Ash, Windsor- and fancy-chair manufacturer. From *Longworth's American Almanac, New-York Register, and City Directory* (June 1820): inside back cover. (Winterthur Museum Library.)

During the nineteenth century, as America underwent vast national growth and internal improvements, advertisements often excluded representations of craftsmen at work. Instead, information notices such as an 1822 trade card for J. and L. Brewster (fig. 10), hatmakers of New York City, simply illustrated the familiar allegorical figure of America seated with shield, eagle, and packing crates before tall masts of ships in the distance. Patriotism, federal protection of trades, and encouragement of commerce are ideas embodied in innumerable engravings of the early nineteenth century.

A wood engraving of a craftsman planing a board at his bench (fig. 11), published in *Parley's Magazine* in 1836 is a fairly representative image for its period. Accompanying an article titled "The Joiner," it illustrates a master and his apprentice or journeyman surrounded by a typical clutter of tools and materials. It is highly simplified in its composition, almost to the point of abstraction from reality. Several interesting observations can be made about the picture. The most obvious is the prominence given to the workbench in front of a window. Almost all early illustrations of workbenches feature this arrangement, as it was necessary to shed daylight on the work at hand. With the invention of

Figure 10.   Trade card, J. and L. Brewster. New York, 1822. (Winterthur Museum Library.)

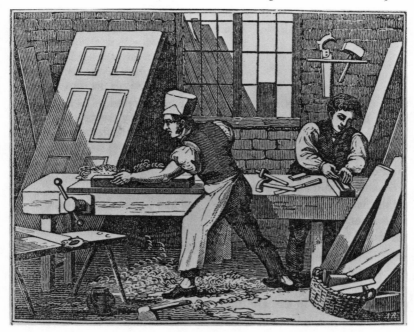

Figure 11. [Alexander Anderson], *The Joiner.* From *Parley's Magazine*, pt. 15 (New York and Boston: Charles S. Francis and Joseph H. Francis, [1836]), p. 249. (Winterthur Museum Library.)

the incandescent electric light bulb in 1879, the necessary relationship between workbench and window began to change, as did working hours. Greater efficiency of production came not only through changing alignments of working spaces with conveyor belts but also through continuous use of shop machinery at all hours, day and night.

The illustration in *Parley's Magazine* brings to mind another basic issue associated with using early pictorial materials to glean historical data about early craftsmen. Most illustrations derive from secondary sources unrelated in time or location to the specific subject pictured. Although this wood engraving shows an American craftsman at work, there is no reason to believe that it was based on actual observation of an American scene. Indeed, the print, by wood engraver Alexander Anderson (1775–1870), composed in the long-standing tradition of quick hack illustrating, may have been based on an earlier, more detailed

CABINET MAKER'S

GUIDE.

illustration, like the one etched in London in 1825 to face the title page of a book printed in Dublin entitled *The Cabinet Maker's Guide* (fig. 12).

Historians should be wary of the historical accuracy of illustrations that modern picture editors often provide for texts. More often than not, the illustrations most readily available are most misleading. It is advisable to steer clear of—or at least to question—the generalized, often inventive illustrations frequently ornamenting the pages of old trade books such as Edward Hazen's *Popular Technology*, published in New York in 1842, the first trade book to feature illustrations by an American artist of American craftsmen at work. Although quaint, decorative, and visually compelling, these cuts fail to render specific details about the nature of the crafts depicted because their imagery is generalized and sometimes overly propagandistic. Their accuracy is often further compromised by interpretive translations from the draftsman to woodcut artist and finally to printer.[8]

In contrast to such prints of doubtful accuracy, a wonderful example of *specificity* is provided by an early nineteenth-century oil painting in the collection of the Newark Museum (fig. 13). Attributed to Johann Heinrich Jenny, the painting portrays the home, shop, and store of fancy-chair maker David Alling (1777–1855) on Broad Street, Newark. In front of the shop and store are painted side chairs similar to, but not quite identical with, those made by Alling, also now in the collection of the Newark Museum. This unusual and welcome historical convergence of image with documented object—especially in the same collection—often stimulates the development of instructive exhibitions.

In an 1842 Boston almanac, a view appears of a portion of S.N. Dickinson's printing office (fig. 14). The legend at the base of this woodcut

[8] Edward Hazen, *Popular Technology; or, Professions and Trades*, 2 vols. (New York: Harper and Co., 1842). Generous use of pictorial sources showing craftsmen at work and their products continues to gain favor with book publishers despite rising printing costs. See Breeden et al., *Craftsman in America*, as an indication of the public taste for illustrated books on craftsmen; and a more historically directed book, Edward Lucie-Smith, *The Story of Craft: The Craftsman's Role in Society* (Ithaca: Cornell University Press, 1981).

Figure 12 *(facing page).*   Frontispiece, George A. Siddons, *The Cabinet Maker's Guide; or, Rules and Instructions in the Art of Varnishing, Dying, Staining, Japanning, Polishing, Lackering, and Beautifying Wood, Ivory, Tortoiseshell & Metal* (Dublin: Printed for Knight and Lacy, 1825).

Figure 13.   *House and Shop of David Alling, Newark Chair Maker,*
1777–1855, attributed to Johann Heinrich Jenny. Newark, N.J., early
nineteenth century. Oil on canvas; H. 21", W. 30". (Newark Museum.)

print informs the reader that the business has expanded from one to five
stories on Boston's Washington Street over a ten-year period, suggesting
that it is now large enough to do all manner of printing required by the
most skilled workmen in the trade. To demonstrate the kind of fancy
printing available, Dickinson cleverly exhibits a specimen page in his
ad, embellished in ornamental classical fashion. Dickinson apparently
was proud of his up-to-date rotary press and what it could accomplish.
The illustration of the shop interior combined with an example of the
shop's product is a powerful evocation of the craftsman's world. The
shop interior and its legend, as well as the specimen page, are obviously
advertising propaganda for the printer, but we can sense the presence of
the printer here, who probably supervised the execution of his advertis-

Figure 14 *(facing page).   View of One Section of Dickinson's Printing*
Office. From S. N. Dickinson, *The Boston Almanac for 1842* (Boston:
Thomas Groom, 1842), facing p. 8. (Winterthur Museum Library.)

View of one Section of Dickinson's Printing Office.

No. 52 Washington St., Boston.

From the above view the beholder may gather some idea of the results of our labor. Ten or twelve years ago, we commenced our business in one small room. Since then we have added room after room, as our business required, till we have spread ' the implements of the world's intelligence,' over five stores on Washington street, and pushed our *territory eastward* from Washington street, as far back as Wilson's Lane ; and which, for the present, seems to be the *boundary line* to our ambition in that quarter. Well, we begin to think our office large enough, and full enough of every requisite thing for the execution of all the kinds of Printing the world ever saw — certainly enough, we think, to suit the fancy of any customer that may come along : from him whose wants are of the most ordinary kind, to him who aspires to the most costly and elaborate productions of our office. To sum up the whole, WE ARE PREPARED TO EXECUTE ALL KINDS OF PRINTING IN THE BEST AND MOST EXPEDITIOUS MANNER ; having an abundance of room and materials, and some of the most skilful workmen belonging to the trade. Jan. 1842.

ing illustration. The woodcut in *Parley's Magazine*, for example, lacks such immediacy.

Although the crafts of printing books and printing wallpaper are quite different, there are similarities between them in materials and techniques. Both crafts are governed by yet another craft, that of papermaking. As long as papermaking was confined to a reliance on hand-held frames in which paper pulp was scooped and strained, the dimensions of both wallpaper and printing paper were restricted. In the late eighteenth century, however, this process underwent important changes. By 1799 the technology for making a continuous web of paper had been developed by Nicholas-Louis Robert in France. In 1804 the patent for Robert's invention was purchased by Henry and Sealy Four- drinier of London, who developed a machine in the early nineteenth century that made printing on a continuous roll practical. This inven- tion enabled Thomas Gilpin to install the first American continuous papermaking machine along the Brandywine Creek near Wilmington, Delaware. Soon a diversity of papermaking machines vied for popular- ity, as suggested by the numerous illustrations of these devices featured in *Knight American Mechanical Dictionary* of 1874. Edward Knight's three-volume dictionary provides for decorative arts scholars a rich source of pictorial images of machines and explanations of their operation.[9]

Continuous papermaking was a precursor of the moving produc- tion line in other crafts. Obviously, the production of wallpaper in large quantities depended upon the availability of paper in rolls. The com- mercial advantage lay in the elimination of much hand labor that had been necessary in block printing designs onto individual sheets of paper. Web-fed rotary presses were the new means of producing designs on paper for decorative purposes—virtually the same machines, of course, that made possible large-scale printing of books, magazines, and news- papers. Note, however, that an 1881 view of a twelve-color printing machine shows that Fr. Beck and Company failed to realize fully the advantages of continuous printing (fig. 15). At the end of the line, the paper is shown looped for drying. A more enterprising manufacturer would have kept the line moving by using a drying chamber or other fast-drying method to insure that the finished product could be imme- diately readied for shipping.

[9] Edward H. Knight, *Knight's American Mechanical Dictionary*, 3 vols. (New York: J. B. Ford and Co., 1875).

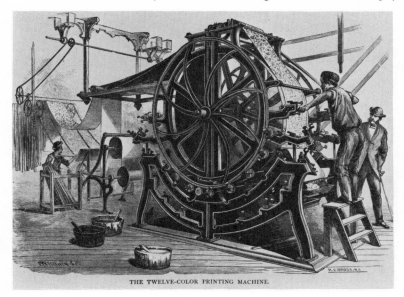

THE TWELVE-COLOR PRINTING MACHINE.

Figure 15. *The Twelve-Color Printing Machine.* From Fr. Beck and Company, *Artistic Wall Papers Designed and Manufactured by Fr. Beck and Company* (New York: New York and Brooklyn Publishing Co., 1881), n.p. (Winterthur Museum Library.)

By the late nineteenth century the continuous manufacture of goods made possible, through standardization of machine parts, the development of precision tooling. The efficient use of employees—the so-called American system of manufacture—now became the wonder of the modern industrial world. But the story of mass production, which led to automation in the twentieth century, carries us away from our focus on handcraftmanship.

Not all historical images celebrate industrial progress. Toward the end of the nineteenth century there was a renewed interest in the handicraft tradition. Two illustrations make this point (figs. 16, 17). In both paintings the central figures are old, wise men who have something important to teach their viewers. *The First Lesson,* by Henry Alexander (1860–94), shows an old taxidermist skinning a meadowlark as a young boy watches him. The interior of his shop is rendered with intense sensitivity. The room is filled with exotic stuffed birds and animals,

Figure 16.   Henry Alexander, *The First Lesson*. San Francisco(?), 1890.
Oil on canvas; H. 25″, W. 34″. (M. H. de Young Memorial Museum,
Mildred and Anna Williams Fund.)

translucent bottles, and light that streams through a window across the
workbench. Splendid beams of prismatic light rake across the taxidermist's hands and fall in a white splash on the floor. The dusty windowpanes are meticulously rendered; every detail in the room seems magically
alive and real. Yet for all the brilliance of his observation, the painter
has committed technical errors. No skillful taxidermist would handle
the bird as we see here, nor would he hold his knife in such a peculiar
manner to slit the skin on the bird's sternum. The specimen would be
positioned on a table with some sawdust or cornmeal readily available
to dust the opening made as the bird was skinned. No doubt the artist
has taken some liberty with his subject for the sake of clarity and poetic
emphasis; criticism of the artist's observations in no way detracts from
the remarkable luminosity of the painting and its authoritative treatment of detail, texture, depth, and character.

   The second painting, executed in 1899 by Jefferson David Chalfant, is entitled *The Old Clockmaker*. An obvious tribute to old age and

Figure 17. Jefferson David Chalfant, *The Old Clockmaker.* Wilmington, Del., 1898 or 1899. Oil on copper; H. 13⅛″, W. 9½″. (M. H. de Young Memorial Museum, Collection of Mr. and Mrs. John D. Rockefeller 3rd: Photo, O. E. Nelson.)

antiques, it was painted in the heyday of the colonial revival, an era of nostalgic taste. Conceived at a time when mass production and large factories were becoming increasingly dominant in the world of the American craftsman, the painting represents a reaction against progress. The scene, although particular in detail, embodies a universalized notion of craftsmanship. The image reflects what was considered the simple dignity and personal control of life and product that craftsmen of bygone days enjoyed. The painting pays homage to the era of handcraftmanship that the painter must have felt was jeopardized by the modern world, and to some degree the success of its message rests on our own curiosity about past craft processes.

While it is impossible to turn with full confidence to early pictures as trustworthy sources for precise information about early American crafts, this does not mean that early pictorial sources are useless in understanding and appreciating our past. Indeed, early pictures serve as mirrors to the past, sometimes distorted or imperfect, but nonetheless means by which we may reflect upon and, in part, enter into a visual world now gone.

Index

Page numbers in **boldface** refer to illustrations.